Socio-Philosophical Perspectives of Education

J.C. Aggarwal
Noushad Husain

SHIPRA

(First Published in india in 2016)

Rs. 1050, US$ 32

ISBN: 978-81-7541-873-8

2021 Impression

Socio-Philosophical Perspectives of Education

Published by:

SHIPRA PUBLICATIONS
LG 18-19, Pankaj Central Market,
I.P. Ext., Patparganj, Delhi 110092
Ph.:91 47322068; 9650028065
info@shiprapublication.com
www.shiprapublication.com

Preface

The sociological and philosophical dimensions influence education as a whole and are reflected in the aims, processes and practices of education. This book introduces the sociological and philosophical perspectives on education with a view to initiate inquiries and discussions on significant facets, themes and questions regarding education in India, that is, how education is both the means and product of social change, how multiculturalism and the concept of composite culture have impacted educational policies and how the movements of human rights education and children's rights have reshaped the content and processes of education.

This book provides a detailed discussion on the sociological and philosophical perspectives of education in the context of Indian Society. It suggests practical measures for fulfilling the objectives of secularism, socialism and democracy as envisaged in Constitution of India. The role of different types of formal, informal and non-formal agencies of education in this regard is highlighted. Suitable quotes of great thinkers on education enrich the subject matter. The subject matter of the book is explained in a simple and easy language. Material in this book has been drawn from the reports of different Committees and Commissions, Resolutions and National Policy on Education. All possible efforts are made to provide authentic and latest information.

The present book is prepared in the light of the new curriculum and syllabus of D.El.Ed. Many topics are from the book 'Philosophical and Sociological Perspectives on Education' of the author, Sh. J.C. Aggarwal and I am pleased to up-to-date this volume by working on the remaining gaps.

Planned as a textbook for students, this can also serve as a handy reference manual for practicing teachers and other interested in sociological and philosophical issues of democratic society. The authors extend their thanks to all the authors and publishers whose works have been used in preparing of this book.

I am thankful to Mr. D. Kumar, Shipra Publications for providing me an opportunity to get ready and up-date this textbook of late Sh. J.C. Aggarwal according to the new curriculum and syllabus of D. El. Ed.

Hope this book proves useful to students for their quality education.

Dr. Noushad Husain

Contents

1

Meaning, Nature and Scope of Education

1.1 SIGNIFICANCE OF EDUCATION

According to thinkers of ancient India, education is the 'third eye' of a person. It gives him insight into all affairs. It teaches him how to act justly and rightly. It leads him to realise the true significance of life. It removes darkness and shatters illusion.

A person without education is really blind.

In the words of Rousseau, "Plants are developed by cultivation and men by education."

Education increases our fame. It makes us cultured and pure.

Education nourishes us like a mother. It directs us to the proper path like the father. It guides us to reach our destination like a teacher.

The 'Upanishadas' consider education as a means of Salvation.

सविधा या विमुक्तये

or

सविधा या विमोक्षधति प्रदा

The following is a traditional common saying in India:

Swadesh pujyate raja,
Vidvan sarvatra pujyata

A king is respected in his own kingdom while a learned man is worshipped everywhere.

The Hindu law-givers even go further and lay down that the very sight of a learned man is sacred.

Joseph Addison (1672-1719), has very rightly stated, "What sculpture is to a block of marble, education is to a human soul."

The Education Commission (1964-66), the first Commission in India which examined all aspects of education, very aptly began its report with these words, "The destiny of India is now new being shaped in the classroom." It further observed, "In a world based on science and technology, it is education that determines the level of prosperity, welfare and security of the people." The National Policy on Education (1992) has emphasised, "Education is fundamental to our all-round development, material and spiritual."

1.2 MEANING OF EDUCATION

The meaning of education may be explained by stating its origin. The term education is derived from the following three Latin words:

1. *Educare*: This means: to bring up, to nourish, to rear and to train.
2. *Educere*: This implies: to draw out, to lead out.
3. *Educo*: The letter 'E' means out of and 'duco' to lead. This denotes: to extract out, to lead forth.

Thus education implies:

(i) Act of bringing up
(ii) Act of drawing out
(iii) Act of extracting out
(iv) Act of leading forth
(v) Act of leading out
(vi) Act of nourishing
(vii) Act of rearing
(viii) Act of training

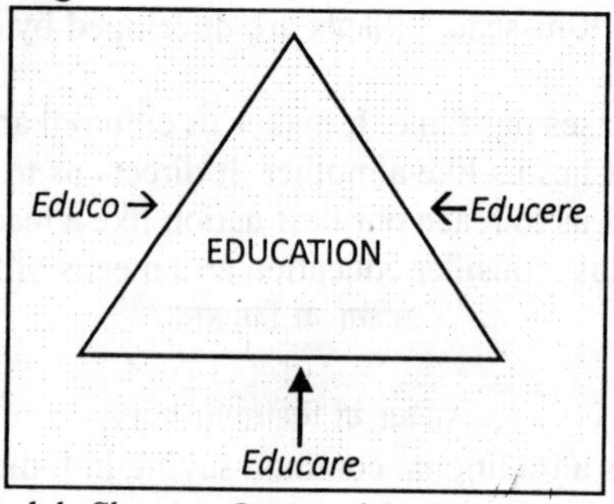

Fig. 1.1: Showing Origin of the Term Education (Derivation or Etymology of Education)

A synthesis of the above words relating to the origin (derivation) of education provides us a comprehensive view of the meanings of the term education. Several great educators and thinkers have followed this approach of synthesis. Plato (427-347 B.C.) stated, "Education develops in the body and in the soul of the pupil all the perfection he is, capable of." A great Swiss educator, namely Pestalozzi (1746-1827) has expressed the meaning of education in these words, "Education is the natural, harmonious and progressive development of man's innate powers." According to Froebel (1782-1852), a German educator, "Education is unfoldment of what is already enfolded. It is the process through which the child makes internal, external." Tagore (1861-1941) has observed, "Education gives us the wealth of inner light." Aurobindo (1872-1950) states, "Education means helping the growing soul to draw out that is in itself." Swami Vivekananda (1863-1902) has said, "Education is the manifestation of divine perfection already existing in man."

Gandhiji (1869-1948) gives the meaning of education as, "By education I mean an all-round drawing out the best in child and man—body, mind and spirit."

Meaning of the term 'Drawing Out': It is accepted by all educators that the nature has given (endowed) children a tremendous energy. They have within them the springs of action, joy and vigour. They have the God-given curiosity to know and explore things for themselves. It will be wrong to suppress these powers. They must be 'drawn out'.

Meaning of the term 'Best in the Child': This implies that maximum use should be made of the innate powers of the child—body, mind and soul.

How to draw out the best? Now the key question arises as to how the innate powers are to be brought out, developed, nourished and trained. Here comes the environmental factor which includes the family, the neighbourhood, the school, the community and the society. Thus, education is a means to provide the proper environment for the all-round development of the individual. The development of the individual has to be a balanced one and not lop-sided. An individual is one whole.

The following figures illustrates the overall meaning of education.

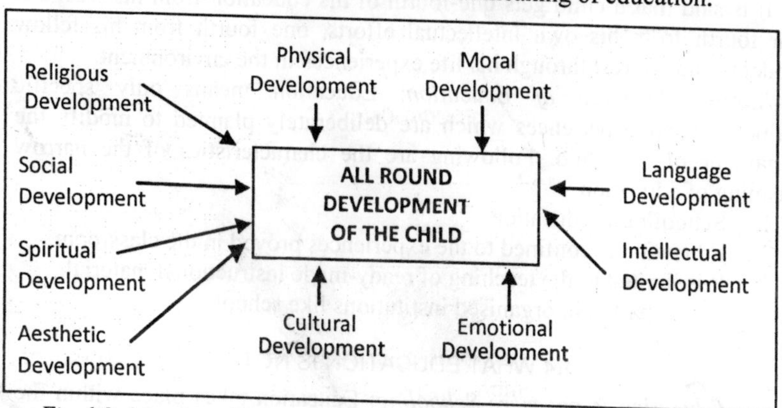

Fig. 1.2: Meaning of Education as the All-Round Development of the Child

The all-round concept of education has been explained by Gandhiji in his book '*Basic Education*' as "I hold that true education of the intellectual can only come through a proper exercise and training of the bodily organs, e.g., hands, feet, eyes, ears, nose etc. In other words an intelligent use of the organs in a child provides the best and quickest way of developing his intellect. But unless the development of the mind goes hand in hand with a corresponding awakening of the soul, the former alone would prove to be a poor lop-sided affair. By spiritual training I mean education of the heart. A proper and an all-round development of the mind, therefore, can take place only when it proceeds 'pari passu' with education of the physical and spiritual faculties of the child. They constitute an indivisible whole."

Summing up: Education implies drawing out the best in the child with the aim of producing individuals who are aesthetically refined, culturally well behaved, emotionally stable, ethically sound, mentally alert, morally upright, physically strong, religiously pious, socially efficient, spiritually enlightened and vocationally self-sufficient.

1.3 WIDER AND NARROW MEANING OF EDUCATION

Wider Meaning of Education: In the wider sense all experience is educative. R.C. Lodge in his book *Philosophy of education* even includes the experience of bite of a mosquito, the taste of watermelon, falling in love, flying in the aeroplane etc. in the educative process. Everything we say, think or do educates us. Likewise what others say to us or do to us should be treated as educational experiences. Consciously or unconsciously, we always learn and receive education.

John Stuart Mill states that every environment, every surrounding and every activity is educative to some extent. Every interaction results in education.

It is said that a child gets one-fourth of his education from his teachers, one-fourth from his own intellectual efforts, one fourth from his fellow students and the rest through his life experiences in the environment.

Narrow Meaning of Education: Education means only specific influences and experiences which are deliberately planned to modify the behaviour of the child. Following are the characteristics of the narrow meaning of education.

1. Schooling is education.
2. Education is confined to the experiences proved in the classroom.
3. It is limited to the teaching of ready-made instructional material.
4. It is imparted in organised institutions like school.

1.4 WHAT EDUCATION IS NOT

1. *Education is not mere Schooling*: Education takes place within the four walls of the school and outside also. Education is not mere spending a few hours in the school and learning some subjects.
2. *Education is not Information*: Information must lead to constructive thinking and wisdom.
3. *Education is not Instruction*: Instruction is confined to classroom. Education is life-long and ends with death.
4. *Education is not Indoctrination*: Indoctrination is confined to a particular belief but education is very broad and leads to broad mindedness.
5. *Education is not merely Training of mind*: Education is concerned with the development of body, mind and soul.

1.5 NATURE OF EDUCATION

Following are the chief characteristics of the nature of education:

1. *Education is Purposive* i.e. there is a definite purpose underlying all educational activities.
2. *Education is Deliberate* i.e. education involves care and guidance.
3. *Education is Planned* i.e. education is not haphazard. It is systematic.
4. *Education is Life-long* i.e. education starts from the time of conception and goes on till death—education from cradle to grave as is sometimes said.
5. *Education is Influence Exerted* i.e. the mature person (parents, elders and teachers) influence the learners.
6. *Education is Balanced Development* i.e. education is concerned with the development of all faculties of the child.
7. *Education is Bi-polar* i.e. both the teacher and the pupil influence each other. Of course, the influence of the teacher is very prominent.
8. *Education is Tri-polar* i.e. education involves the teacher, the taught and the environment or the subject-matter.
9. *Education is Psychological as well as Social* i.e. the endowments or the capacities of the child—his needs, interests etc. must be interpreted in a social setting.
10. *Education is Growth* i.e. education modifies the behaviour of the child.

1.6 SCOPE OF EDUCATION

Scope of education is as vast as life itself. There is no aspect or dimension of life which is not covered under education. In fact all education is life and all life is education. Education is a life-long process. Education is formal, non-formal and informal. Likewise agencies of education are formal, non-formal and informal.

Every year, every month, every day, every moment, step by step we learn from every source.

Education is concerned with the aesthetic, cultural, ethical, intellectual, physical, religious, social, spiritual and vocational development of the individual.

Education has moved away from preparing pupils to fit into a particular society but it seeks to make them feel they belong to the larger world family.

1.7 FUNCTIONS OF EDUCATION

Education is expected to perform the following functions:

1. Individual development functions.
2. Social development functions.

Individual Development Functions of Education: These functions of education are:

(i) Maximum development of the innate or natural abilities and powers of individuals.
(ii) Development of character and personality of the individuals.
(iii) Preparing individuals for living present life amicably and happily.
(iv) Preparing individuals for taking up gainful employment/self-employment.
(v) Development of suitable leisure time activities.
(vi) Development of qualities of followership and leadership.
(vii) Development of emotions of individuals so that they are emotionally stable.

Social Development Functions of Education: These may be stated as:

(i) Development of skills of the individuals that help them to harass the natural resources of the country.
(ii) Development of community sense among the students.
(iii) Conservation of social heritage by providing suitable curriculum to the students.
(iv) Promotion of cultural heritage by broadening the outlook of students.
(v) Involvement of students in community service and welfare activities.
(vi) Development of ideals and values of emotional integration and national unity.
(vii) Development of social awareness.
(viii) Development of values of secularism, socialism and democracy.

1.8 MAIN DIMENSIONS/ELEMENTS OF THE PROCESS OF EDUCATION

1. *Why to Educate*: This includes aims of education. The educator and the educand must be clear about the aims of education so that efforts are made in the right direction. Aims of education depend upon a host of factors: political, economic, social, geographical, religious etc. In a nutshell, education must produce socially efficient individuals.

2. *Whom to Educate*: The educator must understand the educand child thoroughly—his aptitudes, interest, temperaments etc., so that the 'best of him' is 'drawn out'.

3. *Who is to Educate*: The teacher is to educate and he must thoroughly understand himself also. He must get rid himself of all the blemishes and remember 'Woe to the teacher who teaches one thing with the lips and carries another in the heart.'

4. *Where to Educate*: The child is to be educated in a school which must 'simply', 'purify' and 'idealise' the environment. Likewise, there are several other agencies that supplement school's work.

5. *What to Educate*: This leads to the contents of the curriculum which has been described as 'the environment in motion'. In a broader sense it includes all the courses, readings, associations and activities that go in the

school—in the classroom, library, laboratory, workshop, playgrounds and in the numerous informal contacts between teachers and pupils.

6. *How to Educate*: This involves the knowledge and technique of various methods of teaching for making the teaching-learning process dynamic, effective and inspirational.

7. *When to Educate*: This is concerned with the different stages of the child so that 'motivational' aspects may be handled and attended to psychologically.

1.9 MEANING OF FORMAL, NON-FORMAL AND INFORMAL EDUCATION (FORMS OR TYPES OF EDUCATION)

Education

(1) Formal Education (2) Non-formal Education (3) Informal Education

Fig. 1.3: Forms or types of education

Comparative Study of Formal and Non-formal Education

Aspect	*Formal Education*	*Non-formal Education*
Aim	Aim is generally clear and specific. It is examination oriented.	No specific aim. Not examination-oriented. Enrichment of knowledge and skills.
Contents	Fixed curriculum	Flexible curriculum
Period	There are several stages of schooling like elementary, secondary etc.	There is no fixed stage.
Agencies	Educational institutions like schools and colleges.	`Clubs, radio and T.V., social education centres.
Admission Requirements	Points of entry and exist, age and entry qualifications.	Flexible points of entry and exist. No special qualifications
Employment	Usually employment-oriented	Usually growth aspect.
Role of theTeacher	Very predominant	Process of sharing
Lessons	Fixed according to syllabus	Very flexible
Mental strain	Heavy mental strain on the teacher and pupil	Little mental strain
Formalities	Several	Very few
Time Table	Specific and fixed	Flexible
Time	Usually full time	Usually part-time

A Balanced View: The use of new information technology in education has narrowed down the difference between formal and non-formal education. T.V., once a medium of non-formal education, is gradually used in the normal classroom teaching. Distance education, correspondence education and open education employ formal approach to teaching. Homes are becoming educational institutions with the use of computers and internet modes of learning.

Meaning of Informal Education

The following characteristics of informal education bring out its meaning:

1. Informal education is 'not planned' education.
2. Informal education is 'not deliberate' education.
3. Informal education is 'incidental'.
4. Informal education has 'no boundaries'.
5. Informal education is 'spontaneous'.
6. Informal education is not imparted in specialised institutions.
7. Informal education does not involve any conscious effort.
8. Informal education does not follow 'any prescribed time-table.'
9. Informal education has 'no set syllabi'.

Informal education is that education which an individual acquires without attending any educational organisation, system or institution.

Examples: Courteous manners, gentleness etc. learnt even in a market place or in a hotel or in one's sitting room talking with others constitute informal education. We get lot of informal education through films, radio and television. It consists of experiences and actual living in the community.

1.10 IMPORTANT DEFINITIONS OF EDUCATION

Definitions and Meanings of Education Given by Indian Thinkers

(i) *Yajnavalkya* (6th Century B.C.). Education is that which makes a man of good character and useful to the world.

(ii) *Kautilya* (4th Century B.C.). Education means training for the country and developing love for it.

(iii) *Sankraacharya* (788-820). Education means the realisation of the self.

(iv) *Swami Dayanand* (1824-1883). Education is a means for character formation and righteous living.

(v) *Swami Vivekananda* (1863-1902). Education is the manifestation of divine perfection already existing in man.

(vi) *Gandhiji* (1869-1948). By education I mean an all-round drawing out the best in child and man—body, mind and spirit.

(vii) *Tagore* (1861-1941). Education is that which makes one's life in harmony with all existence.

(viii) *Aurobindo* (1872-1950). Education means helping the growing soul to draw out that is in itself.

Definitions and Meanings of Education as Given by Western Thinkers

(ix) *Plato* (427-347 B.C.). Education develops in the body and in the soul of the pupil all the perfection he is capable of.

(x) *Aristotle* (384-322 B.C.). Education is the creation of a sound mind in a sound body.

(xi) *Pestalozzi* (1746-1827). Education is the natural, harmonious and progressive development of man's innate powers.

(xii) *Froebel* (1782-1852). Education is the process through which the child makes internal, external.

(xiii) *Nunn* (1870-1944). Education is the complete development of the individuality of the child so that he can make an original contribution to human life according to the best of his capacity.

(xiv) *Dewey* (1859-1952). Education is the development of all those capacities in the individual which will enable him to control his environment and fulfil his possibilities.

(xv) *Montessori* (1870-1952). Education means helping in the complete unfolding of the child's personality.

1.11 BEST DEFINITION OF EDUCATION

Going through the various definitions of education, one finds that there is a wide difference among the scholars and thinkers. This difference has arisen as education has been defined in the light of the needs of times in different countries. Keeping into account all the definitions, an attempt is made here to give a comprehensive definition of education. Education is a conscious as well as unconscious, deliberate or non-deliberate process of balanced harmonious and maximum development of the innate powers of the individual—aesthetic, cultural, emotional, intellectual, physical, religious, social, spiritual and vocational, according to individual and social needs.

Chief merits of the above mentioned definition are:

1. It takes note of the innate powers of the individual i.e. heredity.
2. It accepts that education may be formal, informal and non-formal i.e. an individual receives education in educational institutions and even without them.
3. It attaches due importance to the environment—environment may be specially designed as is provided in educational institutions or may be natural and unplanned.
4. It includes all aspects of the individual i.e. it treats an individual as a whole.
5. It is based on the needs of the individual as well as of the society.
6. It stresses the words 'balanced and harmonious'.
7. This definition is based on the fact that 'drawing out' of the innate powers i.e. hereditary and 'pouring in' i.e. environmental influences are complementary and supplementary.

1.12 FOUR PILLARS OF EDUCATION: EDUCATION FOR THE TWENTYFIRST CENTURY

Present Tensions: The International Commission on Education (IEC) for the twenty-first century (1993-96) appointed by UNESCO that considered various aspects of education needed for the 21st century, listed the following tensions that should be taken note of.

1. Global *vs.* Local tension
2. Universal *vs.* Individual
3. Tradition *vs.* Modernity
4. Long-term consideration *vs.* Short-term consideration
5. Need for competition *vs.* The concern for equality
6. Spiritual *vs.* Material

Four Pillars of Education: The Commission proposed the following four pillars of education to meet the changes.

Learning to Know: This means 'learning to learn' so as to benefit from the opportunities education provides throughout life. It also implies to acquire education by combining a sufficiently broad general knowledge with the opportunity to work in depth on a small number of subjects.

Learning to Do: This means to acquire not only an occupational skill but also competence to deal with many situations and work in teams. It also implies learning to do in the context of young people's various social and work experiences. These social and work experiences may be formal or informal.

Learning to Live Together: This means (i) Developing an understanding of other people, (ii) Carrying on joint projects, (iii) Managing conflicts, (iv) Developing a spirit of respect for the values of others' culture.

Learning to be: This means developing one's personality and to be able to act with full sense of responsibility. In this connection education pays due regard to all aspects of individual's potential: aesthetic sense, communication skills, memory, reasoning and physical capacities.

2

Aims of Education

2.1 WHY AIMS OF EDUCATION? OR SIGNIFICANCE OF AIMS OF EDUCATION

It is accepted by all that without the knowledge of aims, the educator is like a sailor who does not know his destination and the child is like a rudderless vessel which will be drifted along somewhere ashore.

Educational aims are important for the following reasons:

1. Educational aims given direction to educational activity.
2. Educational aims provide meaning to the educational programme.
3. Educational aims help in acting intelligently.
4. Educational aims provide motivation to take up educational programmes.
5. Educational aims are necessary for efficient school organisation, administration and supervision.
6. Educational aims are necessary to assess the outcomes or results of the process of education.
7. Educational aims are useful for parents, students and teachers to contribute their best to achieve these aims.
8. Educational aims give continuity and significance to education.

2.2 FACTORS AFFECTING AIMS OF EDUCATION

Aims are related to the needs of the individual and the society. Education to be effective must meet the many-sided needs of the individual and the society. Since change is the law of nature, needs also undergo changes. A child is educated in a society. So to become a useful member, he must be educated according to the changed needs. Educational aims change with the cultural, economic, geographical, political, philosophical, religious and sociological changes in the society. Thus, educational aims may differ from time to time and country to country.

The moral and religious aims dominated education in ancient India.

There were two diametrically opposed aims of education in ancient Greek states. On account of internal as well external in security, Sparta, aimed at developing courage, endurance, obedience and above all, physical strength of its pupils under the supreme control of the State. The immediate aim of education was to train Spartan youth as good soldiers. On the other hand, Athenian education was finer and richer. It laid more stress on inculcating in pupils such qualities as obedience to elders, ability to discern the beautiful and to enjoy life, fortitude and truthfulness. The sophists' overstressed system aimed at acquainting the pupils with several subjects. Ability to argue and debate was strengthened.

The educational system of the Romans was more utilitarian in nature. Moral aim was also given due attention. It was more state welfare oriented than individual development oriented.

Education in middle age was on the whole religion-dominated.

During the 18th, 19th and first half of the 20th century, the imperialists' powers of Europe had established their rule in several parts of the world. Accordingly, their interest was to establish that system which catered to their needs and those of the conquered nations. It was natural that after gaining independence, the independent countries established third educational system which suited their aspirations and needs.

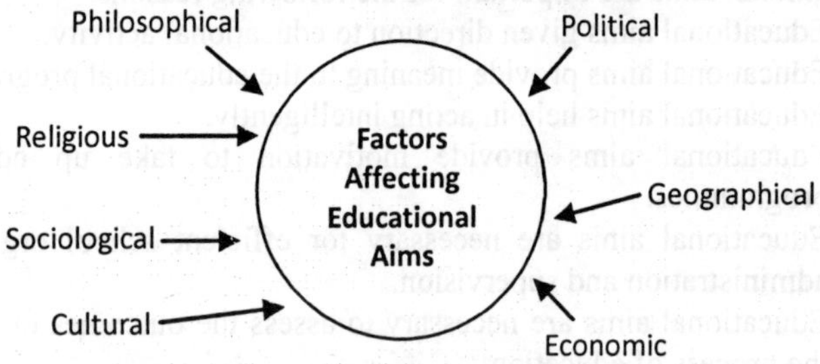

Fig. 2.1: Factors affecting educational aims

2.3 GENERAL AIMS OF EDUCATION

1. Aesthetic aim.
2. Complete living aim.
3. Cultural aim.
4. Harmonious and all-round development aim.
5. Happiness aim.
6. Individual aim.
7. International understanding aim.
8. Knowledge aim.
9. Leisure aim or recreational aim.
10. Moral aim.
11. Physical health and well-being aim.
12. Political aim.
13. Religious aim.
14. Self-realisation aim.
15. Social aim.
16. Spiritual aim.
17. Vocational aim.

Summing up: Education to be effective cannot have a single aim. An ideal balance among various aims has to be struck.

Aesthetic Aim of Education: It consists of developing the aesthetic senses of the child, for instance, appreciation of the beauty of the sun-set or song or an object of art etc.

Cultural Aim of Education: Although culture has different meanings, here it is taken as a way of communicating with others i.e. use of refined etiquettes and manners.

Knowledge Aim of Education: Some sort of knowledge is necessary for a well-adjusted life.

Moral Aim of Education: It is related to the development of values like honesty etc.

Vocational Aim of Education: According to this aim, education must enable an individual to earn his livelihood.

Physical Strength Aim of Education: Sparta, a Greek State followed the physical strength as the chief of education in ancient times. This was account of the reason that it faced external as well internal dangers to its freedom. So, the state prepared its citizen to become efficient soldiers and fighters.

2.4 INDIVIDUAL AIM AND SOCIAL AIM OF EDUCATION

Individual Aim of Education

Meaning of Individual Aim: Individual aim of education implies that education should train the individual first. The primary task of education is to provide such an environment in which the individuality of the pupil is most completely developed.

Supporters of Individual Aim of Education

1. *Biologists' Support to Individual Aim*: Prof. G. Thompson is the ardent supporter of this aim. According to him education must enable the individual to survive.

2. *Naturalists' Support to Individual Aim*: Rousseau's is the champion of this view. According to him, "Everything is good as it comes from the hands of nature but everything degenerates in the hands of man." Likewise Percy Nunn states, "Nothing good enters into the human work except in and through the free activities of the individual."

3. *Psychologists' Support to Individual Aim*: According to psychologists, each individual is a separate and unique identity. Accordingly, education should be in accordance with individual needs.

4. *Spiritualists' Support to Education*: The spiritualists, in general, stress that the aim of life is self-realisation. Education, therefore, must provide opportunities for self-development and self-realisation.

Criticism of the Individual Aim of Education

1. According to Raymont, an individual is only a figment of imagination. An individual cannot be conceived in isolation from society.

2. Absolute freedom to the individual should not be given. The individual may begin to assert that 'I must have what I want.'

3. The critics of individual aim believe that the individual left to himself is an animal, selfish and undisciplined. The animal instinct of man, if given, a loose rein is sure to lead him to the state of primitive barbarism where the law of jungle prevailed.

4. The exaggerated claim of the individual may have an adverse effect in the politics and economy of a country. The policy of '*Laissez faire*' i.e. 'let things go alone' is not conducive to national interests in the modern times.

Social Aim of Education

Meaning of Social Aim of Education: Social aim has several dimensions. (1) Society is supreme and an individual exists in the society and for the society, (2) State should provide for citizenship training, (3) Social efficiency should be the main aim of all training.

Social aim of education finds expressions in such terms 'education for citizenship' and 'education for social service'.

Supporters of the Social Aim of Education

1. According to Prof. Dewey, a socially efficient individual is an asset to himself as well as to society. He is able to earn his livelihood. He conforms to moral and social standards of conduct.

2. Raymont says that an individual is a social being. An isolated individual is 'a figment of imagination'. An individual lives in the society. So, he should be trained through social contacts.

3. The Education Commission 1984-66 emphasised that education cannot be considered in isolation. It is to be planned in social settings. It must contribute to national development.

Criticism of the Social Aims of Education

1. Social aim of education ignores the fact that every individual has his unique individuality.

2. Undue stress on social aim of education is against the concept of universal brotherhood.

3. Extreme form of social aim has led to the concept. "My country! Wrong or right". This emphasis became responsible for the rise of Nazism in Germany and Fascism in Italy. As a result of this, Second World War took place. Rise of communism led to lot of bloodshed.

4. Social aim of education envisages the individual as a non-entity and leaves little scope for his personality development.

Synthesis between Individual and Social Aim of Education

The individual and the society, both be regarded as realities. Neither of the two is absolutely independent of the other. Instead of being regarded as isolated entities, the individual and the society should be considered as related to each other. The individual acts on the society, and the society reacts on the individual. The individual is the product of society. The society in its own turn finds its advancement in the development of its individual members. In the words of John Adam, "Individuality requires a social medium to grow. Without social contact we are not human."

According to Ross, "Individuality is of no value and personality is a meaningless term apart from the social environment in which they are developed." Self-realisation can be achieved only through social service. Social ideas of real value can come into being only through free individuals who have developed valuable individuality. The circle cannot be broken.

Following points should be noted in this regard:

1. Individuality and society are interdependent.
2. Equal importance should be given to the individual and the society.
3. Synthesis is always an ideal condition.
4. The good of all is the good of each and the good of each is the good of all.

2.5 CHARACTER DEVELOPMENT AIM OF EDUCATION AND VOCATIONAL AIM OF EDUCATION

Character Development as an Aim in Education

Meaning of Character: Broadly speaking, each letter of the word as given below signifies some characteristics of a man of character:

C denotes – Cooperativeness, Constructiveness, Creativity, Clarity.	C denotes – Cleanliness (Ethical)
H denotes – Hard work, Humility, Honesty.	T denotes – Truthfulness, Tolerance
A denotes – Affectionate	E denotes – Ethics
R denotes – Rational.	R denotes – Reasonable
A denotes – Adaptability	

Character has two aspects: personal and relationship with society

Importance of Character as an Aim of Education

Gandhiji has observed, "All our learning or recitation of the Vedas, correct knowledge of Sanskrit, Latin, Greek and what not will avail us nothing if they do not enable us to cultivate absolute purity of heart. The end of all knowledge must be building up of character."

According to Swami Vivekananda, "We want that education by which character is formed."

Dewey has stated, "The formation of character is a comprehensive aim of education."

The Secondary Education Commission has observed, "Education is the training of character to fit the students to participate creatively as citizens."

Building of Character: It is very difficult to build character.

Character is the product of daily, hourly actions and words and thoughts; daily forgiveness, unselfishness, kindness, sympathies, clarities, sacrifices for the good of others, struggles against temptations. What is character without elementary personal purity?

In India, today we find a lack of character at various levels so much so that the actions of the V.I.P.'s also create doubts in the mind of the common man. State of affairs is very shocking. The present saying is 'As the ruler, so that people'. Perhaps after independence, morality or character has been the greatest causality. Education, therefore, must be devoted to character building activities.

Criticism of Character Development Aim: The aim is one-sided. A man of character but empty stomach will face frustration.

Vocational Aim of Education

Meaning of Vocational Aim: It implies preparing students for livelihood. It is also called 'bread and butter aim'.

Importance of Vocational Aim in Education

(i) An individual must be prepared to earn his livelihood, otherwise he will not be a happy man.
(ii) Vocational education contributes to increase production and national wealth.
(iii) As Gandhiji observed, "True education ought to be for them (boys and girls) a kind of insurance against unemployment.
(iv) Vocational education develops values of dignity of labour.
(v) Vocational education reduces verbalism and memorisation.
(vi) Vocational training is also suitable for persons with low intelligence.

Criticism of Vocational Aim of Education: Man does not live by bread alone. This aim is very narrow.

Synthesis of Character Formation and Vocational Aim of Education: Vocational aim in education has its own importance but man does not live by bread alone. Education must take into consideration the entire personality of the pupil and not one segment of it. Man has to develop himself aesthetically, intellectually, morality, physically, socially and vocationally. The University Education Commission 1948-1949 has very rightly observed, that vocational aim alone would starve the spirit and lead to '*Rakshas Raj*'.

Pt. Nehru had stated, "Education has mainly two aspects, the cultural aspect which makes a person grow, and the productive aspect which makes a person do things. Both are essential. Everybody should be a producer as well as good citizen." Gandhiji, it is true, stressed the vocational aspect but at the same time he was very emphatic, "By education I mean an all-round drawing out of the best in child and man—body, mind and spirit". He was convinced that without character, vocational efficiency had no meaning.

2.6 AIM OF EDUCATION IN INDIA THROUGH THE AGES

Aim of Education in Ancient India: Aim of life in the Vedic period and the Buddhist period was '*mukti*' or '*nirvana*' i.e. salvation. Accordingly, education was imparted for the realisation of this aim. Development of personal purity was the common feature. Of course, contents and methods of education differed in both the periods.

Aim of Education during the Medieval Period: Religious aim was the supreme aim.

Aim of education during the British period: Aim of education was to prepare individuals who would serve the British rulers faithfully.

Aims of Education in Democratic Free India: The ideals and values embodied in the Preamble to the Constitution of India are the guiding sources of educational aims in India. These may be expressed as under:

1. Development of democratic values.
2. Development of egalitarian values (values of equality).
3. Development of secular values.
4. Development of values related to dignity of individual.
5. Development of values conducive to the unity of the country.
6. Development of skills and values related to vocations/professions.
7. Development of values related to universal brotherhood and understanding.

(*Details are discussed in the subsequent chapters*).

2.7 IMMEDIATE AND ULTIMATE AIMS OF EDUCATION

Immediate or Functional Aims of Education: The specific aims or immediate or functional aims which need immediate attention are:

1. Development of language abilities of listening, reading, writing and thinking and communication skills needed for social living.
2. Development of mathematical abilities to develop a logical mind that would help learn perform mathematical operations and apply them in daily life.
3. Development of scientific temper.
4. Development of environmental understanding
5. Development of qualities necessary for self-learning.
6. Development of appreciation of small families.
7. Development of healthy sex related attitudes.
8. Development of the capacity to process, understand, reflect and develop insight.
9. Development of qualities needed for living a harmonious social life.
10. Development of attitudes and skills necessary for keeping physically and mentally fit.
11. Development of understanding and appreciation of composite culture of India and diversity in language etc. of the people of India.
12. Development of respectful attitude for freedom fighters.
13. Development of appreciation for the need of a balanced synthesis

between technological advancements and humanistic values.

14. Development of appreciation for the need of a balanced synthesis between globalisation and localisation.
15. Development of respect for the national symbols.
16. Development of patriotic ideals to preserve national unity.

Ultimate or Universal Aim of Education: The ultimate or universal aim of education is the emotional, ethical, intellectual and physical integration of the individual into a complete individual. In other words 'education is for complete living'.

Concluding Observations: The immediate aims of education should become the stepping stones for the ultimate aims of education.

2.8 PRINCIPLES AND GENERAL OBJECTIVES OF EDUCATION

India's commitment to the spread of knowledge and freedom of thought among all citizens is reflected in its Constitution, promulgated in January 1950. The Directive Principle contained in Article 45 ensures that "the State shall endeavour to provide within a period of ten years from the commencement of this Constitution, for free and compulsory education for all children until they complete the age of fourteen years."

Article 29 (1) ensure that any citizen having a distinct language, script or culture will have the right to conserve it.

Article 350-A stipulates that "it shall be the endeavour of every state and of every local authority within the state to provide adequate facilities for instruction in the mother tongue at the primary stage of education to children belonging to linguistic minority groups."

Moreover, special care of the economic and educational interests of the underprivileged sections—in particular, the Scheduled Castes and Scheduled Tribes—is a declared obligation of the State under Article 46.

Article 29(2) ensures that no citizen shall be denied admission into any educational institution maintained by the State or the receipt of aid from State funds on grounds of religion, race, caste, or language.

In accordance with the principles contained in the Constitution, the Government has to provide free and compulsory education for all children in the age group 6-14 years.

One of the major developments during the 1990s has been decisive step to decentralise the management of education through two Constitutional amendments made in 1993. They mandate states to enact laws developing powers to elected bodies at urban, district and village levels for developmental administration.

The eighty-sixth Constitutional Amendment Act of December 2002 has made elementary education a fundamental right for all children in the age group of 6-14 years.

3

Informal, Formal and Non-Formal Agencies of Education and Social Change

3.1 NEED FOR DIFFERENT TYPES OF AGENCIES OF EDUCATION

It is rightly observed by Counts that "The school is but one among many educational agencies." The common belief that education is confined to schools and colleges is not entirely true. No doubt schools and colleges do occupy the most predominant place in the society as educational institutions. But when we use the word 'education' to denote the idea of the all-round development of the personality of the individual, we must recognise the role of other agencies of the society besides the schools and the colleges. Schools function for a short time daily. They function for nearly seven months only during the year. The rest of the time of the students is spent outside the school premises – in the family, in the neighbourhood and with the peer groups. They are influenced by mass communication media and other agencies like class, social education centres, libraries etc.

According to some educators, of all the education we receive, we learn one-fourth from our teachers, one-fourth from books, one-fourth from our colleagues and one-fourth from the overall environment. This indicates the type of education and the multitude of agencies of education.

Education in a wider sense takes place from the womb to the tomb i.e. from the conception to cremation. Education is a life-long process. Education goes on whether we are aware of it or unaware of it. Thus, there are several types of social institutions that impart education. There are active as well as passive agencies of education. Likewise there are formal, non-formal and informal agencies of education. They are agencies of education run and managed by the Government. Private agencies are also involved in running different types of educational institutions.

Education imparted in formal agencies is called formal education. Education given in non-formal agencies is called non-formal education. Education received in informal ways is called informal education.

While discussing different types of agencies, it may be borne in mind that teachers are not the only educators. As observed by T. Ramount, "Let us agree to recognise explicitly that in a real sense teachers are not the only educators. In other words it is life that educates, the school provides a part of life's experience".

3.2 BROAD CLASSIFICATIONS OF AGENCIES OF EDUCATION

Broad Classification of Agencies of Education: No. 1

1. *Formal Agencies of Education* (Active Agencies of Education)	2. *Informal Agencies of Education* (Passive Agencies of Education)	3. *Non-formal Agencies of Education* (Active-Passive Agencies of Education)
1. School	1. Art Gallery	1. Adult and Social Education Centres
2. College	2. Cinema	2. Play-ground (when regular physical education is organised)
3. Home or Family (in the Past)	3. Home/Family	3. Radio (Educational Programmes)
4. Church (in the past)	4. Library	4. T.V. (Educational Programmes)
5. Adult school (on regular basis)	5. Museum	5. Professional Organisations like Teachers' Associations when they organise seminars, workshops etc.
6. Open school (when contact classes are also arranged)	6. Peer group	6. Clubs when educational talks etc. are organised.
7. T.V. (When used as an integral part of the curriculum and pre-telecast and post-telecast teaching is organised)	7. Play-ground (when not supervised by the teacher)	7. Cinema (When educational pictures are organised)
8. Radio (When used as an integral part of the curriculum and pre-broadcast and post-broadcast lessons are organised)	8. Press	8. Internet (When some educational course is organised)
	9. Reading Room	9. Correspondence Institutions
	10. Radio (Normal Programme)	10. Open Learning Institutions
	11. Television (Normal Programme)	11. Distance Learning Institutions
	12. Voluntary Organisations like Bharat Sewak Samaj, Boy Scouts etc.	
	13. Internet	

Agencies of Education: Classification No. II

Active Agencies of Education	*Passive Agencies of Education*
1. The Family	1. Cinema
2. The School	2. Radio
3. The Community	3. T.V.
4. The Religion	4. Internet
5. The State	5. Library
6. Social Clubs	6. Magazines
7. Peers	7. Newspapers
8. Neighbourhood	8. Market places

Formal Agencies of Education and Formal Education

Formal agencies of education like schools and colleges impart formal education. These agencies are consciously and deliberately planned to bring about specific influences on the educand. They have regular working hours. They prepare students for taking public examinations on regular basis. Usually they employ full time staff. They follow prescribed curriculum and textbooks. They have to conform to rigid departmental rules and regulations.

Informal Agencies of Education and Informal Education

The informal agencies do not follow any set pattern of instruction or education. In fact they impart education incidentally. Education is not organised deliberately in these institutions. These are informal groups. Education is indirect. One may learn without being conscious of it. Nevertheless influence of informal agencies of education is quite significant.

Non-Formal Agencies of Education

'Flexibility' is the key-word in the case of non-formal agencies of education. The system is an 'open one' with regard to: (1) Admission (2) Curricular work (3) Place of instruction (4) Mode of instruction (5) Time and duration of instruction (6) Regular/temporary/part time staff. Open School, Open University, Open Learning Institutions and agencies imparting correspondence education come under non-formal agencies of education. Adult education agencies are usually placed under this category.

3.3 NO WATERTIGHT DIVISION OF AGENCIES OF EDUCATION

There is no clear-cut dividing time in classifying educational agencies into formal, non-formal and informal agencies. Even a school can take the form of a non-formal agency of education when it organises adult education classes and programmes. Students in the school acquire a good deal of education through informal contacts with the peers and the teachers. The press, the radio and the T.V. are normally termed as informal agencies of education. However, when they take up occasional programmes of formal education, they assume the form of non-formal agencies of education. Regular school broadcasts and T.V. lessons based on the school curriculum may be considered as programmes of formal education and radio and T.V. as agencies of formal education.

The entire programme of correspondence/distance education/open education may be classified into both formal as well as non-formal, depending upon the type and mode of educational activity.

An adult school which follows a regular programme of education comes under the category of formal agency of education. However, when it is used for educational work, for sometime it is placed under the category of non-formal agency of education. Recreational programme of an adult school may be placed under the category of informal education. Now this comes under the category of an informal agency of education.

3.4 BROAD COMPARISON BETWEEN FORMAL AND NON-FORMAL AGENCIES OF EDUCATION

Item	Formal Agency of Education	Non-Formal Agency of Education
1. *Learners*	It caters to learners who can attend full time courses	It caters to those learners who cannot attend full time courses or have dropped from school. It also includes learners who want to improve their qualifications
2. *Aims*	To get a certificate, diploma or degree needed for a job or self-employment	(i) To increase knowledge (ii) To better skills (iii) To improve qualifications
3. *Place*	An educational institution with more or less permanent location. School or College	No specific place, can be home, factory, farm library, open space etc.
4. *Age*	Usually prescribed age	Usually no age limit
5. *Grade/Class*	Students are grouped into classes	Usually flexible groups
6. *Curriculum*	Almost fixed and rigid	Almost flexible
7. *Text books*	Prescribed text books as well as recommended text books	Usually general books on the subjects
8. *Teachers*	Normally almost all teachers on full time basis	Very few full time teachers. Mostly part time teachers or on contract basis
9. *Examinations*	Examinations at regular intervals Tests of different kinds	Normally no examinations or very few examinations, assignments
10. *Methods of Teaching*	Face to face teaching	Contact programmes, correspondence lessons Radio, T.V.
11. *Status*	Normally high status	Usually not considered at par with regular full time courses.

12. *Degrees/ Diplomas*	Degrees/Diplomas awarded to successful candidates	1. Normally certificates awarded 2. Degrees and diplomas are awarded for cour-ses planned in accor-dance with the pres-cribed syllabi – B.Ed., M. Ed., M.A. etc.

With the increasing use of new educational technology and science, it has become very difficult to divide educational agencies into water-tight compartments.

3.5 MASS MEDIA AS AGENCIES OF EDUCATION

Meaning of Mass Media. Mass media are means or instruments of communication that reach large number of people or pupils. The media may be printed like newspapers or may take the form of cinema, radio and T.V. Now, new media like Internet and e-mail etc. are also increasingly being used. As observed by Erickson and others, "In recent years technology has swept through society from research laboratories into manufacturing communications, the space age and finally now, into education".

Prof. Marrshall MC Luhan (1911-1980) who has written extensively on 'Understanding Media' observes, "Education will no longer depend entirely on obtaining knowledge through the print media. The visual approach to learning is fast changing to total sensory involvement (visual auditory, mots etc.) in the process of acquiring knowledge". His slogan was 'Medium is the message'.

Earlier the teacher was the only medium of communication for children. Now we see new media like radio and T.V. making their inroads into education. A close look at the use of new media of education indicates that they are supplementary to teacher's work. They do not and cannot replace the teacher.

Importance of Mass Media in Education

1. Mass media is very helpful in spreading literacy.
2. Mass media is very useful in social education.
3. Mass media provides very useful information on almost all matters of significance in life.
4. It can bring the entire world in the classroom.
5. It sends information to remote places and helps in distant learning.
6. It helps in providing a simplified and vivid description even of complicated skills like performing of operations, experiments etc.
7. It helps in the modification of attitudes and values of individuals.
8. It provides information very speedily.

9. It is useful in reinforcing group dynamics.
10. It appeals to various senses and this is helpful in developing motivation.

3.6 RADIO AS AGENCY OF EDUCATION

In the words of R.G. Reynolds, "Radio is the most significant medium of education in its broadest sense. As a supplement to classroom teaching its possibilities are almost unlimited". Frederic Wittis has observed, "I like to think of education by radio as a timely, vital and dramatic thing".

Merits of School Broadcasts

1. They enrich the school programmes.
2. They provide latest information on a variety of topics of interests to students.
3. They bring the school into contact with the world around.
4. They develop leisure time interests among students.
5. They provide opportunities for student participation.
6. They impart vocational skills.
7. They develop scientific temper of mind.
8. They promote emotional and national integration.
9. They provide useful information on population education, energy conservation, preservation of wild life etc.
10. They serve as instruments of teacher training.
11. They reach the masses, conquering the barriers of space and time.
12. They are very helpful in adult education programmes.
13. Various radio programmes like 'Children's programme', 'University Broadcast', 'Youth Programme', etc. reach varied sections of society and provide informal but effective and meaningful education.

Deficiencies and Limitations of Radio Broadcasts

1. Broadcast exposition leaves some gaps.
2. Broadcast time may not be suitable.
3. Radio sets may develop defects and need immediate repairs.

Suggestions for the Improvement of School Broadcast Programmes

(i) The broadcasts should have a wider horizon of application in day-to-day life.
(ii) The school broadcasts should also be designed according to the needs of the syllabus.
(iii) Teachers should be actively involved in various dimensions of broadcasts meant for the students.
(iv) The radio programmes should be intended to give supplementary information on the various topics in the curriculum.

(v) Teachers should occasionally meet, discuss and plan the type of assistance required in producing effective broadcast programmes.
(vi) Students should be asked to give suitable suggestions to make further improvement in broadcasts.
(vii) Every school should have one teacher trained in the electronic media.
(viii) Proper follow-up may be taken up on school broadcasts.
(ix) Suitable listing facilities should be provided to the students in the school.
(x) Broadcasts should be made in a pleasing style.
(xi) Language used in school broadcasts should be easy, simple but forceful.

History of School Broadcasts

Since 1920 when the British Broadcasting Corporation (BBC) started the programme of school broadcasts, it has made rapid strides in making sound contribution to formal education.

In U.S.A., broadcast programmes in accounts were planned from New York in 1923, programmes in arithmetic and literature from Oakland in 1924, music appreciation lessons in 1925 from Cleveland. By 1952, 20 States in U.S.A. had made provision for educational broadcasting.

Around 1952, nearly 98 per cent of the schools in U.K. were equipped with radio and there were regular daily programmes.

January 1929 was the beginning of radio programmes of interest to students from the Bombay radio station. From April 30, the Corporation of Madras had regular school broadcasts for half an hour on all working days. Similar programmes were introduced by Calcutta Station in 1932.

At present, following types of programmes are produced by Akashvani Stations:

a) Programmes for children of primary classes.
b) Programmes for children of secondary and higher secondary classes.
c) Review lessons for secondary and higher secondary classes on the eve of annual examinations.
d) Programmes for teachers
e) General enrichment programmes for children

3.7 TELEVISION AS AN EDUCATIONAL MEDIUM

Importance of Television. For a country like India which has vast and inaccessible areas, T.V. can serve as one of the important media of educating the masses. It can be used as formal, non-formal and informal agency of education. It attracts attention which is essential for learning. Following are the important merits of T.V.:

1. T.V. comes to the assistance of those persons who are unable to acquire education through the traditional system.

2. It promotes the goal of equalisation of educational opportunity by reaching the remote areas.
3. It provides technical advantages which normally are not readily available in normal classroom for demonstration or illustration.
4. It makes possible close-up magnification of small objects, components, intricate mechanisms, diagrams, etc. by providing students a 'front-row-seat automatically.
5. It makes quick and lasting visual and aural impressions.
6. It makes possible to bring large, scarce or new equipment into the classroom electronically.
7. It saves time, effort and cost of setting up classroom projection equipment.
8. It brings into the classroom demonstration, videotape or film presentations at the instant or immediately after they occur.
9. It allows relationship between two illustrations or time lapse between two stages of a process by dissolving one picture into another.
10. It directs the attention of the student to the exact details of an object.
11. It permits inclusion of up-to-the-moment information, modifications, new equipment or techniques into classroom instruction.
12. It permits the use of the services of the best available teachers to teach a subject to a large member of viewer students.
13. It permits to preserve the expert teaching skills on video tape or film for later use.
14. It provides a uniform experience to all students when they see the basic ideas or techniques on television.
15. It provides classroom teachers the opportunity to observe the teaching process of the best teachers and to increase their skills of teaching.
16. It incorporates useful film sequences, slides, graphic art and makes teaching aids available within the T.V. presentation, tailored to meet the needs of a particular topic.
17. Educational telecasts can re-create the past through dramatisation, films or lectures.
18. Educational telecasts can explain several scientific phenomena which are too small, too slow, too fast or too dangerous to be observed first hand, by sound films.
19. Educational T.V. has both amusement and instruction value.
20. Education T.V. reduces dependence on the classroom teachers.
21. It bridges the gap between the private school and public school to some extent by making the best teachers available to all students.
22. Educational T.V. helps in the in-service training of teachers.
23. In case of distance learning, television reduces cost of instruction.
24. On account of the combination of audio and video components, T.V. has great appeal than radio and print media.

Limitations of T.V. Instruction

1. There is one-way communication from teacher to students.
2. It does not provide opportunity for question-answer, discussion and interaction of the viewers with the T.V. teacher at the time of telecast.
3. Educational T.V. expects thousands of students who view telecasts to be of the same educational standard.
4. T.V. teachers cannot cater to the individual differences of the students.
5. Teaching through T.V. is a costly affair. It is not within the reach of every school.
6. All schools do not have the proper viewing facilities.
7. T.V. lessons to large number of students in the hall may create disciplinary problems.

Suggestion for Making T.V. Instruction More Effective

1. Effective arrangement for pre-telecast and post-telecast should be made.
2. There should be interaction among the students, subject teachers and the teachers who telecast, irrespective of the fact whether teachers who telecast are practising teachers or not.
3. There should be proper seating arrangements so that all the students have a proper view of the lesson.
4. Provision for T.V. repairs should be made suitably.

History of T.V. Instruction

Regular T.V. programmes began by B.B.C. in1936. By 1958, more than 98 per cent population in U.S.A. and U.K. was covered by television transmission. By 1962, American engineers succeeded in bouncing T.V. waves across the Atlantic on Satellite Telestor. In 1967, the first regular service of colour T.V. began on BBC-2 in Europe.

On October 2, 1961, the Delhi School T.V. Project was launched by the 'All India Radio (AIR), in collaboration with the Directorate of Education, Delhi and the Ford Foundation. The project was taken up in 140 schools with 300 T.V. sets. It covered nearly 29,000 students.

3.8 PEER GROUP AND EDUCATION

Meaning of a Peer Group. Broadly speaking, a peer group may be thought of as a social group with limited number of members who have same common objects of loyalty. Social relations are fundamental to peer group.

Chief Characteristics of a Peer Group. Some of the salient characteristics of a peer group are as under.

1. The group has a feeling of oneness and unity.
2. The members of the group possess 'we feeling'.

3. There is a similarity of behaviour among the peers.
4. The members have common interests.
5. The members are expected to obey the social norms.
6. The members have mutual obligations.
7. The members have common interests.
8. The members have common values.
9. The members have high expectations.
10. The members of a peer group are interrelated in various respects.

Peer Group as an Informal Agency of Education. The peer group primarily operates in the area of recreational, social and vocational activities. Members of the peer group become sources of sex education. A peer group attempts to assist its member i.e. the teenager in the process of self-identification and individualisation. It also helps in socialisation. It develops a co-operative spirit. Members learn to appreciate difference of opinion. Qualities of followership and leadership are strengthened.

A peer group serves as an important social agency of education during adolescence.

4

Role of the Family, School, Community, NGOs and State in Education and Social Change

4.1 ROLE OF THE FAMILY IN EDUCATION

Views of Great Philosophers and Thinkers on the Role of the Family

Home/family is the first social institution where a child learns his first lessons of living together, working together, helping each other and learning lessons of mutual help and adjustment. Originally, the family was the all-inclusive social institution. It is only recently that the role of the school has expanded.

Following views of great thinkers reflect the role of the family/home on the education of the child:

Froebel – Mothers are the ideal teachers and informal education given in home is the most affective and natural.

Mazzini – Child leans the first lesson of citizenship between the kiss of mother and care of father.

Pestalozzi – Home – a centre of love and affection, is the best place and the first school of the child.

Raymont – The home is the soil in which spring up those virtues of which 'sympathy' is the common characteristic. It is here that the warmest and most intimate affection flourishes. It is here that the child learns the difference between generosity and meanness, considerateness and selfishness, justice and injustice, truth and falsehood, industry and idleness.

Rousseau – Education begins at birth and proper nurse is the mother.

Frank states – It is the only institution which is an essential agency for child rearing, socialisation, and for introducing the child to the culture of the society thereby shaping his basic character – structure and personality.

Henderson remarks – A child's education begins in his home.

Swami Dayanand – Blessed is the family, fortunate is the child whose parents be godly and learned.

Saiyidain – The education of man depends on the environments that he enjoins. If the environments are based on good customs and traditions of the family, they will spread beneficial influence on his ideas and development and his education will be useful not only to him but to the whole community.

Important Educational Functions of the Family

1. Providing environment and necessary facilities for proper physical development of the child.
2. Providing suitable moral environment for the moral development of the child.
3. Exploring and developing aesthetic and intellectual interests in the child.
4. Providing opportunities to the child for participation in routine household responsibilities.
5. Understanding the nature of the child and acting accordingly.
6. Understanding the importance of the individual differences of their children and treating accordingly.
7. Providing opportunities for self-expression.
8. Following a proper code of discipline.
9. Providing learning equipment at the proper time.
10. Realising the limitations of the school.

Effects of Industrialisation on the Role of the Family

1. Very few opportunities for vocational guidance.
2. Less opportunities for social contacts.
3. Less time available for looking after the child.

Summing up. In spite of the limitations of the role of the family, it can still play a prominent role in providing proper care, guidance and learning experiences to the child. There is no doubt that home can do a lot in 'making the man'. As the popular saying goes, "A wise father is more than a hundred school masters. The mother's face is the child's first lesson-book."

The great scientist J.C. Bose got an insight into his scientific in-genuity from his mother's conservation during childhood.

4.2 SCHOOL AS AN AGENCY OF EDUCATION

Importance of School as a Social Institution and a Formal Agency of Education: Select views

A school is one of the most important formal agencies of education. It plays a very significant role in discovering, and moulding the innate capacities, attitudes, habits and ideas of the children with a view to producing well balanced personalities: aesthetically rich, culturally refined, emotionally stable, mentally alert, morally sound, physically strong, socially efficient and spiritually enlightened.

Following quotations of the eminent thinkers illustrate suitably the importance of the school:

1. In the words of Kandel, "The school exists to accelerate the impact of the essential aspects of culture which prevails in the society."

2. J.S. Ross observes, "Schools ought to stress the duties and responsibilities of individual citizen. They ought to train their pupils on the spirit of cheerful willing and effective service."
3. H.G. Wells has remarked, "A world whose schools are unreformed is an unreformed world."
4. According to Dewey, "The school is primarily a social institution – an effective agency in bringing the child to share in the inherited resources of the race, and to use his own powers for social ends."
5. Nunn has stated, "A nation's school are an organ of its life, whose special function is to consolidate its spiritual strength, to maintain its historic continuity, to secure its past achievements, and to guarantee its future."
6. In the opinion of the Secondary Education Commission (1952–53), "The school must be transformed into an activity school – whose main concern is training its pupils in the gracious art of living."
7. The Education Commission 1964-66 remarked, "The destiny of India is being shaped in her classrooms."
8. Harold Rugg thinks of school as an "enterprise in living, both social and personal".

Functions and Roles of the School in the Society

The school is expected to perform the following functions and roles:

1. School as the transmitter of cultural heritage of the society.
2. School as the conserver of cultural heritage of the society.
3. School as the promoter of cultural heritage of the society.
4. School as the connecting link between home and the community.
5. School as the provider of special environment for the all-round development of the child.
6. School as the provider of a planned scheme of things for the child.
7. School as the promoter of cultural pluralism i.e. tolerance of all cultures.
8. School as the promoter of ideals of the State.
9. School as the promoter of social development of the child.
10. School as the promoter of democratic values in the child.
11. School as the promoter of secular values in the child.
12. School as the promoter of ethical, moral and spiritual values of the child.
13. School as the promoter of scientific values in the child.
14. School as the promoter of professional and vocational skills and values in the child.
15. School as a promoter of egalitarian values in the child.
16. School as a promoter of innate abilities of the child.
17. School as a promoter of values of international understanding and peace.

18. School as a centre of community.
19. School as a trainer in the art of living together.

Summing up. In the words of S. Balakrishna Joshi, "In a word, a well-conducted school is a happy home, a sacred shrine, a social centre, a State in miniature and bewitching Brindavan – all beautifully blended into a synthetic structure."

Measures to be Taken by the School to Perform Its Functions

1. *Balanced and simplified environment.* The school discharges this function through curriculum. The school becomes a 'miniature community'.
2. *Art of living together*. The school provides a number of group activities through which students get a lot of training in the art of living together.
3. *Training in democratic living*. School incorporates activities like student self-government.
4. *Opportunities for Vocational Training*. School includes several programmes and activities like work experience and vocational subjects.
5. *Development of Child's entire personality*. The school makes all possible efforts to provide a pleasant and stimulating intellectual, physical and spiritual environment which will evoke the manifold interests of the students and develop them creatively and constructively. It formulates a programme of hobbies, occupations and projects that cater to the varying aptitudes and temperaments of the students.

   The school library, laboratory and workshop become the humble of stimulating activities.
6. *Spirit of co-operation.* The head of school should develop an environment of co-operation and harmony among staff members so that the students also imbibe this attitude.
7. *Co-operation with Several Agencies of Education.* School enlists the co-operation of the various formal, non-formal and informal agencies wherever considered necessary.
8. *School as a Centre of Community Service*. School can organise adult education classes. It can take up community service programmes.

4.3 FUNCTIONS OF THE SCHOOL IN BEHAVIOURAL TERMS: HISTORICAL LETTER OF ABRAHAM LINCOLN (1809-1865), 16th PRESIDENT OF THE U.S. (1861-1863), TO THE HEADMASTER OF THE SCHOOL IN WHICH HIS SON WAS STUDYING

The word of wisdom stated more than one hundred years ago are still valid to-day. (Extracts)

He will have to learn, I know that all men are not just, all men are not true. But teach him also that for every scoundrel, there is hero; that for every selfish politician, there is a dedicated leader.

It will take time, I know; but teach him, if you can that a dollar earned is of more than five thousand ...

Teach him to learn to lose and also to enjoy winning.

Steer him away from envy if you can.

Teach him to learn that the bullies are the easiest to lick.

Teach him if you can, the wonder of books but also give him quite time to ponder over the eternal mystery of birds in the sky, bees in the sun and flowers on a green hillside.

Teach him it is far more honourable to fail than to cheat.

Teach him to have faith in his own ideas, even if anybody tells him they are wrong.

Teach him to be gentle with gentle people and tough with the tough.

Try to give my son the strength not to follow the crowd when everyone is getting on the band-wagon.

Teach him to listen to all men. Teach him also to filter all he hears on a screen of truth and take on the good that comes through.

Teach him, if you can how to laugh when he is sad.

Teach him there is no shame tears

Teach him to scoof at cynics and to be beware of too much sweetness.

Teach him to sell his brawn and brain to the highest bidders, but never to put a price tag on his heart and soul.

Teach him to close his ears to a howling mob.

Teach him to stand and fight if he thinks he's right.

Teach him gently but do not cuddle him because only the tests of fire make fine steel.

Let him have the courage to be impatient. Let him have the patience to be brave.

Teach him always to have sublime faith in himself because then he will always have sublime faith in mankind.

4.4 COMMUNITY AS AN AGENCY OF EDUCATION

Meaning of a Community. In simple words, a community may be defined as a cluster of people living within a small area and sharing a common way of life to a considerable extent. Some of the important definitions of a community are:

According to Mac Iver and Page, "Community is an area of social living marked by some degree of social coherence. The bases of community are locality and common sentiment."

Alvin Goods defines a community as, "A community is a primary group resulting from social contacts, largely direct of those residing in a small area."

Ottaway states, "A community is everybody – adults and children, social and non-social persons living in a certain territory where all share a mode of life."

In the words of Brownell, "Community is meant a small diversified group of people, males and females with different skills and abilities living together as kin-neighbours."

From above, we note the following characteristics of a community:

(i) Community has a population.
(ii) Community lives in a territory.
(iii) Community has a historical heritage.
(iv) Community shares a common mode of life.
(v) Community provides different kinds of services to its members through its various institutions.
(vi) The members of the community work in co-operation and help each other in times of need.

Role of the Community in Education

Community is an important agency of education. It is child's laboratory which provides him first hand learning experiences of different kinds. The community with its various resources can enrich and supplement learning. Community socialises the child through its various institutions. It provides 'concrete', 'seeable' and 'tangible' resources which are dynamic, interesting and meaningful for the learners (children).

A community performs some specific functions as an agency of education. These are as:

1. It provides educational facilities in the locality/territory in the form of schools.
2. It co-ordinates the efforts of various agencies working in the field of education.
3. It undertakes several school improvement projects.
4. It establishes, libraries and social education centres.
5. It takes steps for promoting democratic attitudes among the people through organising conferences.
6. It conducts fairs, festivals and exhibitions which are of great cultural, educational and recreational values.
7. It sometimes encourages experimentation in the curricula and methods of teaching.
8. It co-operates with the school in providing better and effective teaching-learning experiences.

4.5 INTERACTION BETWEEN THE COMMUNITY AND THE SCHOOL

Community	*School*
1. The community opens and maintains schools.	1. The school fulfills the educational needs of the community.
2. The community has a certain philosophy or objective of life.	2. The school translates the philosophy of the community into practice by educating the children accordingly.

Community	*School*
3. Community requires various categories of works, doctors, engineers, lawyers, scientists, etc.	3. The school prepares the children for taking up various jobs and services needed by the community.
4. Community provides the traditional culture.	4. The school balances, purifies and simplifies the complex activities of the traditional community. It also enriches its traditional culture.

There is a great need of co-operation between the home/family, the community and the school. The home/family and the school are an integral part of the community.

4.6 NON-GOVERNMENTAL ORGANISATIONS (NGOs) AND EDUCATION

Significant Role of NGOs

From time immemorial, non-voluntary effort has played an important role in the promotion of education. In earlier times, private enterprise in education was by and large unorganised.

Since the 19th century several non-governmental organisations have been playing a major role in the field of education in India. The beginning of British system of education in India may be traced to the efforts of several Christian missionaries who worked singly or under the auspices of some voluntary organisation.

Philanthrophists, religious and social organisations, social workers, etc. have set up a number of voluntary organisations which work in different dimensions of education i.e. primary, middle, secondary, higher secondary and college level education. They also work in the field of adult and social education. There is a net-work of D.A.V. educational institutions under the D.A.V. Management. Ramakrishna Mission, Sanatam Dharam Sabhas, Shromani Gurudwara Prabandank Committee, Christian Association, Muslim Associations, Parsee Associations etc. are running several types of educational institutions. There are also several educational institutions run by Delhi Public School Society, Modern School Society etc.

Recently some Non-Governmental Organisation have come up for the promotion of environmental education, family planning, population education etc.

The area of operation of voluntary organisation is as broad as the life itself.

The Ministry of Human Resource Development, Department of Education and Government of India is providing grants and other assistance to hundreds of non-governmental organisations for the following purposes:

1. Promotion of adult education.
2. Promotion of literacy among women.
3. Promotion of vocational education.
4. Environmental orientation to school education.

5. Improvement of science education in schools.
6. Strengthening culture and values in education.
7. Strengthening of boarding/hostel facilities for girl students.
8. Integrated education for disabled children.
9. Promotion of yoga.
10. Languages development.
11. Non-formal education.

Several other Ministries of the Government of India also are encouraging non-governmental organisations to work in the educational and social field.

Likewise State Governments are also seeking the co-operation of several non-governmental organisations in undertaking programmes for community development.

Classification of Non-Governmental Organisations

Following are the important ways of classifying non-governmental organisations.

Classification of NGO-I

Work limited to one community | Work extended to several communities

Fig. 4.1: Classification of NGO according to territory of operation

Classification of NGO-II

Religion based NGO | Secular NGO

Fig. 4.2: Classification of NGO: Religious or Secular

Classification of NGO-III

Formal Education | Non-formal Education | Informal Education

Fig. 4.3: Classification of NGO according to type of education

Classification of NGO-IV

Government recognised | Not recognised by the government

Fig. 4.4: Classification according to recognition

Classification of NGO-V

Government aided | Non-government aided

Fig. 4.5: Classification of NGO according to grant

Classification of NGO-VI

- Single purpose
- Manifold purpose

Fig. 4.6: Classification of NGO according to purpose

Classification of NGO-VII

- Community level NGO
- District Level NGO
- State Level NGO
- National Level NGO
- International Level NGO like UNICEF etc.

Fig. 4.7: NGO according to level

4.7 POLICY STATEMENTS ON THE ROLE OF NGOs

Education Commission (1964-66) on the Role of NGOs

The Education Commission (1964-66) recognised the role of the non-governmental organisations (private enterprises) in the development of education in India. It, therefore, recommended that all possible use of their assistance must be made by the Government/State. It felt that the growing educational needs of a modern society cannot be met by government efforts alone. Nevertheless, it should be ensured that the non-governmental organisations, do not include in malpractices.

National Policy on Education (NPE) (1986 and as amended in 1992) on the Role of NGO

In Part X, the NPE has laid down that

"Non-government and voluntary effort including social activist groups will be encouraged and financial assistance provided. Of course, their work and management would be supervised."

4.8 ROLE OF THE STATE IN EDUCATION

Form of State and Educational Enterprise

In a totalitarian State, the entire responsibility of education is of the State. It establishes and manages all educational institutions. It determines the aims, contents, methods of teaching and discipline etc. in the field of education. There is no scope for private enterprise in education.

In a Laissez-faire State, there is an attitude like 'as you please' i.e. the State does not interfere in education and in fact in almost all areas of national life.

Education, a Joint Enterprise in India

It is universally accepted that a democratic State should not claim monopoly in running and managing educational institutions. It should encourage private enterprise in education also.

The National Policy on Education (1986 and as amended in 1992) has laid down the following directions in the management of education:

1. Decentralisation and the creation of a spirit of autonomy for educational institutions.
2. Giving pre-eminence to people's involvement, including association of non-government agencies and voluntary effort.

Merits of State Control of Education

1. State having large funds at its disposal, can make huge investment in education.
2. State control can ensure universal, compulsory and free education to all children of a certain age group.
3. State can ensure a uniform system of education.
4. State can prescribe a common curriculum.
5. State can introduce an egalitarian element in the provision of educational opportunities.
6. State can ensure suitable standard of education.
7. State can ensure suitable service conditions for teachers.
8. State can ensure secular education.
9. State can ensure quality in teacher training and also availability of the required number of teachers.

Demerits of State Control of Education

1. Education will be politicalised.
2. Indoctrination, brain washing and brain storming would become the order of the day.
3. Teachers committed to a particular ideology will be recruited.
4. Individuality of the students is likely to be made subservient and not allowed to develop harmoniously and naturally.
5. Individual differences of children are likely to be ignored.
6. Qualities like initiative and enterprise would tend to receive set-back.
7. There will be regimentation. Democratic ideals would recede to the background.
8. Work ethics may wither away.
9. The family will be deprived of its fundamental right to look after its children.
10. A narrow view of education will predominate.

Educational Functions of a Modern Democratic State

A democratic State like India is expected to perform the following functions:

1. Provision of adequate educational facilities in institutions.
2. Raising the quality of education.
3. Making primary education compulsory, universal and free.
4. Assisting private enterprise in education.
5. Providing adult education to all illiterate adults.
6. Exercising general control and guidance.
7. Training young men and women in citizenship.
8. Providing competent educators.
9. Evolving a national system of education.
10. Ensuring availability of adequate teaching-learning material to students.
11. Encouraging research in education.
12. Awarding sufficient number of scholarship to the talented.
13. Preparing and implementing educational plans.
14. Preparing suitable manpower for various technical, vocational, professional and other fields.
15. Appointing education committees and commissions for suggesting suitable changes in the light of new developments in economy industry, science and technology etc.
16. Instituting cadres of Indian Education Service (IES) and State Education Service (SES) to manage the educational enterprise.
17. Constituting working groups and advisory bodies of cross–section experts to link education with various disciplines and fields.
18. Organising boards and committees relating to framing of curriculum, preparation of teaching material, recognition of educational institutions and conduct of examinations.

5

Meaning, Nature, Functions and Scope of Philosophy: Philosophy and Education

5.1 SIGNIFICANCE OF PHILOSOPHY

The subject matter of philosophy is as wide as human experience. It is as old as human life. There is no aspect of life, natural or supernatural, animate or inanimate which falls outside its domain. This wide scope in itself indicates the significance of philosophy. On account of this fact, Francis Bacon (1561-1626), a great English philosopher considered philosophy as the 'great mother of the sciences'. Philosophy is so deeply involved into human life that Aristotle (384-322 B.C.), the great Greek philosopher remarked, "Everyone follows a philosophy, whether he is aware of it or not."

Thousands of years ago, Indian seers and thinkers developed a very comprehensive and well-organised system of philosophy for the guidance of an individual.

5.2 MEANING AND NATURE OF PHILOSOPHY

Sanskrit word '*Darshan*' (philosophy) means 'direct perception' of the truth. Seers of ancient India used to see or perceive the truth. The same thing may be said about Socrates (469-399 B.C.), Plato (427-347 B.C.) and Aristotle (384-322 B.C.)—trio of Greek philosophy.

The word 'philosophy' has a Greek origin. '*Philosophia*' a Greek word consists of two words, i.e. '*phileo*' meaning love and '*sophia*' meaning wisdom. Therefore, the literal meaning of philosophy is 'love of wisdom'.

The following definitions of philosophy help us to understand the true meaning of philosophy.

1. In the words of Plato, "Knowledge of the true nature of different things is philosophy."

2. According to Aristotle, "Philosophy is a science which discovers the real nature of supernatural elements."

3. Kant (1724-1804) regards philosophy as "the science and criticism of cognition."

4. Dr. Radhakrishnan (1872-1970) considers philosophy as a "logical inquiry into the nature of reality".

5. Henderson (1947) thinks that philosophy is a search for "a comprehensive view of nature, an attempt at a universal explanation of the nature of things".

From above we conclude that:

1. Philosophy is a search for reality and truth.
2. Philosophy is based on enquiry.
3. Philosophy is local.
4. Philosophy is a dynamic and living force.
5. Philosophy is an art as well as a science.
6. Philosophy is closely related to education.
7. Philosophy is an intellectual attempt to interpret and understand nature.
8. Philosophy is love of knowledge.
9. Philosophy is love of wisdom.
10. Philosophy is a guide to a way of life.

5.3 WHY DO WE NEED PHILOSOPHY

Philosophy gives a direction to life. Philosophy in India emerged as a result of reflection over the experiences and problems of life. Dr. Radhakrishnan, the great Indian philosopher has suggested this meaning of philosophy through the titles of two of his books. "*The Indian View of Life*" and "*The Idealist View of Life*". Human life is always purposeful. The purpose of life is determined by the philosophy of life.

We need philosophy to take decisions wisely and to act consistently. One needs wisdom to distinguish between two extremes—falsehood and truth, ugliness and beauty, right and wrong, etc. Philosophy enables us to live by values for we do not live only by bread, vitamins and technological discoveries.

5.4 SCOPE OF PHILOSOPHY

Scope of philosophy is so vast that Cicero (106-43) B.C., a Roman scholar called it as 'the mother of all arts" and "the true medicine of mind". Francis Bacon, a great English philosopher regarded the philosophy as, "the great mother of the Sciences". Coleridge (1772-1834) a noted poet considered it as the 'Science of Sciences'.

Broadly speaking following types of problems come under the scope of philosophy.

1. Problems of reality
2. Problems of knowledge
3. Problems of value

5.5 IMPORTANCE OF PHILOSOPHY

Philosophic thought is an inescapable part of human existence. Almost everyone has been puzzled from time to time by such essentially philosophic questions as "*What does life mean?*" "*Did I have any existence before I was born?*" and "*Is there life after death?*" Most people also have some kind of philosophy in the sense of a personal outlook on life. Even a person who claims that considering philosophic questions is a waste of time is expressing what is important, worthwhile, or valuable. A rejection of all philosophy is in itself philosophy.

The importance of philosophy can be best understood with the help of the following points:

- A philosophy is a system of beliefs about reality. It is one's integrated view of the world.
- It includes an understanding of the nature of existence, man, and his role in the world.
- Philosophy is the foundation of knowledge.
- It is the standard by which ideas are integrated and understood.
- Philosophy is a necessary product of man's rational mind. To live, man must gain knowledge of the world. To understand the world, man must form conclusions about its very nature. For instance, to gain knowledge of particular objects, man must recognise that objects have identity. He must recognise that conclusions are possible because the world does exist, and exists in a particular way.
- Philosophy provides the framework for which man can understand the world.
- It provides the premises by which man can discover truth, and use his mind to support his life. Every man has an understanding of the world. Every man must have a philosophy, even if it is never made explicit.
- By studying philosophy, people can clarify what they believe, and they can be stimulated to think about ultimate questions.
- A person can study philosophers of the past to discover why they thought as they did and what value their thoughts may have in one's own life. There are people who simply enjoy reading the great philosophers, especially those who were also great writers.
- Philosophy has had enormous influence on our everyday lives. The very language we speak uses classifications derived from philosophy. For example, the classifications of noun and verb involve the philosophic idea that there is a difference between things and actions. If we ask what the difference is, we are starting a philosophic inquiry.
- Every institution of society is based on philosophic ideas, whether that institution is the law, government, religion, the family, marriage, industry, business, or education.
- Philosophic differences have led to the overthrow of governments,

drastic changes in laws, and the transformation of entire economic systems. Such changes have occurred because the people involved held certain beliefs about what is important, true, real, and significant and about how life should be ordered.

- Systems of education follow a society's philosophic ideas about what children should be taught and for what purposes. Democratic societies stress that people learn to think and make choices for themselves. Non-democratic societies discourage such activities and want their citizens to surrender their own interests to those of the state. The values and skills taught by the educational system of a society thus reflect the society's philosophic ideas of what is important.
- Philosophy is a study that seeks to understand the mysteries of existence and reality.
- It tries to discover the nature of truth and knowledge and to find what is of basic value and importance in life.
- It also examines the relationships between humanity and nature and between the individual and society.
- Philosophy arises out of wonder, curiosity, and the desire to know and understand. Philosophy is thus a form of inquiry--a process of analysis, criticism, interpretation, and speculation.

5.6 FUNCTIONS OF PHILOSOPHY

The functions of philosophy are the uses of the subject to us as individuals and as members of a society. The functions of philosophy are explained as follows:

Analytical Function

This has to do with the analysis and clarification of ideas, issues and statements to enable us understand the subject matters of other disciplines. This analytical function is considered to be the primary function of philosophy.

Speculative and Normative Function

The mind is a very essential instrument for doing philosophy. The mind is one gift to man, which enables him think about himself, the people around him and the world, in general. With it he can speculate about things he is not sure of; he can imagine things that are possible and even those that are not possible. It is to be noted however, that, when we think about things or speculate on issues it is done within the context of our social and cultural environment.

Inspirational Function

The educational process is constantly inspired by philosophers. Such works, as Plato's Republic and other like it have become the reference book for many educators because they obtain a lot of insight from these books to guide their activities. For one thing, every society has its ideal and thus, strives to attain it. Plato's ideal in the Republic is one in which education serves as an important criterion for assigning social positions and responsibilities. It is, therefore, believed that people should be educated in order to enable them achieve self-fulfillment.

Prescriptive Function

Every nation has its problems, which calls for solution. It is expected that everyone would contribute to the best of his ability. Although philosophy has a lot to contribute, philosophers are sometimes excluded from the decision-making process. This appears to have made the situation worse. For example, before adopting a new educational or social policy in the country, one would expect that philosophers would be included in the planning. Such contributions would benefit all concerned.

Co-coordinating Function

Since it is well known that all other disciplines are generated from philosophy, philosophy cannot be seen as competing with its offspring. In view of the fact that these disciplines have established their knowledge base solidly, philosophy has mapped out for itself other responsibilities. The fact that there exist at present such area as philosophy of science, philosophy of social science, philosophy of law and philosophy of education among others shows the contribution that philosophy still makes to learning. Consequently, the coordinating role of philosophy in articulating the knowledge base of these disciplines should not leave anyone in doubt about the prescriptive function of philosophy.

5.7 RELATIONSHIP BETWEEN PHILOSOPHY AND EDUCATION

Education and philosophy are inseparable. This is explained as:

1. Education and life are interdependent. The aim of education is the all-round development or promotion of life. Likewise philosophy and life are inseparable. It is, therefore, natural that education and philosophy are inseparable. It is aptly remarked that without philosophy, education would be a 'blind effort' and without education, philosophy would be 'cripple'.

2. Philosophy points out the way, and education follows it. Education, thus, becomes the best means for the promotion of philosophy. For the good of life, for the good of the individual and for the good of society, we need direction. This direction is provided by philosophy, which is the mother of all sciences including education. This, however, does not mean that education is a slave of philosophy. The field of education provides a testing ground to test the truth of wisdom or direction provided by philosophy. Without the testing ground of education, philosophers would remain arm-

chair theorists. A constant mutual interaction goes on between the two.

It is stated that when we define education as the modification of behaviour, the direction in which modification is to be carried out is determined by philosophy. Philosophy deals with the end and education with the means.

3. Education and philosophy are two sides of the same coin—life. Sir John Adams said that education is the dynamic side of philosophy. As Ross put it, "Education is the active aspect of philosophical belief, the practical means of realising ideals of life." T.P. Nunn has also said, "Educational aims are correlative to ideals of life." Henderson has expressed similar views, "Educational aims cannot be determined apart from the ends and aims of life itself for educational aims grow out of life's aims. To determine what constitutes worth living has been one of the chief tasks of philosophy."

Gentile feels that "Education without philosophy would mean a failure to understand the precise nature of education."

4. Fichte right rightly observed, "The art of education will never attain complete clearness without philosophy." Dewey said, "Philosophy is the theory of education is its most general phrases. Education is a laboratory in which philosophical directions become concrete and are tested."

5. If education is a set of techniques for imparting knowledge, skills and attitudes, philosophy is the foundation to vitalise these. Philosophy is the foundation and education is the super-structure.

6. Philosophy determines what is worth-living. Education then prepares for that.

Almost all Great Philosophers are Great Educators and Great Educators as Great Philosophers

A close analysis of the concept of education as given by various philosophers and educators will make clear that their views on education are based on their varying concepts of reality, of knowledge, of wisdom and of values. The great philosophers of all times have also been great educators. Most of the educational movements were the outcome of their philosophical beliefs. Views of great thinkers like Socrates, Plato, Aristotle, Comenius, John Locke, Rousseau, Froebel, Dewey, H.G. Wells, Bertrand Russell, A.N. Whitehead and Aldous Huxley, offer an interesting example of the intimate connection between philosophy and education. The ancient sages in India were all educational philosophers. In recent times, this is fully illustrated in the case of Swami Dayananda, Swami Vivekananda, Sri Aurobindo, Rabindranath Tagore, Dr. Radhakrishnan, Mahatma Gandhi, etc.

5.8 CONTRIBUTION OF PHILOSOPHY TO EDUCATION

The contribution of philosophy to education may be taken up under the following heads:

1. Philosophy and Educational Aims
2. Philosophy and Curriculum
3. Philosophy and Textbooks
4. Philosophy and Methods of Teaching
5. Philosophy and the Discipline
6. Philosophy and the Teacher
7. Philosophy and Educational Organisation, Administration and Supervision

1. *Philosophy and Educational Aims*: The aim of education has a reference to the ideals or philosophy of a nation. In independent India, philosophy of life is enshrined in the Preamble of its Constitution. Educational aims, accordingly, draw their inspiration from it. The aims of education in U.S.A. are based on its democratic philosophy. The philosophy of fascism determined the aims of education in Germany during Hitler's time. The philosophy of communism influenced the aims of education in Russia and China.

2. *Philosophy and Curriculum*: The philosophical approach to life is the guiding factor in the determination of the curriculum. Gandhi's scheme of basic education was an expression of his philosophy. He was against the lop-sidedness of the system of education as propounded by Lord Macaulay and was moved by the illiteracy and poverty of the people. His scheme of studies, therefore, emphasised crafts and the environment. He was very keen to make education self-supporting besides developing moral character. The National Policy on Education 1986 lays stress on a Core Curriculum keeping in view the needs of emotional and national integration.

Introduction of self-government in school programme is the outcome of democratic philosophy.

Various philosophies like humanism, idealism, pragmatism and naturalism have influenced curriculum in varying degrees.

3. *Philosophy and Textbooks*: The contents of the textbooks must mirror the philosophy or way of life of the people. In a socialist society textbooks emphasise socialist philosophy. In a state dominated and ruled by religious leaders, textbooks reflect tenets of scriptures. In India, since independence, there has been a great stress on emotional integration and national unity. Accordingly, textbooks are being screened from time to time to ensure that they include only that matter which promoters emotional integration and national unity.

4. *Philosophy and Methods of Teaching*: Every school of philosophy has its own methods of teaching. According to the philosophy of idealism, question-answer method, lecture method and discussion method are the most suitable methods of education. Naturalism recommends learning by doing, learning by self-experience and direct experience. Pragmatic philosophy advocates project method, problem solving method and socialist techniques.

5. *Philosophy and Discipline*: Philosophy has a great bearing on discipline in educational institutions. In a democratic set up, discipline is viewed as inner discipline as well as social discipline based on group work. In the totalitarian state, discipline is regimented and assumes the form of a military discipline, and is based on fear of the teacher and the head. There is little concern for the individuality of the child in a totalitarian type of discipline. The idealists emphasise the impact of impression of the teacher on his students. 'Free discipline' is the slogan of the naturalist.

6. *Philosophy and the Teacher*: A teacher is said to play an important role in shaping and moulding the ideals, habits, manners, tastes and ways of life and above all the character and personality of the students. It is, therefore, very essential that he must have a consistent and sound philosophy in accordance with the philosophy of the nation to which he belongs.

A teacher with fatalistic negative philosophy cannot help in the realisation of such an aim as 'complete living' or 'harmonious development'. A teacher without a democratic philosophy would not be able to develop democratic ideals in his students. There is no doubt that the philosophy of a teacher affects everything with which he is connected—the educand, the aims, the curriculum, the textbooks, the methods of teaching, the discipline and the class management.

Philosophy helps the teacher in the following ways:

It provides a way of life to the teacher.

It provides direction to the teacher.

It provides insight to the teacher to comprehend the problems of education in general.

It guides the teacher to undertake experiments.

It enables the teacher to think constructively and rationally.

It serves as a guide to the teacher to solve disciplinary problems.

7. *Philosophy and Educational Organisation, Administration and Supervision*: Democratic philosophy lays emphasis on the participation of the staff and the students in running some programmes of the educational institutions. Philosophy of communism provides little scope for such involvement and the head decides everything.

6

Idealism

6.1 MEANING OF IDEALISM

Idealism contends that spiritual aspects are the chief aspects of human life. Natural or scientific facets of life are subordinate to spiritual ones. When the emphasis is on the spiritual aspect, it is called idealism or philosophy of idealism. The idealist 'idolise' the mind beyond everything. Idealism exalts human personality.

Idealism in India is as old as the Vedas. The Vedic seers were great idealists. The Upanishads and the *Bhagwad Gita* made a very comprehensive analysis of idealism. In the West, Plato—a Greek philosopher (427-347 B.C.) was a great idealist.

According to *Kathopanishad*, an idealist is one who possess supreme knowledge by concentration of mind.

Brubacher states, "It is the mind that is central in understanding the world."

6.2 CHIEF EXPONENTS OF IDEALISM

1. *Eastern Idealists*: (i) Vedic seers, (ii) The Upanishads and the Gita, (iii) Swami Dayanand, (iv) Swami Vivekananda, (v) Mahatma Gandhi, (vi) Rabindranath Tagore, (vii) Sri Aurobindo.
2. *Western Idealists*: (i) Plato—a Greek philosopher (427-347 B.C.), (ii) Kant—a German philosopher (1724-1804 A.D.), (iii) Froebel—a German philosopher (1772-1852 A.D.), (iv) William T. Haris—an American philosopher (1835-1909 A.D.)

6.3 MAIN PRINCIPLES OF IDEALISM

Following are the main principles of idealism:

1. God is the source of all creation.
2. God is the source of all knowledge.
3. Spirit and mind constitute reality.
4. Material and physical universe is not a complete expression.
5. The universe of ideas and values i.e. spiritual universe is superior to material and physical universe.
6. Spiritual aspect is more important than material aspect.

7. Values are absolute, eternal and unchanging.
8. What is ultimately real, is not the object itself, but the ideal or idea behind it.
9. Man being spiritual is a supreme creation.
10. Man needs some encouragement and light in the face of darkness.
11. They are intrinsic moral and spiritual values.
12. Reality is to be found in man's mind rather than in material nature.
13. Study of man's mind and his nature is more important than the study of material universe.
14. Man has a superior nature and it is expressed in the form of intellectual culture, morality and religion.

6.4 IDEALISM AND VARIOUS ASPECTS OF EDUCATION

1. *Idealism and Aims of Education*: Idealism provides us clear aims of education and this is considered to be the most important contribution of idealism to education.

According to Froebel, "The object of education is the realisation of a faithful, pure, inviolable and hence holy life. Education should lead man to unity with God." Sri Aurobindo in this context has observed, "The central aim of education is the building of the powers of the human mind and spirit."

R.W. Emerson has expressed this view in the following verse.

Not gold but only men can make a people great and strong
Men who for truth and honour's sake stand fast and suffer long.

The aim of education has been very beautifully stated by the University Education Commission in these words, "If we wish to bring about a savage upheaval in our society, a '*Rakshasa Raj*', all that we need to do is to give vocational and technical education and starve the spirit. We will have a member of scientists without conscience."

According to Rusk, "Education must enable mankind to enter into the spiritual realism."

According to idealism, following are the aims of education:

1. Unfolding the Divine in man.
2. Universal education with universal individual.
3. Self-realisation.
4. Transmission of cultural and spiritual heritage.
5. Development of moral values which falls into two categories:
   (i) Duties to self which include industriousness, self-culture etc.
   (ii) Duties to others i.e. respect for and appreciation of the opinion of others, cooperativeness' generosity etc.
6. Development of rational attitude.

While discussing aims of education, it must be kept in view that idealism does not ignore the vocational aim of education. If simply gives it secondary importance.

2. *Curriculum and Idealism*: Idealism stresses three values of 'truth', 'goodness' and 'beauty'. These three values determine three types of human activities—intellectual, moral and aesthetic. Each type of activity is represented by studies or subjects that should form a part of the curriculum. The following arrangement of the curriculum is recommended by idealism.

Value	*Subject/Activity*
1. Truth	1. It is represented by intellectual subjects or activities. This includes subjects like humanities, languages, social sciences and physical sciences.
2. Goodness	2. This includes subjects like ethics, metaphysics and religion etc.
3. Beauty	3. Aesthetic subjects or activities like art and poetry etc. relate to this part of the curriculum.

Ross's scheme for a complete curriculum in the light of idealism is as under:

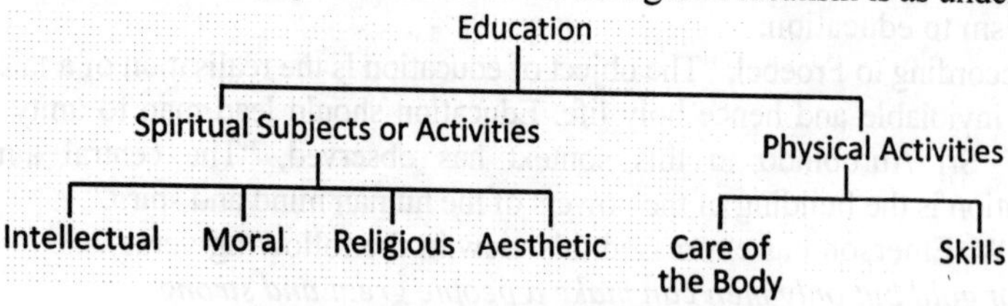

Fig. 6.1: Complete Ideal Curriculum

3. *Idealism and Methods of Teaching*: The idealist suggests the following techniques and methods of teaching:

(i) Narration
(ii) Explanation
(iii) Exposition
(iv) Questioning
(v) Discussion
(vi) Practice and Repetition

4. *Idealism and Discipline*: While 'freedom' is the slogan of the naturalists, 'discipline' is that of idealists. Disciplining the mind and body of the child are the watchwords of the idealists. An idealist attaches great importance to the guidance of the teacher to the child for realising his 'self'. Suggested features of discipline according to idealists are:

(i) Idealism believes in inner discipline.
(ii) Inner discipline can be obtained through guidance as well as restrain—inner as well as outer or external.
(iii) There is need for restricting freedom of the child. A child cannot be given a long rope with which he may hang himself.
(iv) The teacher should win over the child through 'impression' i.e. good personal examples of behaviour and conduct. The child

especially in the plastic period of his early life considers the teacher to be an ideal person to be emulated by the pupils.

(v) Participation in social service activities develops spirit of sacrifice—an important feature of the life of an ideal person.

5. *Idealism and the Teacher*: Teacher assumes an important place of idealism. He is the key figure in the educative process. His personality is the most vital influence on the education of the child. A child is greatly influenced by his conduct, his way of speech, his etiquette etc.

Idealism considers the teacher a friend, philosopher and guide to his pupils. He guides them in such a way as they may attain 'self-realisation'. Character development and value development are the most important concerns of the teacher.

Froechel's metaphor of the 'Kindergarten' perhaps, explains best the role of the teacher in idealism. The school is regarded as a garden, the child as the plant and the teacher as the gardener. The gardener i.e. the teacher tends the little plants (human plants) in his charge carefully and helps them to grow to perfection. The gardener makes all efforts to ensure that the plant attains its finest form in all respects.

The main functions of the teacher are:

1. To understand the pupil thoroughly.
2. To have a deep knowledge of his subject.
3. To inculcate the students an attitude of hard work.
4. To use thought provoking questions and other techniques to encourage his pupils to think for themselves.
5. To develop in the students the habit of self-study.
6. To present high standards of moral behaviour.
7. To influence the pupils with his ideal behaviour and conduct.
8. To inculcate in the students higher values of life.
9. Above all to be a personal friend, guide and philosopher to his students.

6.5 LIMITATIONS AND WEAKNESSES OF IDEALISM IN EDUCATION

1. Undue stress on gaining knowledge is likely to turn educational institutions into 'information mongers' workshops.
2. Under the impact of idealism in education, curriculum is likely to be overloaded.
3. Obsolete knowledge may create hindrance in infusing new spirit in the curriculum.
4. For the classroom teacher, 'mind', 'soul' and spirit have little relevance.
5. The modern scientific view, by and large, does not support the concept of spiritual universe.
6. The idealist in education stresses the imitation of the teacher's model behaviour. Such a model behaviour is quite often not

available in our educational institutions.

7. The present generation prefers to experiment and innovate rather than to imitate.
8. In general, the idealist view in education pays less attention to the present environment dominated by electronic development.

6.6 CONTRIBUTION OF IDEALISM TO EDUCATIONAL THEORY AND PRACTICE

1. The present world is threatened by materialism which ignores higher values of life. Idealism aims to restore man to his proper place.
2. Idealism holds that the past culture must be given its due place in any scheme of educational reconstruction.
3. The present machine and electronic age treats the human being as a machine. Idealism warns against this type of approach.
4. Idealism assigns an important place to the teacher in the educative process.
5. Idealism insists that for the realisation of the 'self', every human being must receive a chance to be educated. Thus the goal of the idealist in this context is universal education.
6. Emphasis of the idealist on personality development has provided a fresh look at human relations in teaching.
7. Idealism provides clear guidelines for determining aims in education, curricular, teacher's role and methods of teaching-learning.

6.7 SUMMING UP

In a world threatened by materialism, the philosophy of idealism provides light and direction to man for restoring his proper place. The need of the hour is to develop higher values among students. This lead must come from leaders—political, religious and all those who occupy high places in different walks of life. They must set good examples. Educational institutions alone cannot develop higher values of life.

7

Naturalism

7.1 MEANING OF NATURALISM

'Return to nature', 'break the chains of society' are the important slogans raised by the naturalists. Following are the important definitions of naturalism which thrown adequate light on the concept of naturalism:

In the words of George Haward, "Naturalism is the exclusion of whatever is spiritual."

Hocking states, "Naturalism considers nature as the whole of reality."

James Wards writes, "Naturalism separates nature from God."

7.2 CHIEF CHARACTERISTICS OF NATURALISM

1. Nature alone is the source of all knowledge.
2. Mind is subordinate to nature.
3. Material world is the real world.
4. There is nothing like 'supernatural'.
5. All values exist in nature.
6. Scientific knowledge is final.
7. Values are created in terms of specific needs.
8. Senses are the gateways of knowledge.
9. In the natural order of things all human-beings are equal.
10. Everything that comes to us from nature is good but it generates in the hands of man.
11. Man creates societies to meet some of his needs.
12. Moral instinct, innate conscience, providence, power of prayer and freedom of will etc. are all illusions.

Types of Naturalism

(1)	(2)	(3)
Biological Naturalism	*Mechanical Naturalism*	*Physical Sciences Naturalism*
This type of naturalism assumes man as a product of evolution.	According to it, man is like a machine.	It lays stress on external nature.

7.3 PROMINENT NATURALIST PHILOSOPHERS

1. Bacon, Francis (1561-1626 A.D.), English philosopher
2. Comenius, John (1529-1670 A.D.), Czechoslovakian philosopher
3. Democritus (460-370 B.C.), Greek philosopher
4. Rousseau, Jean Jacques (1712-1877), French (Swiss born) philosopher
5. Spencer, Herbert (1820-1903 A.D.), English philosopher
6. Tagore, Rabindranath (1861-1941), Indian philosopher

7.4 NATURALISM AND ITS VARIOUS DIMENSIONS IN EDUCATION

1. Principles of Education according to Naturalism

1. Naturalism accords an importance place to the child in the educative process.
2. Naturalism advocates education in accordance with the nature of the child.
3. Naturalism considers natural environment as an important source of education.
4. Naturalism gives an important place to the present life of the child and makes it the basis of education.
5. Naturalism states that adequate freedom should be given to the child in the educative process.
6. Naturalism has an insignificant place for acquiring knowledge from books.

2. Naturalism and Aims of Education

It is generally accepted that naturalism has very little to offer as regards aims of education. Naturalists differ in this respect. However, following aims of education can be deduced from the writings of the naturalist philosophers.

1. Developing the child in accordance with his nature.
2. Sublimating of redirecting and co-ordinating the natural tendencies of the child.
3. Equipping the child for the struggle of existence and ensuring his survival.
4. Enabling the child to live in harmony with his surroundings and environment.
5. Laying stress on the autonomous development of the individuality of the child.

3. Naturalism and Curriculum

Although there are divergent views of the naturalists on curriculum contents, they agree on the following points:

1. Curriculum should cater to the aptitudes, interests and needs of the child.
2. Curriculum should be constructed to meet the needs of the child according to the nature of development at each stage.

Rousseau, the prominent exponent of idealism in education recommended the following curriculum at four stages of the development of the child.

Curriculum Stages for Child Development (Rousseau)

Stage	*Years of Duration*	*Aim*	*Curriculum*
1. Infancy	From birth to 5 years of age	Physical development	Physical education in a natural way. No set curriculum.
2. Childhood	5 to 12 years of age	Providing strength to the child with which he may prepare himself for freedom.	Negative education (Explained below)
3. Boyhood or pre-adolescent period	12 to 15 years	To make the child functionally useful.	Period of intellectual development. Curriculum to include astronomy, science and art. Learning of manual and industrial arts.
4. Adolescence period	15 to 18 years of age develop	To enable the students. Complex social relationships.	1. Study of economics, history, politics and society. 2. Moral education through activities and occupations.
Education of Woman		1. Since woman is made to please the man, her education would be quite different. 2. Preparing her for pleasing the man and for household work..	1. Teaching details of house-keeping. 2. Cooking 3. Cleaning 4. Maintaining accounts 5. Cleanliness 6. Moral education through examples so that she remains chaste.

Characteristics of Curriculum

The chief characteristics of curriculum according to naturalism in general are:

1. Curriculum is based on the nature of the child, his interests etc.
2. It lays stress on the subjects which are helpful in the self-preservation of man.
3. It stresses basic sciences.
4. It gives importance to physical and health sciences.

4. Naturalism and Methods of Teaching

1. *Experience is the Best Teacher*: Rousseau advises, "Give your scholar no verbal lessons; he should be taught by experience."

2. *Observation method*: The child should observe things and discover for himself.
3. *Individualised Instruction*: According to a naturalist, every child's ability to acquire knowledge and to benefit the individual. Hence the method of class teaching is not useful.
4. *Self-Education*: The naturalist advocates that the child is expected to acquire information, knowledge and ideas by himself.
5. *Things rather than Words*: Rousseau says, "Teach by doing whatever you can, and only fall back upon words when doing is out of question."
6. *Social Learning through Participation*: A child acquires social learning when he takes part in the social activities.

5. Naturalism and Discipline

1. *Discipline by Natural Consequences*: The concept of discipline, according to idealists may be expressed in four words, "Discipline by natural consequences". Natural consequences are those experiences which the child receives by following an activity. When the child runs its head against the table, it feels pain. The remembrance of pain makes the child disciplined.
2. *No Punishments*: Rousseau states, "Children should never receive punishment as such, it should always come as the natural consequences of his action." If a child is late for a picnic party, let him learn from this experience of being late.
3. *Full Freedom to the Child*: A naturalist starts with the assumption that the nature of child is essentially good. Therefore, he should be given freedom of expression and development.

6. Naturalism and the Teacher

Naturalists make the following observations regarding the role of the teacher:

1. *Art of Observing*: Rousseau states, "I wish some discreet person would give us a treatise on the art of observing children."
2. *Art of Suggesting*: Rousseau writes, "To know how to suggest is the art of teaching."
3. *Art of Stimulating*: Rousseau says, "The highest function of the teacher consists not so much is imparting knowledge as on stimulating the pupil in its love and pursuit."
4. *Free development of the child*: The teacher should not impose himself on children. He should provide an environment full of freedom.

7. Idealism and the Child

A naturalist accepts the child as a 'hero' or 'star' in the drama of education. Tender regard for the child is very essential in his education.

7.5 NEGATIVE EDUCATION ACCORDING TO ROUSSEAU — A PROMINENT NATURALIST

1. *No Book Learning*: Rousseau said, "I hate books because they are curse to children."

2. *No Habit Formation*: According to Rousseau, habits make children 'slaves'.
3. *No Direct moral Instruction*: "A child should be left free to act and learn what is right or wrong."
4. *No formal discipline*: A child should learn from the "natural consequences of his actions."
5. *No Sticking to Traditional Procedure of Education*: Rousseau said, "Follow the reverse of the current procedure and you will almost do right."
6. *Nature a Great Teacher*: According to Rousseau, the nature of the child is good. Hence, he should have the freedom to learn from nature and natural surroundings.

7.6 LIMITATIONS OF NATURALISM IN EDUCATION

1. *No Clear Cut Goals*: Naturalism does not offer definite aims of education.
2. *Neglect of Books*: There is a very minor place for books. We cannot neglect the treasure of knowledge contained in the pointed materials.
3. *Negligible Importance to Higher Values*: Naturalism by and large, ignores the higher ends in the process of education.
4. *Undue Emphasis on Education through Nature*: It is certain that physical nature alone cannot be considered adequate for providing all education.
5. *Absolute Freedom a Myth*: Absolute freedom does not exist. It never existed. It will never exist in a civilised society. "Child cannot be given the long rope to hang himself."
6. *Very Little Role for the Teacher*: Naturalism minimises the role of the teacher in the educative process. Even in the electronic age, a teacher occupies an important place in the teaching-learning process.
7. *Neglect of Moral and Spiritual Values*: Naturalism ignores the moral and spiritual development of the child.

7.7 CONTRIBUTION OF NATURALISM TO EDUCATION

1. Naturalism has brought to the forefront the importance of the recognition of child in the process of education.
2. Naturalism has very clearly drawn the attention of the educators to study child carefully and provide education accordingly. It advocates that education, should be 'child centred'.
3. Naturalism has stressed that the educative process should be made pleasurable and enjoyable.
4. Naturalism indicates that educational institutions should be set up in natural surroundings.
5. Naturalism brings to light the significance, of progressive methods of teaching like 'learning by doing', 'learning by observing' and 'learning by inductive approach'.
6. Naturalism has given birth to new movements and new types of educational institutions like A.S. Neill's Summer School and Visvabharati.

8

Pragmatism

8.1 MEANING OF PRAGMATISM

Pragmatism is also known as 'Practical Philosophy', 'Worldly-wise Philosophy', 'Utilitarian Philosophy', 'Down to Earth Philosophy' and 'Cash Philosophy' on account of its emphasis on 'utility' aspect.

The word 'pragmatism' is derived from a Greek word '*Pragma*' which means 'to do', 'to make', and to 'accomplish'. Therefore words 'doing', 'making', 'accomplishing' etc. are used while referring to pragmatism. Expressions like 'action', 'practice' and 'activity' have become popular in education in account of pragmatism.

Pragmatism stands between idealism and naturalism.

Chief Promoters of Pragmatism

C.S. Pierce (1839-1914 A.D.) was the first to use the word pragmatism in philosophical thought. Pragmatism, first appeared in 1878 in the essay, '*How to Make Our Ideas Clear*', written by Pierce. Pragmatism was popularised by William James (1842-1910) and John Dewey (1859-1959), both American philosophers.

Origin of Pragmatism

Pragmatism represents the American way of life and thinking. The (Puritans) foreigners who came to U.S.A. from Europe had to face several new problems. They had no readymade solutions of their problems. The application of the well-known ideals of Europe would not serve the purpose. Consequently, they built up a philosophy of life through 'experience'. This philosophy of experience became popular as pragmatism.

8.2 FUNDAMENTAL PRINCIPLES OF PRAGMATISM

1. Experience is the central idea in pragmatism. According to John Dewey, "Truth is made just as health, wealth and strength are made in the course of experience."
2. William James sees no difference between 'pragmatism' and 'practicalism'. Truth is that which works in institutions. It changes with times.

3. There are no absolute values of life.
4. Action is real and ideas are tools.
5. Man is an active being.
6. Man has the ability to solve his problems.
7. Man solves his problems though the logic of experiments and scientific methods.
8. Knowledge is functional and tentative.
9. Utilitarian aspect is supreme.
10. Past has little value.
11. Present and future are more important.
12. Spiritual character of existence has little significance.
13. Pragmatism rejects all types of authoritarianism whether in government or religion or education.

8.3 BROAD FEATURES OF PRAGMATISM IN EDUCATION

1. Educational practices have to be experimental.
2. Values are created through experimentation.
3. Child learns by doing more than by reflection.
4. Education is a continuous process. Education is a constant reorganising or reconstructing of experience.
5. Education should enable the child to learn new techniques to cope with new situations.
6. Curriculum is activity centred.
7. Curriculum is integrated.
8. Moral values cannot be imposed by the elders upon the younger generation.
9. Life situations should be made the basis of education.
10. Education is a social necessity. It is the means by which it renews itself.
11. Suitable environment is needed for the development of the personality of the child.
12. Freedom should be given to the child for the development of his all-round personality.
13. Educational experiments lead to the development of philosophy of education.

A. Pragmatism and Aims of Education

1. There are no pre-conceived aims of education.
2. Aims of education are not final and fixed.
3. Aims of education arise out of situations
4. Education is its own end.
5. Education should enable an individual to adapt to the environment.
6. Education should provide more and more purposeful experience.
7. Dewey lays on emphasis in preparing a socially efficient individual.

B. Pragmatism and Curriculum

Pragmatism points out the following criteria for curriculum construction.

1. *Principle of Utility*: This is the first concern. The school must provide those experiences that are useful to the child. The utility aspect requires direct training for the later stage of the school.
2. *Principle of Child's Natural Instincts*: The curriculum should be based on the natural instincts of the child.
3. *Principle of Graded Curriculum*: The curriculum should take into account the successive stages of child's development.
4. *Principle of Child's Occupations and Activities*: Curriculum attaches limited importance to book learning. Besides the subjects, the curriculum includes purposive, productive and socialised activities.
5. *Principle of Integration*: Subjects are not treated water-light compartments. Subjects are presented as modes of activities. Integration, for the pragmatist is of life, with activity of the learner.
6. *Principle of Social Worth*: A pragmatist also recognises that the subjects and experiences provided to the child must make him socially useful.
7. *Principle of Dynamism*: The pragmatist does not believe in the rigidity of the curriculum. So, the curriculum is not static. Curriculum changes according to the needs of the pupils and the society. The main aim of knowledge i.e. human progress should not be overlooked.

Curriculum includes tools of knowledge as reading, writing, counting, nature study, drawing, handwork, hygiene, physical training, history, geography, science—domestic science for girls and agricultural science for boys. Vocational training is an indispensable part of the curriculum.

C. Pragmatism and Methods of Teaching

1. *Learning by doing*: The pragmatists regard learning as a by-product of activity. This is explained as:

   Child's activities are:

   —Spontaneous activities.

   —Purposeful activities.

   —Socialised activities

   The teacher's job is to keep him alive to:

   —His purposes.

   —His capacities.

   —His limitations.

   So that the child evolves:

   —His own discipline.

   —Makes his own adjustment.

   —And thus realises himself.

2. *Project Method*: William Kilpatric, an ardent follower of Dewey, the most prominent pragmatist, originated the Project Method of Teaching. According to him a project is a whole-hearted, purposeful activity, preceding in a social environment.

The Project Method considers the school, the curriculum and the contents of studies from the point of view of the child. Subjects and activities are integrated round a project which relates to a real situation.

The teacher provides suitable and interesting situations, preferably social ones. Children study many subjects while undertaking the project. For instance, a project on 'know your country' involves several activities and experiences relating to many subjects. Likewise, a project on 'Village Survey' provides lots of information and experiences.

D. Pragmatism and Discipline

The pragmatism holds that discipline should be social through and through. Free, purposeful and co-operative activities organised in the school lead to social discipline. These activities inculcate attitudes of co-operation and consideration. Besides, these keep the students busy in worthwhile tasks. Moral development taken place through such activities. Students develop a sense of self-control.

E. Pragmatism and the Teacher

Pragmatism regards the teacher as a helper and guide. The teacher assumes the role of an 'arranger of experience'. According to Dewey, "The teacher is a guide and director, he steers the boat, but the energy that propels it must come from those who are learning."

8.4 LIMITATIONS OF PRAGMATISM

1. Pragmatism, by and large, ignores eternal values.
2. Pragmatism pays little attention to spiritual values.
3. Pragmatism lays too much emphasis on material things.
4. Pragmatism advocates a utilitarian approach only.
5. Pragmatism provides very insignificant place to cultural values.
6. Pragmatism believes that experience is all in all. It ignores the knowledge accumulated through the ages.
7. Pragmatism does not give due importance to regular and systematic instruction.
8. The entire knowledge and experience needed by the child cannot be obtained through projects.
9. Pragmatism places heavy demands on the teacher.
10. Pragmatism does not indicate fixed educational goals.

8.5 CONTRIBUTION OF PRAGMATISM TO EDUCATION

1. Pragmatism saves the child from the burden of education which is too much centred on books.

2. Pragmatism helps us in realising the value of to-days' life by experiencing it.
3. Pragmatism advises us to have a balanced approach towards the past, present and future. The past may be glorious and rich but it must guide for living a glorious and rich life in the present. Thus, too much emphasis on cultural heritage should not be laid.
4. Pragmatism rightly advocates that the present experiences of the child should not be sacrificed for the future which is very uncertain.
5. Pragmatism contributes to the development of a system which is vocation-centred. In India this aspect remained ignored for a long time.
6. Pragmatism recognises that an individual should be socially efficient and productive. The curriculum duly takes note of it.
7. Another important principle which has been given by the pragmatism in the curriculum is that of integration of knowledge.
8. The pragmatism's contribution to the method of teaching is commendable. Project method can serve several educational tasks.
9. The pragmatic approach is neither teacher-centred, nor examination centred, nor curriculum centred but pupil-centred. Of course, this approach considers the teacher a friend and guide of the child.

9

Humanism: Comparative Study of Idealism, Naturalism and Pragmatism

9.1 MEANING OF HUMANISM

Humanism is a very old philosophy but it emerged as a modern philosophy in the sixteenth century A.D. Scholars and writers during Renaissance in Europe brought to focus the main features of humanism. Humanism is an 'ism' that gives prominence to the human being.

The word humanism is derived from the Latin word 'Homo', meaning human being.

Humanism has been interpreted in the following ways:

1. Humanism is a reasonable balance in life.
2. Humanism takes vivid interests in all sides of life.
3. Humanism is free from religious bigotry.
4. Humanism is responsive to all passions.
5. Humanism regards man or the human being as the centre and measure of all activities.

9.2 PRINCIPLES OF HUMANISM

Following are the main principles of humanism:

1. Man is the maker and master of his own destiny.
2. Man is competent to solve all his problems.
3. Man's happiness lies in this world.
4. Man should be made free in this world for the achievement of his happiness.
5. Humanism believes in the interests and welfare of all human beings.
6. Humanism stands for brotherhood of man.
7. Humanism stands for international friendship.
8. Humanism does not believe in supernaturalism.

9.3 HUMANISM AND MODIFICATION OF HUMAN NATURE

Humanism believes that human nature is flexible. Human nature may have to be reconditioned and reshaped to face the new challenges. Humanism does not believe in the dictum, "You cannot change human nature". This task of reconditioning, reshaping and transforming human nature has to be directed towards the good of the individual and society. Humanism wants to check the egoistic nature of man.

Humanism wants that the life of the human being should be so transformed that welfare of all should become the goal. Humanism states that for the achievement of this goal, an individual may have to renounce some of his desires. He must have strict control over himself in the interest of human happiness on this earth.

9.4 HUMANISM AND DEMOCRACY

Humanism accepts that the growth of the human being must always be seen in the context of social welfare. Humanism believes that democracy has a permanent value and validity for mankind.

9.5 EDUCATIONAL IMPLICATIONS OF HUMANISM

The humanistic approach is based on understanding the needs of the learners. This is the first step towards the fulfilment of learning objectives. The learner is competent to solve his problems provided he is properly guided. A suitable environment has to be created for this. Watchwords of humanism in education are: 'better learner', a 'better human being' and a 'well-adjusted personality'.

Following are the main educational implications of humanism:

1. Betterment of each learner or all learners is the chief concern of education.
2. Learning becomes effective when it is need-based.
3. It aims at increasing the learner's self-direction.
4. Its focus is on learning at a higher level i.e. self-actualisation.
5. It stresses self-discipline and self-control.
6. It points out that education should develop values so that the learners become broad-minded.
7. It advocates co-operation, mutual toleration and social understanding.
8. It points out that the qualities of brotherhood and international understanding must be given their due attention.
9. Teacher is considered as a guide and helper to the students.

9.6 HUMANISM AND CURRICULUM

Following are the chief characteristics of curriculum in humanism:

Due Regard for Ancient Cultures: Educational programmes should foster an admiration and love for ancient cultures. Ancient cultures are important sources for the growth of humanistic values.

Respect for Scholars: The younger generation must be taught to learn to respect the wisdom of scholars as it relates to important human values.

Group Work: Adequate opportunities should be provided to the learners for group work so that they develop an attitude of tolerance.

9.7 COMPARATIVE IMPACT OF IDEALISM, NATURALISM AND PRAGMATISM ON EDUCATIONAL THEORY AND PRACTICE

Idealism	*Naturalism*	*Pragmatism*
1. Basic Philosophical Features		
1. Idealism believes in the existence of God.	Naturalism has no belief in the existence of God.	Pragmatism has some belief in the existence of God.
2. Ultimate reality is spiritual.	Ultimate reality is physical.	Ultimate reality is utility.
3. Universe is God's creation.	Universe is man's creation.	Universe is natural creation.
4. Eternal spiritual values never change.	Values are not eternal.	Values are changeable.
5. Truth, beauty and goodness are eternal values.	There are no such values.	The nature of these values undergoes changes.
6. Spiritual laws are Universal.	Physical and natural laws are Universal.	No law is universal.
2. Aims of Education		
1. Self-realisation aim.	1. Self-expression aim.	1. Social efficiency aim.
2. Spiritual development aim.	2. Autonomous development of the individuality aim.	2. Adjustment with present aim.
3. Character development aim.	3. Adjustment to environment aim.	
3. Curriculum		
1. Emphasis on ethics and humanities.	1. Emphasis on sciences.	1. Stress on utilitarian subjects and vocational subjects.
2. Study of cultural heritage.	2. Curriculum band on the need, ability and aptitude of the individual nature.	2. Life experiences. 3. Integrated curriculum.
4. Methods of Teaching		
1. Lecture method.	1. Direct observation.	1. Learning by doing.
2. Question answer method.	2. Heuristic method.	2. Project method.

5. Discipline

1. Emphasis on regulated freedom.	Uncontrolled freedom.	Social discipline.
2. Self-discipline.	Discipline through natural consequences.	Discipline through co-operative activities.

6. Teacher's Role

1. Important role of the teacher.	Limited role of the teacher.	Teacher as a guide.
2. Importance of teacher's personality.	Very little importance to teacher's personality.	Limited importance.
3. Teacher as an ideal person.	Teacher as an observer.	Teacher as a friend and philosopher.

Summing up: We cannot remain wedded to a particular philosophy. Each philosophy contributes something to educational theory and practice. We must make a balanced and rational use of each type of philosophy according to needs.

10

M.K. Gandhi (1869-1948)

10.1 BRIEF LIFE SKETCH

Mohandas Karamchand Gandhi (Karam Chand was his father's name) is popularly known as 'Gandhiji' out of reverence, '*Bapu*' out of affection, '*Mahatma*' on account of saintly nature and '*Father of the Nation*', for his role in the freedom of India from British rule.

Early Life and Education: Gandhiji was born on October 2, 1869 at Porbander in Gujarat. His father was a Dewan (Chief Administrator and Chief Revenue Officer) of a small state. At school, he was slow, hesitant and shy. He was married to Kasturba at the age of 13. His mother was very pious and he was greatly influenced by her.

Education in England: When 18 years old, he was sent to London to study law where he remained for three years. His mother made him promise that in England, he would not take meat and alcohol and indulge in sex. Gandhiji kept his promise.

Work in South Africa: After returning from England, he started his law practice at Bombay. However, he was not very successful.

In April 1893, he went to South Africa in connection with a civil law case of a firm. In 1893 itself, he was thrown out of a first class compartment in Durban (South Africa) for he was a coloured man. He stayed there for about 20 years. This was a turning point in his life. Gandhiji found that the Indians in South Africa were treated very cruelly and in fact like animals. They had no political rights. Gandhiji took up cases which were not entirely political but touched intimately the life of the people. Gandhiji gave up his legal practice. He completely devoted himself to the service of the people. He put into practice 'Satyagraha' and 'Ahimsa'.

10.2 GANDHIJI'S EDUCATIONAL EXPERIMENTS

1. Gandhiji's philosophy of life including philosophy of education took shape in South Africa. His educational experiences at the Tolstoy Farm at Transwal in South Africa proved very valuable to him in formulating a new system of education suited to the needs of masses. On the Farm, he undertook the responsibility of educating his own sons and other children. The children had to devote 8 hours

a day for vocational training and only 2 hours to book learning. 'Learning by doing' and 'learning by cooperation' became the chief methods of education.

2. Gandhiji came to India in 1914. Thereafter, though he was deeply involved in the freedom struggle. He continued his educational experiments for a short time at Shantiniketan, then at Sabarmati Ashram and finally at Sewagram Ashram established by him. Sewagram Ashram is located 16 km from Wardha. This place has a great significance as Gandhiji not only formulated his scheme of Basic Education but also fought the battle for freedom from here.

10.3 GANDHIJI'S PUBLICATIONS ON EDUCATION

Important publications on education and having hearing on education are:

1. *My Experiments with Truth.*
2. *Basic Education*
3. *Towards Need Education*
4. *True Education*
5. *To the Students*
6. *Task Before Indian Students*
7. *India of My Dreams*
8. *Medium of Instruction*
9. *Tasks for India*

Gandhiji also wrote extensively on education in '*Harijan*'—a paper founded by him.

10.4 PRINCIPAL FEATURES OF GANDHIJI'S PHILOSOPHY OF LIFE

1. *Supreme God*: He said, "God pervades everything. God is life, Truth and Light."
2. *Truth and Ahimsa* (Non-violence), According to Gandhiji, "Truth and Ahimsa are the two sides of a coin. They are interwined and it is practically impossible to separate them." '*Satyagraha*' impliesholding of truth, through love and purity.
3. *Service of Humanity*: Gandhiji observed, "The immediate service of all human beings becomes a necessary part because it is the only way to see Him in his creation."
4. *Self-discipline and Self-purification*—Gandhi always held the high ideals of purity, sacrifice and service.
5. *Righteousness and truth as the highest religion*: Gandhiji was of the firm view that 'true religion and true morality are inseparably bound up with each other'.
6. *Ram Rajya as the Concept of a Society*: He wanted to establish Ram Rajya which he identified with justice, peace, happiness and welfare of all.

10.5 FACTORS THAT INFLUENCED GANDHIJI'S PHILOSOPHY OF LIFE AND PHILOSOPHY OF EDUCATION

Following were the chief influences which had a great effect on Gandhiji's philosophy of life and philosophy of education.

1. *Mother's Influence*: Gandhiji's mother taught him the lessons of simplicity and piety.
2. *Three Great Thinkers*: (i) Rayachand Bhai Patel who taught Gandhiji the first lesson in non-violence.
   (ii) Ruskin, through his book '*Unto the Last*' drew his attention to the principle of dignity of labour.
   (iii) Leo Tolstoy's '*The Kingdom of the God is within you*', greatly influenced his spiritual outlook.
3. *The Phoenix Settlement (South Africa)*: Gandhiji conducted experiments here.
4. *The Tolstoy Farm*: In 1911, Gandhiji started an Ashram in Transwal. It was here that Gandhiji helped children in their all-round development. He taught vocations such as cooking, digging and massage work. The medium of instruction was mother-tongue. English was also taught. Children learnt by doing. Textbooks were not used. No punishment was administered. Creed of non-violence was put into practice in letter and spirit.
5. *The Sabarmati Ashram*: After returning to India in 1914, Gandhiji started the Sabarmati Ashram. A school was attached with the *Ashram* which Gandhiji wanted it to make a model school.
6. *The Sevagram Ashram and the Evolution of Basic Education*: In April 1935, Gandhiji founded the Sevagram, a village with an ideal, near Wardha. Gandhiji had earlier written a few articles on education in '*Harijan*' a paper started by Gandhiji. Here, Gandhiji convened a conference in October 1937 which was attended by the leading educationists of the country. Gandhiji's views on education were considered and a Committee under the Chairmanship of Dr. Zakir Hussain was appointed. The Committee gave a concrete shape and finalised the programme of Basic Education or *Bunyadi Shiksha* or *Nai Talim*. This Scheme is also known as Wardha Scheme.

10.6 GANDHIJI'S VIEWS ON DIFFERENT ASPECTS OF EDUCATION

1. *Concept of Education*: Gandhiji summed up his ideas on education in these words, "By education I mean an all-round drawing out of the best in child and man—body, mind and spirit."
   'All round' implies the harmonious development of the individual. Man is neither mere the gross animal body, nor intellectual and nor the heart and soul alone. A proper and harmonious combination of all these three is required for making the whole man. Any

programme on education which puts exclusive emphasis on one of these aspects of the human personality is against the principle of education.

2. *Objective of Education*: "The ultimate objective of education is not only a balanced and harmonious individual but also a balanced and harmonious society—a just social order in which there is no unnatural dividing line between the havens and have-nots and everybody is assured of a living wage and right to freedom."
3. *Education and Character*: Gandhiji said, "What is education without character and what is character without elementary purity?"
4. *Learning by Earning*: According to Gandhiji, students should learn and side by side earn by doing some work in the school.
5. *Craft Centred Education*: Craft should become the source and centre of learning. Gandhiji suggested crafts like weaving and spinning etc. About spinning Gandhiji said, "Just as we cannot live without eating, so it is impossible for us to attain economic independence and banish pauperism."
6. *Self-sufficient Education*: Education should be imparted in such a way through crafts that their products/manufactured articles by the students should meet some expenditure in running the school.
7. *Dignity of Labour*: Love for work with hands should be developed in the students.
8. *Medium of Instruction*: Mother-tongue should be the medium of instruction. The foreign medium has made our children practically foreigners in our own land.
9. *Freedom but under Discipline*: The highest form of freedom comes through humility and self-control.
10. *Women Education*: Gandhiji advocated same facilities for women as for men and special facilities where necessary.
11. *Ideal Teacher*: According to him a teacher has to be both father and mother to his pupils. He stated, "Woe to the teacher who teaches one thing with the lips and carries another in the heart."

10.7 GANDHIJI AS AN IDEALIST, NATURALIST AND PRAGMATIC EDUCATIONIST

Idealism: Gandhiji's emphasis on truth, non-violence and character development clearly indicates that he was an idealist.

Naturalism: Gandhiji's views of making mother-tongue as the medium of instruction and providing freedom to the child reflect his naturalism.

Pragmatism: Gandhiji had an experimental approach to educational and other issues. He also emphasised learning through real life activities.

10.8 CRITICISM OF GANDHIAN APPROACH TO EDUCATION

1. *Based on Unsound Psychological Foundations*: It ignores cognitive (intellectual) and affective (feelings etc.) aspects of child's development.
2. *Cruelty on the Child*: It is nothing short of cruelty to make the child learn when he ought to be playing and enjoying himself.
3. *Craft as the only Basis of Correlation*: It is absurd to hang all knowledge from the peg of a single craft.
4. *Not Suited to the Age of Industrialisation*: With industrialisation of India, knowledge of science and technology assumes far more importance than the skills in crafts.
5. *Self-sufficiency Aspect not Practicable*: Education imparted in schools cannot meet the expenditure on it. Now the policy is to provide free and compulsory education to all children upto the age of 14 years.

10.9 CONTRIBUTION AND RELEVANCE OF GANDHIJI'S VIEWS ON EDUCATION IN MODERN TIMES

1. The most important point in Gandhi's scheme of education is its emphasis on relating school education to the needs of the society. He wanted to achieve this objective through a system of 'Learning while earning'. He gave an important place to the learning of craft. It will be seen from the curriculum of the present day schools that work experience and socially useful productive work find an important place.
2. His emphasis on education through the mother-tongue is the accepted principle by all thinkers.
3. Gandhiji's stress on inculcating dignity of labour is the need of the hour.
4. There is the dire need to develop elements of spirituality in our life which is dominated by materialism.

11

Rabindranath Tagore (1861-1941)

11.1 BRIEF LIFE SKETCH

Early Life and Education

Tagore was born on May 6, 1861 at Calcutta. The family of Tagore was known for its enlightened and progressive views. He was the youngest son of (Maharshi) Devendranath and grandson of Dwarkanath Tagore. His father was a prominent leader of the Brahmo Samaj. He studied Sanskrit, astronomy and the Upanishadas from his father. He attended the seminary and the Bengal Academy for his other studies. However, his school days were not happy. About his school he wrote, "All of a sudden I found my world vanishing." Regarding school, he uses the words "cage, dreadful and lifeless." It glorified 'mechanical memorising of facts without original thinking'. Hence in disgust, he left the conventional studies.

After private education, in India, he was sent to England in 1877 to study law for becoming a barrister but he soon returned to India. While still young, he started writing for Bengali magazines. He wrote his first verse in English while he was just eight.

Educational Experiments: In 1901, he established his school with five students at Bolpur, about 150 km from Calcutta. This school, later on developed into the famous 'Shantiniketan'—a World University called "Visbabharati".

Bursting into International Fame: Tagore become a world figure when his book '*Gitanjali*' won him the Nobel Prize in 1913. Tagore utilised the entire amount of the award of £8000 for the upkeep of his school.

Renouncing Knighthood (Title of Honour): The British Government made him 'Knight' in 1915 but he was so pained and stirred by the Jallianwalan Bagh Massacre of Amritsar in 1919, that he returned the Insignia of Knighthood. At that time he wrote to the Viceroy of India. "The time has come when badges of honour make our shame glaring in their incongruous context of humiliation, and I, for my part wish to stand, shorn of all special distinctions, by the side of those of my countrymen who, for their so-called insignificance, are liable to suffer a degradation not fit for human beings."

Founding of Educational Institutions: On December 22, 1921, Tagore founded the Visvabharati—an international university to being about understanding between eastern and western cultures.

From 1921 to 1941 i.e. till his death, he laboured hard to develop a number of institutions such as Kala Bhawan, Sangit Bhawan and Cheena Bhawan etc.

Multi-splendoured Personality: Tagore has left his deep impression on several facets of life i.e. artistic, cultural, educational, intellectual, political and social. There is no field of literature which he has not enriched by his contribution. He was a great artist, educationist, a poet, a patriot, a philosopher and social reformer.

11.2 TAGORE'S PHILOSOPHY OF LIFE

1. *Tagore's Humanism*: Tagore observed, "He (God) is there where the tiller is tilling the hard ground and where the pathmaker is breaking stone."
2. *Tagore's Naturalism*: He said, "He lives in a prison house whose walls are alien to him." Tagore loved nature immensely.
3. *Tagore's Spiritualism*: Tagore said, 'I believe in the spiritual unity of man and therefore I ask you to accept this task from me."
4. *Tagore's Individualism*: Tagore believed that every being has the right to shape his life in his own way.
5. *Tagore's Universalism*: He wanted to break down barriers between cultures. He said, "Before we are in a position to stand a comparison with the other cultures of the world, or truly co-operate with them, we must base our own culture on a synthesis of all the different cultures we have."
6. *Tagore's Internationalism*: Tagore advocated synthesis between the East and the West. The Visvabharati at Shantiniketan is an embodiment of his international outlook.

11.3 EDUCATIONAL PHILOSOPHY OF TAGORE

Sources of Information: Apart from his several publications on different aspects, we get valuable information about Tagore's views on education from the following sources relating to education. Essays were written mostly in Bengali.

1. '*Shiksar Herpher*' (Our Education and Its Incongruities)
2. '*Shiksha Samasya*' (The Problem of Education)
3. '*Abaran*' (Culture or Covering)
4. '*Tapovan*' (Forest Colony)
5. '*Dharmashiksha*' (Religious Education)
6. '*Hindu Visvavidyalay*' (Hindu University)
7. '*Strishiksha*' (Women Education)
8. '*Shiksar Bahan*' (The Vehicle of Education)
9. '*My School*'
10. '*Shiksar Milan*' (The Meeting of Cultures)
11. 'A Poet's School'
12. 'Shiksar Vikiran' (Diffusion of Education)
13. '*Ashramer Shiksha*' (Education in Ashram)

14. '*Bodher Sadhana*' (Education of the Feeling)
15. '*Several Convocation Addresses*'

Factors Influencing Tagore's Philosophy of Education: Tagore's philosophy of education was influenced by the following factors:

1. Influence of the Home Environment
2. Influence of the School Environment.
3. Love for Nature.
4. His Extensive Visits.

11.4 TAGORE'S VIEWS ON DIFFERENT ASPECTS OF EDUCATION

On account of the above influences, Tagore may be described as an idealist, a naturalist, a modernist, a pragmatic, a traditionalist and above all a humanist and an internationalist.

1. *Aims of Education*: Following were the other aims of education according to Tagore:

(i) Education should develop a creative mind.
(ii) Education should aim at developing aesthetic sense.
(iii) Education should develop values of simple living.
(iv) Education should prepare an individual for a vocation.
(v) Education should develop international understanding.
(vi) Education should develop freedom of mind.

2. *Curriculum*: Tagore recommended a curriculum for the full man satisfying the spiritual, the creative, the aesthetic and the vocational aims of education. Besides providing for the teaching of ordinary schools, Tagore developed many educational ideas, years ahead of others. Now-a-days educationists talk so much about the educational value of crafts, projects, music, dancing, fine arts, etc. But it is indeed very significant to note that the poet provided for the teaching of most of these subjects from the very beginning in his school at Shantiniketan.

3. *Methods of Teaching*: Tagore strongly criticised the bookish and examination oriented teaching. He stressed movement of the whole body in various learning activities. He followed the activity principle, and advocated constructive and creative activities.

4. *Children as Children*: It is a mistake to judge children by the standards of grown-ups. Adults ignore the natural gifts of children and insist that children must learn through the same process as themselves. This is man's most cruel and most wasteful mistake.

Children's have their subconscious mind which is more active than their conscious intelligence.

5. *Discipline and Freedom*: Living ideals cannot be set into clock-work arrangement. Tagore wrote, "I never said to them. Don't do this, or don't do that... I never punished them."

6. *An Ideal School*: An ideal school is an Ashram where men gather for the highest end of life. Tagore observed. "To give spiritual culture to our boys was my principal object in starting my school at Bolpur."

7. *Role of the Teacher*: In teaching, the guiding spirit should be personal love based on human relations. In education, the teacher is more important than the method.

Tagore pointed out, "A teacher can never truly teach unless he is learning himself. A lamp can never light another lamp unless it continues to burn its own flame."

8. *Religious Education*: Tagore stressed religious education through practice. He wrote, "Teaching of religion can never be imparted in the form of lessons, it is where there is religion in living—where life is simple."

According to Tagore, "Real training consists not in foisting moral teachings but in making religion and morality an integral part of life."

11.5 AN IDEAL SCHOOL

Tagore attempted to make his school at Bolpur as an ideal institution. According to him an ideal school should have the following characteristics:

1. The school should be situated in natural surroundings. There should prevail the atmosphere of nature's own beauty with her varied gifts of colour and dance, flowers and fruits, with the joy of her mornings and the peace of her starry nights.
2. It should cultivate love of nature among the students.
3. It should provide spiritual training to students.
4. It should educate children by providing an environment of freedom.
5. It should impart education in the mother-tongue of the students.
6. It should provide an environment after the fashion of ancient '*tapovans*'—forest schools about which he had read so much in the Upanishads.
7. It should be a community school where there is no distinction of caste and creed.
8. It should teach crafts like sewing, book-binding, weaving, carpentry etc.
9. It should include drawing, art and music as an integral part of the curriculum.
10. It should provide students adequate opportunities for choosing their hobbies and occupations.
11. It should be a self-governing institution—has a dairy farm, post-office, hospital and workshop. Students hold their own courts.
12. It should provide for close personal contact with the teacher. The number of students in classes should be very small.
13. It should have a well-equipped library.
14. It should provide for manual labour.

11.6 EDUCATIONAL INSTITUTES STARTED BY TAGORE

Following institutions were started by him to carry out his experiments in education:

1. Sisu Bhawan (Nursery School)

2. Path Bhawan (School Section—Matriculation Examination)
3. Siksha Bhawan (Higher Secondary)
4. Vidya Bhawan (College of Undergraduate and Post-Graduate Studies and Research)
5. Vinya Bhawan (Teachers' Training College)
6. Kala Bhawan (College of Fine Arts and Crafts)
7. Sangit Bhawan (College of Dance)
8. Sriniketan (Department of Rural Reconstruction)
9. Siksa Satra (Rural High School)
10. Silpa Sadana (College of Industrial Training)
11. Cheena Bhawan (School of Languages, *e.g.*, Chinese, Tibetan etc.)

By and large, all formed part of Visvabharati University.

11.7 VISVABHARATI (WORLD UNIVERSITY)

The word Visvabharati consists of two Sanskrit words. '*Visva*' means world and '*Bharati*' means cultures. Thus Visvabharati would mean world culture. The motto of this university is '*Yatra Visvam bhavati ekamidam*' i.e. where the world meets at one place.

Main Features of Visvabharati: Tagore describes these as:

1. It wants to hold before the world the ideal of the universality of man.
2. The greatest distinction is the direct and immediate emotional contact of pupils with their teachers and with external nature.
3. A speciality of our institution is that it wants to bring up our pupils in inseparable association with nature.
4. It is intended not only to be the intellectual centre of the intellectual life of India but also the centre of her economic life.
5. It is envisaged to be the nucleus of an international university and as one of the means of promoting mutual understanding between the East and the West.

Growth of Visvabharati: In 1863, Rabindranath's Tagore's father founded the Ashram at Bholpur. It was called Shantiniketan (Abode of Peace). It was meant for the seekers of truth. In 1901, Tagore started the experimental school. In 1921, it became the Visvabharati.

11.8 CONTRIBUTION OF TAGORE TO EDUCATION

1. Tagore established a number of educational institutions at Shantiniketan.
2. Tagore founded the Visvabharati.
3. Tagore was a great practitioner. He worked out his ideas and ideals in a constructive way.
4. He drew attention to the listless environment of the traditional school.
5. He tried to synthesise the ancient Indian ideals of education and the western arts and sciences.
6. Tagore pointed out the significance of providing an environment of freedom in the school.

12

Swami Vivekananda (1863-1902)

12.1 BRIEF LIFE SKETCH AND WORK OF SWAMI VIVEKANANDA

Early Life

Swami Vivekananda's original name was Narendranath Dutt. He acquired the new name in 1886 when he took '*sanyasa*'. His father was a lawyer who practised at the Calcutta High Court. As a child he developed great taste for music and was adapt in sports. Under the influence of his mother he made a deep study of the Hindu scriptures. He was provided the best of education. He graduated with honours from Calcutta University.

He had an excellent command over Bengali, English and Sanskrit. He was a voracious reader and had a sharp memory. He could often display a verbatim familiarity with the '*Encyclopaedia Britannica*'. His principal Rev. W.W. Hastie once remarked, "Narendranath is really a genius. I have travelled far and wide but I have never yet come across a lad of his talents and possibilities, even in German Universities, among philosophical students."

Meeting with Shri Ramakrishna—A Turning Point in Life

He was deeply interested in the study of philosophy and religion. He studied eastern and western philosophy and religion. For sometimes he was a classroom teacher also. His search for truth led him to Ramakrishna Paramhansa, at Dakshineswar in 1882. Though not literate, Swami Ramakrishna was an enlightened soul. During the next six years of his association with the master, he had a spiritual transformation and emerged as Swami Vivekananda. He left home and travelled all over India. His wandering left him deeply affected by the despair and poverty of the masses of India.

Swami Vivekanand organised the Ramakrishna Mission in 1886, after the passing away of his master.

Soul-stirring Address at the World Parliament of Religions at Chicago (USA) in 1893: On September 11, 1893, on the opening day of the Parliament, he sat rapt in silent meditation. In the afternoon session he rose to speak. He bowed down to Saraswati, the Devi (goddess of learning) and addressed the audience as, "Sisters and brothers of America". Before he could utter another word, people were so much mesmerised that there was applause for full two minutes. When silence was restored, he began his address. His wisdom coupled with universal message of love and tolerance made him a world teacher.

Message of Spirituality and Social Service: He addressed several meetings in U.S.A., U.K., Sri Lanka and spread the spiritual message.

Swami Vivekananda devoted the rest of his strenuous life in communicating his message of unity and tolerance.

In India, he organised social work also in addition to spiritual pursuits.

12.2 PRINCIPAL FEATURES OF SWAMI VIVEKANANDA'S PHILOSOPHY

1. God resides in every human heart.
2. The best worship of God is service to mankind.
3. Ethics and morality should be the real basis of life.
4. Love and renunciation should permeate the universe.
5. Religion means self-realisation through self-control.

12.3 SWAMI VIVEKANANDA'S PHILOSOPHY OF EDUCATION

Following are the main points of the philosophy of Swami Vivekananda:

1. All knowledge is in the human mind.
2. Education is the manifestation of the perfection already in man.
3. Knowledge is inherent in man. No knowledge comes from outside.
4. Like fire in a piece of flint, knowledge exists in the mind. Man discovers it.
5. The infinite library of the universe is in our mind.

Swami Vivekanand explains this as, "We say Newton discovered gravitation. The falling of an apple gave the suggestion to Newton and then he studied his own mind. He rearranged all the previous links of thought in his mind and discovered a link among them, which we call the law of gravitation."

12.4 SWAMI VIVEKANAND ON VARIOUS ASPECTS OF EDUCATION

I. Aims of Education

1. Development of spirituality in social setting i.e. development of a spirit of fellow-feeling.
2. Development of character which implies doing good to others, courage, fearlessness and strength and above all, strong will-power for a noble cause.
3. Development of balanced human relationships.
4. Development of the attitude of considering work as worship.
5. Development of spirit of service to the poor and the neglected.
6. Development of a spirit of renunciation, giving up pride and ego and acquiring spirit of self-sacrifice.
7. Development of vocational proficiency.
8. Development of physical health.

Character-building as the most important aim of Education: "If you really want to judge the character of man, look not at his great performances, watch a man do his most common actions. Those are indeed the things which will tell you the real character of the great man." 'Intellectuality' is not the highest good. 'Morality' and 'Spirituality' are the things for which we strive'. "Our women are not so learned, but they are more pure". He does not consider a man as educated if he can only pass some examination and deliver good lectures. The basis of all system, social or political, rests upon the goodness of man. No nation is great or good because its Parliament enacts this or that, but because its men are great and good.

II. Role of the Teacher

Vivekananda laid stress on the following qualities that a teacher should have:

1. The first condition is that he should be sinless.
2. The second condition is that he should know the spirit of scriptures.
3. The third condition is the spiritual force of the teacher based on love for the students.
4. The fourth condition is that the teacher should think that he is only helping the child grow. He is the external teacher and he offers the suggestion which arouses the internal teacher i.e. in the mind of the child.

III. Principles of teaching-learning:

Swami Vivekananda emphasised the following:

1. *Self-teaching*—"No one was ever taught by another. Each of us has to teach himself. A child educates itself."
2. *Living Examples of Teacher*—"Words even thoughts, contribute only one-third of the influence in making an impression—the man two-thirds."
3. *Teaching through Positive Suggestions*—"We should give positive ideas. Negative ideas only weaken men. If you speak kind words to them and encourage them, they are bound to improve in time."
4. *Concentration as the only method of education*—"The power of concentration is the only key to the treasure-house of knowledge."
5. *Qualities of the Learner*: "The conditions necessary for the taught are purity, a real thirst after knowledge and perseverance."

IV. Physical and Health Education

"Be strong, my young friends....you will be nearer to Heaven through football than through the study of Gita."

V. Education to be based on Western Science coupled with Vedanta

"Living with the Guru and a similar system of imparting education are needed. What we want is western science coupled with Vedanta—'*Brahmacharya*' as the guiding motto and also '*Shraddha*' (faith) in one's own self."

VI. Education of the masses

Vivekananda gave prime importance to the education of the masses. He asserted, "The chief cause of India's ruin has been the monopolising of the whole education of the land, by dint of pride and royal authority, among a handful of men." He further observed, "If we are to rise again, we shall have to do it in the same way, that is, by spreading education among the masses." He considers that "The great national sin is the neglect of the masses, and that is one of the chief causes of our downfall. No amount of politics would be of any avail until the masses in India are once more well-educated, well-fed, and cared for. They pay for our education, they build our temples, but in return they get kicks. They are practically our slaves, if we want to regenerate India, we must work for them."

VII. Women's education

Vivekananda was an ardent champion of the education of women. He remarked, "Women have many and grave problems but none that cannot be solved by that magic world: education!"

VIII. Secular Education

Vivekanand had great regard for all religions. "Let us take in all that has been in the past, enjoy the light of the present and open every window of the heart for all that will come in the future. Salutation to all the prophets of the past, to all the great ones of the present and to all that are to come in the future."

12.5 CONTRIBUTION OF SWAMI VIVEKANANDA TO EDUCATION: RELEVANCE OF HIS VIEWS TODAY

1. He laid stress on the character development education.
2. He advocated the education of the masses which implies adult education and free and compulsory education regardless of caste, creed or colour. He said, "I consider that the greatest national sin is the neglect of the masses."
3. He revived the spirit of humanism in education.
4. His clarion call to the educated people was, "So long as the millions live in hunger and ignorance, I hold every man a traitor who, having been educated at their expense, pays not the least head to them."
5. He considered the education of women as the chief instrument of national regeneration.
6. He stressed the teaching of western learning.
7. He emphasised social service, "Service to mankind is the highest goal of religion." 'Assimilation' and 'Toleration' were the key points in religion and religious education.
8. Ramakrishna Mission established by Swami Vivekananda is running several educational institutions and spiritual centres, hospitals and dispensaries and doing several types of social work.

Summing up: Swami Vivekananda's views on education may be summed up in his own words, "We want that education by which character is formed, strength of mind is increased, the intellect is expanded and by which one stands on one's own feet."

13

Jiddu Krishnamurthy (1895-1986)

Jiddu Krishnamurthy was born on May 11, 1895 in Madanapalle, a small town in South India. He and his brother were adopted in their youth by Dr Annie Besant, the then President of the Theosophical Society. From then, for nearly sixty years until his death on February 17, 1986, he travelled throughout the world talking to large audiences and to individuals about the need for a radical change in mankind.

Krishnamurthy is regarded globally as one of the greatest thinkers and religious teachers of all time. He did not expound any philosophy or religion, but rather talked of the things that concern all of us in our everyday lives, of the problems of living in modern society with its violence and corruption, of the individual's search for security and happiness, and the need for mankind to free itself from inner burdens of fear, anger, hurt, and sorrow. He explained with great precision the subtle workings of the human mind, and pointed to the need for bringing to our daily life a deeply meditative and spiritual quality.

13.1 EDUCATIONAL PHILOSOPHY OF JIDDU KRISHNAMURTHY

Krishnamurthy's educational philosophy reaches beyond the particularities of culture, and locates it in a universal moral space. 'The function of education,' he said in 1956, 'is not to help the young conform to this rotten society, but to be free of its influences so that they may create a new society, a different world.' In his public talks, Krishnamurthy was a withering critic of social conditions and the ways of life that support those conditions. He often began his talks with comments on the state of the world, followed by a call for change. He traced violence, wars and sorrow back to pre-historic times, as depicted symbolically in art. Then he sketched a way of life that might be possible if individuals would change their lives in certain fundamental ways. A typical description of Krishnamurthy's good society is one 'without violence, without the contradictions of various beliefs, dogmas, rituals, gods, without national and economic divisions.' 'A good society is not possible,' he concluded, 'without good human beings'.

The role of education in any society has been to transmit its culture: rituals, knowledge and values, to future generations and, in the process, to perpetuate traditions. Both primitive societies and traditional ones evolve methods for educating their young in a variety of ways: piety to their gods, reverence for their great men, imitation of heroic role models, implanting rational principles and rules for good government – these are considered well-trodden paths to the good life. The knowledge that educational institutions have sought to transmit is, in some sense, embedded in the larger social fabric.

13.2 AIMS OF EDUCATION ACCORDING TO JIDDU KRISHNAMURTHY

For Krishnamurthy, education is: (i) Educating the whole person; (ii) Educating the person as a whole (not as an assemblage of parts); and (iii) Educating the person within a whole (As part of society, humanity, nature, etc.). For him education is about preparation for the whole life and not preparation for part of life (like work).

Jiddu Krishnamurthy, like Rabindranath Tagore, Mahatma Gandhi, Swami Vivekanand and others founded his own educational institutions to put into practice what he preached. In his educational institutions, he insisted that children must be educated rightly in order to make them religious human beings, of course, according to his interpretation of religiousness. He wanted these centers to be the places of learning the ways of life, which is not based on pleasures, on self-centered activities instead on the understanding of correct action, on the depth of relationships and on the sacredness of a religious life. These places should be meant for only the enlightened ones. Education should awaken the capacity to be self-aware and not merely, indulge in gratifying self-expression. The right kind of education is not concerned with any ideology, however much it offers to future Utopia. It is not based on any system, however carefully thought out, nor is it a means of conditioning the individual in some special manner.

Education in the true sense, is of helping the individual to be mature and free, to flower greatly in love and goodness. That is what we should be interested in, and not in shaping the child according to some idealistic pattern. According to this great teacher, the main aim of education is to enable the child to develop mentally in such a way that he should know himself. Education should help one to feel freedom of mind and fearlessness. For Jiddu Krishnamurthy, the intentions of education must be the inner transformation and liberation of the human being and, from that, society would be transformed. Education is intended to assist people to become truly religious. These intentions must not be just pleasant sounding ideals to which one pays lip service, and they are not to be arrived at by their opposites. And the religious intentions are not for some eventual goal, but for life in educational centers from moment to moment. The function of education is to help us from childhood not to imitate anybody, but to be ourselves all the time. So freedom lies...in understanding what we are from moment to moment. We are not [normally] educated for this; our education encourages us to become something or the other.

To understand life is to understand ourselves, and that is both the beginning and the end of education. Krishnamurthy felt that not only was a person's nature and deepest aspects to be uncovered, but each person also has a unique vocation that needs to be discovered; what he/she really loves to do has to be found and pursued, and to do anything else is a deprivation of the worst kind, especially if such deprivation is in order to pursue success or other such cultural aspirations. The discovery of the natural vocation for an individual student and the student's understanding what he really loves to do may not fit into the plans of the parents or society, but it is an important part of understanding oneself and, consequently, of education.

Modern education is making us into thoughtless entities; it does very little towards helping us to find our individual vocation. To find out what you really love to do is one of the most difficult things. That is part of education. Right education is to help you to find out for yourself what you really, with all your heart, love to do. It does not matter what it is, whether it is to cook, or to be a gardener, but is something in which you have put your mind, your heart.

13.3 SHORTCOMINGS OF THE PREVAILING SYSTEM OF EDUCATION

Krishnamurthy observed the following shortcomings of the Indian education:

The conventional education:

- Makes independent thinking extremely difficult.
- Strangulates spontaneity.
- Leads to dull and lackluster mind.
- Develops fear in the mind to deviate from established standards even if they are legitimate.
- Fails to enable us to understand the higher and wider significance of life.
- Fails to integrate thoughts and feelings.
- Is lopsided and doesn't provide overall growth of the individual.
- Trains us only to seek personal gains and security and fight for ourselves.
- Considers examinations and degrees as criteria for intelligence.
- Merely train the mind to be cunning and avoid vital human issues.
- Helps in making us subservient, mechanical and thoughtless.
- Though it awakens intellectually, leaves us incompetent and uncreative.

13.4 CHARACTERISTICS OF INTEGRAL LEARNING

According to Krishnamurthy, integral education enables a learner for the following:

Development of Capacities to Face Challenges: If the individual is to grapple with life's problems, intricacies, mysteries, and sudden demands, he must be free from theories and particular patterns of thoughts.

Development of Self Knowledge: Education should help an individual discover the true values which come with unbiased investigation and self-expression becomes self-assertion with all its aggressive and ambitions conflicts. To Krishnamurthy the individual is of first importance; not the system, and as long as the individual does not understand the total process of himself, no system can bring order and peace to the world. Understanding comes only through self-knowledge which is awareness of one's total psychological process. Education in the true sense is the understanding of oneself for it is within each one of us that the whole of existence is gathered.

Integrated Experience: Krishnamurthy says "the right kind of education which encourages the language of technique should help man to experience the integral process of life which is of greater importance. It is this experiencing that will put capacity and technique in their right place".

Freedom from Readymade Ideas: According to Jiddu Krishnamurthy, ideas have no place in education for they prevent the comprehension of the present and escaping into the future cannot make one aware of what is to be after an idea indicates sluggishness of mind and a desire to avoid the present. Pursuit of a readymade utopia is denial of the freedom and integration of the individual. What we need is not an idealistic entity or mechanical minds but integrated human beings who are intelligent and free.

Development of Free and Mature Human Beings: To Jiddu Krishnamurthy, the right kind of education is free from ideology and conditioning. Education in true sense should help the individual to be free and mature and to blossom in love and goodness. The conditioning of the child's mind to fit a particular ideology whether political or religious breed's enmity between man and man will not help to bring about brotherhood and change in the society. The Indian scenario gives ample examples of lack of brotherhood understanding and resistance.

Re-education: Right education comes with transformation of ourselves. We must learn to be compassionate, to be content with little and to seek the supreme for, only then can there be the true salvation of mankind.

Development of Right Understanding of Environment: We must realise the fact that we are not conditioned by the environment, but we are the environment. We never see that we are the total environment because there are several entities in us, all revolving round the 'me', the self. The self is made of these entities, which are merely desires in various forms. From this conglomeration of desires arises the central figure, the thinker, the will of the 'me' and the 'mine'. A division, is thus, established between the 'self' and the 'non-self'; between the 'me' and the environment i.e. the society. This separation is the beginning of conflict: inward and outward.

Development of Wisdom and not Acquiring Knowledge: In our desire to acquire more knowledge, we are losing love, feeling for beauty and sensitivity to cruelty. When we become more and more specialised, we are becoming less and less integrated. Wisdom cannot be replaced by knowledge and no amount of explanation or accumulation of facts will free man from suffering. Our education is making us more and more shallow and is not helping us to overcome the deeper meanings of our being and our lives are becoming increasingly meaningless, disharmonious and empty.

Knowledge of facts though ever increasing is limited by its very nature, whereas wisdom is infinite. It includes knowledge and the way of action. What we normally do is holding a branch; assume it is the whole tree. Through the knowledge of the past, we can never realise the joy of the whole. We are like the blind men who tried to describe the elephant after feeling different parts of the elephant. Intellect alone can never give a holistic view because it is only a segment of the whole.

Development of Love towards Others: Only true love and right thinking will bring about revolution within oneself. But it cannot be achieved through pursuit of the ideal of love. What can be done is to keep ourselves free from hatred, greed, exploitation, envy and ego.

Development of Right Relationship: Education should help an individual to cultivate right relationship between individuals and society and this is possible only if he understands his own psychological process. Intelligence lies in understanding oneself and going above and beyond oneself.

Development of Freedom and Integration: To educate a child is to help him to understand freedom and integration. To have freedom, there must be order and order is achieved only through virtue. Integration is achieved through simplicity- simplicity in both our inward life and outward needs.

Development of Creative Intelligence: The spirit of constant inquiry and the feeling of discomfort in the existing system can bring forth creative intelligence. To keep this spirit alive is cumbersome task. Most people do not want their children to have this kind of intelligence, the reason being the uncomfortability they have to face when the established values are questioned.

Development of International Understanding: As long as the glaring disparities like rich and poor, exploiters and exploited, powerful and powerless exist in our society and divisions like nationality, religion, caste, colour and various dividing loyalties prevail, it is not possible to have brotherhood among men. If we are to change radically our present human relationship, our only and immediate task is to transform ourselves through self-knowledge. Thus we come back to the central point which is 'oneself'. We normally dodge this point and instead of owning up the responsibility, put the government, religious and ideologies responsible. The government is what we are. The religious and ideologies are but projection of us. Until we change ourselves fundamentally, there can neither be right education nor a peaceful world.

Freedom from Ideology: Jiddu Krishnamurthy says conditioning of the child's mind to fit a particular ideology, whether political or religious breed's enmity between man and man. In a competitive society we cannot have brotherhood.

Freedom and Discipline: It is only in individual freedom that love and goodness can blossom. Only the right kind of education offers this freedom. One of the dangers of freedom is that this system becomes important than the human beings. Here, discipline becomes a substitute for love. It is because our hearts are empty that we cling to discipline. Freedom can never be achieved through discipline. Freedom is not a goal or an end to be achieved. Freedom is at the beginning and not at the end. A sincere teacher will protect and help the children towards the right kind of freedom. For this, he himself should be free from ideologies and dogmas.

Rewards and Punishments: Sensitivity can never be awakened through compulsion. Compulsion breeds antagonism and fear. Reward and punishment in any form only make the mind subservient and dull. Discipline may be an effective way to control a child, but it doesn't help him to understand the problems in living. If a child persists on disorderliness or is unreasonably mischievous, the educator should inquire into the cause which may be found in wrong diet, lack of rest, family wrangles or some hidden fear.

Spiritual Training and not Religious Education: To him dogmas, mysteries and rituals are not conducive to spiritual life. Religious education in the true sense is to encourage the child to understand his own relationship to people, things and to nature. There is no existence without relationships. It is rather impossible to explain this to a child. But the educator and the parents can grasp its significance and the meaning of spirituality and convey the same to the child through their attitude, conduct and speech. There is hope for a better world only if the youth have the spirit of inquiry and the urge to search out the truth of all things.

13.5 METHODS OF TEACHING ACCORDING TO KRISHNAMURTHY

According to J. Krishnamurthy:

- We should not teach the student 'what to think' and 'how to think'. Allow him freedom to think for himself.
- Study the child thoroughly and employ such methods that suit him best.
- The student should be treated as an equal partner.
- Problem solving and explorative methods should be encouraged. Repetition encourages the mind of the child to be sluggish.

13.6 ROLE OF TEACHER ACCORDING TO JIDDU KRISHNAMURTHY

Understanding the Child

According to Krishnamurthy, "*The right kind of education consists in understanding the child as he is without imposing up on him an ideal of what we think he should be. Ideals are an actual hindrance to our understanding of the child and to the child's own understanding of himself.*"

The right kind of a teacher doesn't depend on a particular method. He will study each pupil closely. He is fully aware of the fact that the pupils are living beings who are impressionable, volatile, sensitive, affectionate and often timid. He knows that he should have a lot of patience and love to deal with them. The absence of these qualities makes a teacher mechanical in his attitude and shirks away the demands of the profession.

Keen Observer

The best way for a teacher to understand a child is to observe him at play, work, and at different moods. The teacher should not be tempted to project upon the child his prejudices, hopes and fears. The ideal teacher will desist from moulding him to fit his idiosyncrasies, prejudices and ideas which gratify him.

Integrated Educator

If a lamp doesn't burn itself, it cannot light other lamps. If the teacher himself/herself is not an integrated personality, we cannot expect him to help the children become integrated personalities.

13.7 THE QUALITIES OF A TRUE TEACHER ACCORDING TO JIDDU KRISHNAMURTHY

According to Krishnamurthy, a true teacher is not simply a giver of information, but is the one who shows the way to wisdom and truth. Truth is more important than the teacher himself. The search for truth is religion. Truth is of no country and of any creed. It is not to be found in any temple or church or mosque. Without the search for the truth, the society will decay. To create a new society each one of us has to be a true teacher. This means that we have to be both the pupil and the master.

If a new social order is to be established, we need teachers who do not work merely to earn a salary. To regard education as a means of livelihood is to exploit the children for one's own advantage. A true teacher is not a subservient to politicians, not bound by the ideals and beliefs of a country, and not a power monger or after positions. He is inwardly rich and above the compulsions of society.

There can be no real hierarchy between the staff and students. There are, of course, differences between staff and students in their responsibilities and experience but in all that is most important in education: the staff and the students, are really in the same boat. Staff members may know more about academic subjects, or gardening, or administration and therefore, have a certain authority in those areas but these are not the central concerns of education. In the central concerns of education which is to do with inner liberation, both the students and the teachers are learners and therefore equal, and this is untouched by functional authority.

According to Krishnamurthy, a good teacher must possess the following qualities:

Self-control as to the Mind: It means control of temper, so that we may feel no anger or impatience; of the mind itself, so that the thought may always be calm and unruffled. The calm mind also means courage and steadiness so that we may face the trials and difficulties of the Path without fear. This will help us to make light of the troubles which come into everyone's life, and avoid the incessant worry over little things. The Master teaches that it does not matter in the least what happens to a man from the outside; sorrows, troubles, sicknesses, losses - all these must be as nothing to him, and must not be allowed to affect the calmness of his mind. They are the result of past actions, and when they come, we must bear them cheerfully, remembering that all evil is transitory, and that our duty is to remain always joyous and serene. 'Think of what you are doing now, rather than the past or future'. Never allow us to feel sad or depressed. Depression is wrong because it infects others and makes their lives harder. Therefore, if ever it comes to us, we must control our thought and we must not let it wander. One must hold back one's mind from pride, for pride comes only from ignorance. The man who does not know thinks that he is great; the wise man knows that only God is great, and that all good work is done by God alone.

Self-control in Action: If your thought is what it should be, you will have little trouble with your action. Yet, remember that to be useful to mankind, thought must result in action. There must be no laziness, but constant activity in good work. Leave every man to do his own work in his own way; be always ready to offer help if need be, but never interfere in others' work. For many people the most difficult thing in the world to learn is to mind their own business; but that is exactly what we must do. Because we try to take up higher work, we must not forget our ordinary duties, for until they are done we are not free for other services.

Tolerance: It is necessary to feel perfect tolerance for all, and a hearty interest in the beliefs of those of another religion, just as much as one's own. But in order to gain this perfect tolerance, one must first be free from bigotry and superstition. We must learn that no ceremonies are necessary. Yet, we must not condemn others who still cling to ceremonies. Let them do as they will; only they must not try to force upon us that which we have outgrown. Make allowance for everything: be kinds towards everything. Now that our eyes are opened, some of our old beliefs, our old ceremonies, may seem to us absurd; perhaps, indeed, they really are so. Yet respect them for the sake of those good souls to whom they are still important. They have their place, they have their use; they are like those double lines which guided us as a child to write straight and evenly, until we learnt to write far better and freely without them. There was a time when we needed them; but now that time is past.

A great Teacher once wrote: 'When I was a child I spoke as a child, I understood as a child, I thought as a child; but when I became a man I put away childish things.' Yet he who has forgotten his childhood and lost sympathy with the children is not the man who can teach them or help them. So look kindly, gently, tolerantly upon all; but upon all alike, Buddhist or Hindu; Jain or Jew; Christian or Mohammedan.

Cheerfulness: 'You must bear your karma cheerfully, whatever it may be, taking it as an honour that suffering comes to you. However hard it is, be thankful that it is no worse. Remember that you are of but little use to the Master until your evil karma is worked out, and you are free. Yet another point, you must give up all feeling of possession. Karma may take from you the things which you like best - even people whom you love most. Even then you must be cheerful - ready to part with anything and everything. Often the Master needs to pour out His strength upon others through His servant; He cannot do that if the servant yields to depression. So cheerfulness must be the rule.

One-pointed Action: The one thing that we must set before us is to do the Master's work. Yet nothing else can come in our way, for all helpful unselfish work is the Master's work. And we must give all our attention to each piece as we do it, so that it may be our very best. That same Teacher also wrote: 'Whatsoever ye do, do it heartily and with all might as to the Lord, and not unto men.' One-pointed action means, that nothing shall ever turn you, even for a moment, from the Path upon which you have entered. No temptations, no worldly pleasures, no worldly affections even, must ever draw you aside. For you must become one with the Path; it must be so much part of your nature that you follow it without needing to think of it.

Confidence: Unless there is perfect trust there cannot be the perfect flow of love and power. We must trust ourselves. If we say we know ourselves too well then we do not know ourselves; we know only the weak outer husk. We are a spark of God's own fire, and because of that there is nothing that we cannot do if we will. Say to yourself: 'I can do this thing, and I will.' Our will must be like tempered steel, if we should tread the Path.

13.8 JIDDU KRISHNAMURTHY'S CONCEPT OF AN IDEAL SCHOOL

According to Krishnamurthy, an ideal school should have limited number of students because mass instruction cannot help develop integrated personality. The school will have teachers who are dedicated, thoughtful and alert. The school takes interest in a careful study to understand the child of his potentials and limitations.

The ideal school is maintained through spirit of self-sacrifice. The school of his vision functions without the influence of any ideology. In his school, there is an atmosphere of collective responsibilities. There is sincere co-operation among all the teachers. A student council is formed to discuss all matters relating to the well-being of the whole group. The school has an atmosphere where the students can discover what is and what he is interested in. There is a provision for proper guidance for all. An atmosphere of confidence and co-operation prevails in the school.

13.9 KRISHNAMURTHY'S CONTRIBUTION TO EDUCATION

Education was always close to Krishnamurthy's heart. He established nearly a dozen co-educational schools in India and abroad to translate his ideas into practice. Ten percent of the seats in these institutions were reserved for non-paying pupils. He used to visit them every year for discussion with the students and teachers. Although the ordinary curriculum was followed in these schools, his main objective in starting these schools was to provide children adequate opportunities and freedom to grow up without any of the national, racial class and cultural prejudice that build barriers between one human being and another and give rise to violence. Krishnamurthy's conception of methods of teaching, school organisation and the role of a teacher is truly progressive of education. His emphasis on the development of an integrated personality through integral approach to education is highly commended by almost all thinkers.

14

Gijubhai Badheka (1885 -1939)

14.1 LIFE SKETCH OF GIJUBHAI BADHEKA

Girijashanker Badheka, generally known as Gijubhai, the most outstanding personality in the field of pre-primary education, was born on 15 November 1885 at Chittal village in Gujarat. He had his early education at a primary school at Vala and later passed the Matriculation from Bhavnagar.

He joined the Shamlals College but had to leave his studies incomplete and go to East Africa in 1907 to earn a livelihood. On his return in 1910, he studied law in Mumbai. He started practice in 1911 as a District Pleader and in 1912, he enrolled himself is High Court Pleader.

Gijubhai's maternal uncle Hargovind Pandya had a great influence in moulding his mind and character. Another strong influence was that of S. P. Stevens, a solicitor for whom Gijubhai worked in East Africa, who taught him self-help and reliance.

Solicitude for the education of his first son, Narendrabhai (February 1913), led Gijubhai to see the child education classes conducted under the guidance of Motibhai Amin at Vaso, Gujarat, where he was presented a Gujrati book describing the Montessori method of education. That first attracted him to organize child education on similar lines. In 1915 he assisted in drafting the construction of the Dakshinamurti, then started as a hostel at Bhavnager. In 1916 he left legal practice and joined the Dakashinamurti as Assistant Superintendent. He drew the attention of the Superintendent, Nanabhai Bhatt to the fact that the boarders had to study in old fashioned schools.

To remove this anomaly the Dakshinamurti was converted into a teaching institution with Gijubhai as the Acharya (Principal). Simultaneously Gijubhai trained his son according to the Montessori system. This convinced him about the need to the begin at the very beginning, and the Dakshinamurti Balmandir, a pre-primary school, came into being August 1920. Gijubhai's contribution was evolution of a system of child education suitable to Indian environment, training teachers and creation of suitable literature for children, teachers and parents. Gijubhai's system liberally borrowed from the educational philosophies of Montessori, Frobell, Dalton and others and oriented the admixture to fit Indian requirements. Freedom and love was the twin principles around which the system revolved. With the introduction of equipment for sensory development, coupled with the use of music, dance, travel, story-telling and play-ground as instantly acquired popularity with children and parents.

In 1925 the first Pre-Primary Teachers Training College (Adhyapak Mandir) was started at Dakshinamurti to meet the need for qualified teachers. Gijubhai also turned his attention to children's literature and wrote simple short stories, nursery rhymes and tales of travel and adventure. He produced more than 100 works which still retain their importance and many of them have been rendered into several other Indian languages.

In 1925 Gijubhai, along with Sm. Taraben Modak, started editing a Gujrati monthly, the Shikshan Patrika. His frank and fearless criticism of the existing methods of education created a sensation in Gujrat. For the propagation of the new system of child education among the masses, conferences wee organized in 1925 at Bhavnagar and in 1928 at Ahmedabad.

Gijubhai was partly responsible for the entry of Harijans into the Dakshinamurti. He also assisted in making arrangements for the farmer families who were abandoning their homes during the Bardoli Satyagraha. He initiated the concept of the 'Vanarsena', a battalion of children satyagrahis who made life impossible for the Government officials in the 1930 Movement. Under Gijubhai, Nanabhai and Harbhai, the Dakshinamurti, located in the territory of sympathetic princes, came to be regarded as the training-centre for dedicated freedom-fighters. Gijubhai also conducted Adult Education Campaign in 1930.

In 1936 Gijubhai left the Dakshinamurti due to a difference of opinion and started the Adhyapak Mandir at Rajkot. Constant overwork had ruined his health, and he died on 23 June 1939. Proverbial affection for the children earned him the title 'Maochhali Ma' meaning mother with whiskers.

14.2 METAPHYSICS OF GIJUBHAI'S PHILOSOPHY

Gijubhai was a devotee to Lord Shiva. He believed that God is the creator of his universe and He is its destroyer too. He considered man as the noblest creation of God and said that the ultimate aim of human life is attainment of God, which can be attained by following religion and morality and devotion to God.

14.3 EPISTEMOLOGY AND LOGIC OF GIJUBHAI'S PHILOSOPHY

Gijubhai had taken birth during Indian renaissance period. It was a time when superstitions were being eliminated and man was coming to know the true knowledge of the material world. Gijubhai was influenced by the attributes of his family on the one hand and that of English education on the other. He considered both types of physical and spiritual knowledge as necessary and said that physical knowledge can be attained through external senses and the knowledge of spirituality can be attained by inner-self.

14.4 AXILOGY AND ETHICS OF GIJUBHAI'S PHILOSOPHY

Gijubhai considered religion and morality as the basis of human life. In his view, every person should follow truth, non-violence and honesty and should practice the feelings of love, affection, mercy, kindness and well-being for all beings. He did not consider pa person devoid of morality as a man. Our contrary was under foreign rule at that time. We had recognized the significance of national spirit. Gijubhai expected every person to be devoted to his country.

14.5 REAL EDUCATION

His works Divaswapna, Mata Pita Se, and others solidifies his thoughts on Education that what does he expect from us as he takes us towards to the real nature of education he has been demanding. His works reminds us of not only goodness of the child, nature of real learning but also critical role and responsibility of adults as parents and teachers to educate the child. His experiment of teaching children in meaningful manner begins with the conflict between theory and practice. He wishes to have the 'first-hand experience' of the classroom.

Real purpose of education that teacher should understand is that children should love their school and teachers. If the children want to come to the school since they are treated with respect and there are enough meaningful learning opportunities, he feels no children would deny coming to the school. Gijubhai cites several of useful learning activities like story telling, drama, games and paper folding to name a few that could serve many objectives of teaching-learning at primary level and make it relevant for children. However, teacher's intuition to link all these methods to curriculum is the real challenge and must. Real learning is also learning where children learn by doing and hence are independent with their learning and do not depend on textbook or teacher as source of information alone. In words of Gijubhai in Divaswapna what he thinks games are "*Games are real education. Great powers are born on the playground.*"

Games means character building.

His ideas on imparting value education to children as against religious indoctrination could be observed in his words "*....we should try to live religion. Parents must try and teachers must try. We could tell children stories from the Puranas, and the Upanishadas, whenever there is a reference to these in their textbooks. Let us tell them stories of saints just as we tell them stories of historical personages. ... .let us not make our children memorise and recite holy verses! Let us not teach religious dogmas and scriptures and the like in the name of moral instruction.*"

This way he tries to argue for meaningful education for children in different areas-History, Language or preparing for exams or school function. He argues that underlying assumptions of methods we follow have flaws hence a need to re-look at it. This will make alternative methods or use of the same method in more effective and correct manner. He believes that for any topic teacher should figure out the underlying concept and then help children identify that through activities.

14.6 EXPERIMENTATION – KEY TO CHANGE

He put a firm faith in alternatives he wishes to try with children and make change possible. We as teachers have stopped to argue for changes and alternatives on arguments say, these are not possible or too idealistic or on several other similar arguments. Gijubhai makes it possible by saying that 'experimentation' is the key to bring the change. A teacher with an untiring spirit to learn, to question the existing system, methods and even failure of individual teacher or student, can try several things that will make 'real' learning takes place and which is not only for exams and some outward reward alone. However, outward rewards of praise, applause and good marks are also achieved by him in his experiment of education.

14.7 PHILOSOPHICAL BASE OF GIJUBHAI

Gijubhai had an intense love for children. His philosophy is based on the following observations made by him:

1. Heaven is in the happiness of the child
2. Heaven is in the health of the child.
3. Heaven is in the pleasure of the child.
4. Heaven is in the playful innocence of the child.
5. Heaven is in the songs and humming of the child.

Gijubhai further said: "*A child is a complete person who has intellect, emotions mind and understanding has strengths and weaknesses-and has likes and dislikes... let us understand the emotions of the child*".

14.8 EDUCATIONAL PRINCIPLES OF GIJUBHAI BADHEKA (ESSENCE OF BAL MANDIR)

The word Mandir has specific connotation of child worship. Gijubhai coined the Slogan Baladev Bhava meaning worship of the child. The following are the educational principles of Gijubhai Badheka:

1. Education should be child/learner-centred.
2. Child's sanctity should be kept intact.
3. Healthy environment should be provided to the learner.
4. There should be maximum involvement of the child in the teaching learning process.
5. Child should learn in an environment which is full of love and understanding of the child.
6. Child should learn by 'living'.
7. Child should learn by 'doing'.

14.9 ENVIRONMENT OF THE BAL MANDIR (CHILDREN'S SCHOOL OR CHILDREN'S TEMPLE OR CHILDREN'S WORLD)

Bal Mandir in the real sense provided an environment which was very healthful and playful. 1t was full of happiness for the child. It provided interesting songs. It gave maximum freedom to the child to develop his potential. The teachers showed real concern for the development of the child.

Following were the chief characteristics of the Bal Mandir of Dakshinamurti School of Bhavnagar in Gujarat. Other schools established by him and his associates also made all possible efforts to follow this.

Mutual Understanding and Cooperation: Here in the school a 'world' is created where children learn from each other. Older children help the smaller ones to climb up the stairs; fill their own cup with water; find their rickshaws while remembering lines of songs and answers or riddles. Children also spend nights here-so that they can together see and understand the sunset and rise, the moon and stars in the sky and also peel potatoes for the collective dinner. The overnight stay of tiny tots might cause anxiety to parents who drop in to see their children, but the latter are happy to be on their own.

Locally made Inexpensive Learning Material: Initially, he implemented the use of tools and methods envisaged by Montessori, but later moved away into thinking of ways that were more inexpensive and he used material which was easily available locally.

Sharing Activity with Children: As he was a man who could play with toys, children could overcome their fear of a strange adult and play with him. He could also tell stories, not only of kings and queens, but of animals, plants and naughty children-and the stories invariably ended in small plays, in which he also acted. Mian Tuski and a King in the Rat's Tale are roles which his contemporaries recollect with glee and amusement.

Understanding Teacher: To be a good teacher one must listen carefully to what a child has to say-and observe him (her) attentively-but without intruding on the child's effort to do things all by herself (himself).

Observing Nature: There was also emphasis on observing nature and walks and outings were a regular feature of the school. Here emphasis was not on tools and techniques of teaching the alphabets or numbers, but on giving the children an atmosphere where they would feel free to express themselves.

Use of the Word Mandir for School: School a sacred place. Evidently, this approach excludes examinations and gradation in the conventional sense. Children have to pass one phase of development before the other. The very fact that labels like 'primary', 'middle' and 'high school' are not used speaks of the attitude of the founders. Instead words like 'Sal Mandir', 'Kishore Mandir' and 'Vinay Mandir' have been preferred; 'Mandir' having specific connotations of worship of the child.

Freedom without Fear: There was no place for punishment to the child. The child was not insulted or jeered. His personality received the utmost respect and care.

14.10 DIWA SWAPNA

Gijubhai's 'Diwa Swapna' written in 1931 in Gujarati, attracted the attention of educators throughout India. Its translations were published in 1934 and 1962. It is a kind of criticism of a primary school. It presents the glimpse of the beautiful and happy nature of school of the future. The whole books are written in the form of a story. The points and events, which have become the theme of this book, are a kind of day-dream for the teachers. In his Bal Mandir, Gijubhai experimented upon principles of psychology and principles of teaching children. How could these principles be made practicable in primary schools was explained in his book 'Diwa Swapna' Gijubhai acknowledge that the teacher of our primary school is ignorant, servant, greedy, money-maker and he does not have self-confidence. By reading this book the teacher may repent, feel sorry and visualize the daydream by raising his level of aspiration.

14.11 LEARNING METHOD

Gijubhai was a man who could play with toys; children could overcome their fear a strange adult and play with him. He could also tell stories, not only of kings and queens, but of animals plants and naughty children-and the stories invariably ended in small plays, in which he also acted. "Mian Tush" and A King. In The Rat's Tale are roles which his contemporaries recollect with glee and amusement. There was also emphasis on observing nature and walks and outings were a regular feature of the school. Here emphasis was not on tools and techniques of teaching the alphabets or numbers, but on giving the children an atmosphere where they would feel free to express themselves. To be a good teacher one had to listen carefully to what a child had to say and observe him (her) attentively but without intruding on the child's effort to do things all by herself (himself).

14.12 GAMES

Gijubhai stressed the usefulness of games for providing joy and pleasures to students. He was not in favour of competitions.

14.13 TEACHER

In the view point of Gijubhai, the profession of teaching is the noblest of all professions in the world. He clarified that while all other professions are related to the present, teaching is relate to the past, present and future, all the three of them. He expected much from infant teachers. Infancy is the period of laying foundation for life. If the foundation is strong, the building will be strong and this work can be performed by the teachers only when they know of nature of infants and have infinite love for the infants; when they know of infant teaching methods and they are full to the brim with the feelings of love, affection, renunciation, others' well-being and dutifulness.

14.14 STUDENT

Gijubhai loved the children most. He emphasized on making education child-centered and basing the whole infant education on the interests, aptitudes and needs of the infants. He has emphasized on this fact that the children have their own world, they want to live free, play and jump, ride the horse made of a stick, they want to dance and take interest in listening and telling stories, therefore they should be given opportunities for all these activities. He instructed the teachers to respect the personality of the children, love them, consider them divine being, serve them and treat them so lovely that they go to school smiling and return from there laughing.

14.15 TEACHING OF LANGUAGE AND OTHER SUBJECTS

One book of Gijubhai is about teaching language in a Primary School. He discusses the method of teaching different aspects of language to the children. The following are the salient features of language teaching advocated by Gijubhai:

1. Reading should precede writing.
2. Writing should start with drawing lines.
3. Child should be taught how to hold the pen with fingers, how to turn it. how to control it and haw to reach the shape of a letter through drawing absurd shapes.
4. Dictation helps to acquire speed and accuracy of writing after hearing.
5. Poetry Teaching should start with teaching of folk songs. The poems should be simple, descriptive and based on stories. No role-learning is needed in poetry. The thrill characteristic of the poem should be stressed. There is no need of word meaning in poetry teaching.
6. Grammar is a part of language and should not be taught separately. In his book on day-dreams the teacher Lakshmi Shankar teaches noun, verb, pronoun, adjective etc. through play. Children recognize them by playing with words.
7. History is to be taught by telling stories.
8. Geography is to be taught by using globe.
9. Montessori Method is used for teaching mathematics.
10. Drawing should be taught by asking the students to draw the shape of things like table, mango, guava etc.
11. Children's books should contain the life-sketch of religious persons. The principles of religion may be postponed at this stage.
12. Gijubhai emphasized games. He said that children should be allowed to play freely and enjoy the play. There is no question of winning and losing in the games.

15

Dr. Maria Montessori (1870-1952)

Dr. Maria Montessori was born in the small town of Chiaravalle, Italy in 1870. At a time when education for girls was not valued, Maria's mother supported the idea of Maria attending college. Maria later attended medical school and became one of the first medical doctors in Italy.

The birth of her son, Mario, changed her life, as did her experience as a doctor for young children. She dedicated her life to creating an educational philosophy that would nurture the lives of children and provide them with a system of education designed for their developmental needs and interests. She established schools throughout Europe, America and India. Along the way she became an entrepreneur, teaching and manufacturing the beautiful materials that she designed for her classrooms. When she died in Holland in 1952 at the age of 82, she had lived through two World Wars and had witnessed the destruction of the lives of families and children. She was nominated twice for the Nobel Peace Prize for her work in education to bring about world peace.

Today, educators recognize both her genius and her dedication to the field of education. Her insights and understanding of children, their needs and their minds, have changed the course of children's education around the world for the past 100 years.

15.1 WORKS BY OR ABOUT DR. MARIA MONTESSORI

- *The Montessori Method* — Maria Montessori
- *From Childhood to Adolescence* — Maria Montessori
- *Montessori*: A Modern Approach — Paula Polk Lillard
- *Montessori: A Comprehensive Approach to Education from Birth to Adulthood* — Paula Polk Lillard
- *The Absorbent Mind* — Maria Montessori
- *The Discovery of the Child* — Maria Montessori
- *The Secret of Childhood* — Maria Montessori
- *Montessori Today* — Paula Polk Lillard
- *Maria Montessori:* A Biography — Rita Kramer
- *Maria Montessori*: Her Life and Work — E.M. Standing
- *The Secret behind the Genius* — Angeline Stoll Lillard

15.2 EDUCATIONAL PHILOSOPHY OF MARIA MONTESSORI

The foundation of Maria Montessori's approach is respect for the child as a worthy individual, occupied with the task of developing himself into a mature human adult. She observed children's need for independence, for self-confidence as adequate people, for control over their own impulses and emotions and a natural curiosity and desire to learn.

She observed in young children a phenomenon she called the "*absorbent mind*". Children can absorb information from their surroundings without any conscious, tedious effort. Learning does not have to be forced upon them. If the environment is orderly and readily accessible and if the children are free to work through their own cycles of activity at their own pace, they can learn to read, write and calculate in the same natural way that they learned to walk and talk.

Dr. Montessori wrote, "*The most important period of life is not the age of university studies but the period from birth to age six.*" It is now commonly accepted that from conception to age 4 the individual develops 50 per cent of his/her mature intelligence; from ages 4 to 8 another 30 per cent. This indicates the rapid growth of intelligence in the early years and the importance of the early environment on this development. It is also true that children mature at very different rates and their periods of readiness for academic subjects vary greatly. Montessori observed that a young child has periods of intense fascination for developing various skills such as climbing stairs or counting. During these sensitive periods it is easier for the child to acquire particular skills than at any other time in his/her life. The Montessori classroom allows each child freedom to select activities which correspond to his or her own periods of interest and readiness.

By answering a child's needs as they arise, some children in a Montessori class begin to read and calculate at a very early age. However, early learning was not Maria Montessori's objective. Her ideal was that the learning experience should occur naturally and joyfully at the proper moment for each individual child. "It is true we cannot make a genius," she wrote. "We can only give each individual the chance to fulfill his/her potential to become an independent, secure and balanced human being".

Montessori environments support the learning of children from birth to middle school:

Infant/Toddler

For children aged birth to three years:

- provide a safe, engaging and nurturing environment for the child
- promote trust in themselves and their world
- develop confidence in their emerging abilities
- develop gross motor coordination, fine motor skills, and language skills
- offer opportunities to gain independence in daily tasks

Primary

For children aged three to six years:

- foster the growth of functional independence, task persistence and self-regulation
- promote social development through respectful, clear communication and safe, natural consequences
- contain a large variety of materials for the refinement of sensory perception and the development of literacy and mathematical understanding
- offer opportunities for imaginative exploration leading to confident, creative self-expression

Elementary

For children aged six to twelve years (Lower Elementary, ages six to nine; Upper Elementary, ages nine to twelve):

- offer opportunities for collaborative intellectual exploration in which the child's interests are supported and guided
- support the development of self-confidence, imagination, intellectual independence and self-efficacy
- foster an understanding of the child's role in their community, in their culture and in the natural world

Adolescence

For adolescents aged twelve to fifteen years:

- ideally a working farm in which adolescents engage in all aspects of farm administration and economic interdependence, but also include non-farm environments in urban settings
- assist the young adult in the understanding of oneself in wider and wider frames of reference
- provide a context for practical application of academics
- emphasize the development of self-expression, true self-reliance, and agility in interpersonal relationships.

15.3 MONTESSORI EDUCATION

Montessori is a method of education that is based on self-directed activity, hands-on learning and collaborative play. In Montessori classrooms children make creative choices in their learning, while the classroom and the teacher offer age-appropriate activities to guide the process. Children work in groups and individually to discover and explore knowledge of the world and to develop their maximum potential

15.4 MONTESSORI METHOD

The Montessori Method is founded on Maria Montessori's educational philosophy. Her basic principle was to "follow the child". A Montessori classroom is carefully prepared to allow the child to work independently and allow for the joy of self-discovery. Teachers introduce materials and children are free to choose them, again and again, working and discovering, and ultimately mastering ideas. Lessons are given, but the goal is for children to discover the answers by using the "auto-didactic", or "self-correcting" materials that are found only in Montessori classrooms.

Children grow academically in the Montessori environment. They discover an ability to complete complex math problems, name the continents, identify geometric shapes, write beautifully and talk about scientific concepts such as "metamorphosis". Just as important in the classroom is the engaging of the child's creative intelligence. Children are exposed to fine art, drama, music, history, and a second language. They might paint their own Impressionist "water lily" one day, participate in the challenges of Sport Day on another, prepare a traditional food from another country, or put on a play based on an ancient folktale.

However, the most important aspect of our educational mission does not concern academics. Our primary goal is to foster and enhance each child's natural sense of joy and wonder. We feel that children should delight in childhood, that the school day must include laughter and the buzz of creative silliness. We want students to love school and the process of learning. The idea that "education is not a chore, but a joyous exploration of life's mysteries", is the most important lesson that we hope to teach our students.

15.5 HIGH QUALITY EDUCATION

The primary goal of a Montessori programme is to help each child reach its full potential in all areas of life. The method of Montessori is based on three key factors; the specialized training of the teacher, a specially prepared environment complete with Montessori apparatus and a multi age grouping of children. When these elements are in place, young children are able to discover their own talents, gain self-confidence, make friendships, experience the joys of learning, and grow in a holistic manner.

Montessori School of Shanghai provides highly trained, credentialed Montessori Teachers and exceptional classroom environments. Mixed age groups are found in our Infant, Toddler, Early Childhood and Junior classes.

Creativity flourishes in an atmosphere of acceptance and trust. Our teachers establish such an atmosphere in their classrooms. Treating each child with love and respect enables the child to trust their teachers. This relationship is the foundation of the learning process. The three-year cycle enables the child, the family and the teacher time to really know one another and work together. Strong bonds are made, and many relationships are long lasting.

For any great accomplishment, the foundation has to be strong, solid and long lasting. That is the opportunity a Montessori education provides. Birth to age six is the most important time of education. It is here that the foundation is firmly established. We build good people!

15.6 MULTI-AGE GROUPING

The Montessori School of Shanghai has classrooms of multi-age children. They are "Multi-Age Learning Communities." Montessori practice has shown that children in multi-year age groupings progress academically while building important social, learning, and character skills.

The multi-age grouping accommodates the child's individualized "biological clock", rather than relying on age as the primary indicator for readiness with lessons. Peer cooperation and peer tutoring increases achievement and self-esteem in both the older and younger child.

The multi-age classroom is a groundbreaking concept for developing community and supporting students of varying levels of academic and social development. By creating a bond between parents, teachers, and children, Dr. Montessori sought to create a closely-knit community where individuals could learn to be empowered; where children could learn to become contributing, sharing members of their school-family; where students could learn to care for younger children, learn from older people, and trust one another; and where children could find ways to be acceptably assertive rather than being aggressive.

15.7 PREPARED ENVIRONMENT

Montessori's idea of the prepared environment was that everything the child came in contact with would facilitate and maximize independent learning and exploration. This calm, well-ordered environment has a lot of movement and activity. Children are free to choose and work on activities at their own pace. Here, they experience a combination of freedom and self-discipline, as guided by the environment and the teacher.

The seven aspects or principles to the prepared environment:

Freedom: A child must be free to explore and follow his own natural impulses, thus developing his potential and increasing his knowledge of the world around him. Within the prepared environment, the child must experience freedom of movement, freedom of exploration, freedom to interact socially, and freedom from interference from others. This freedom ultimately leads to a greater freedom: freedom of choice.

Structure and Order: While Structure and Order seem counter-intuitive to the aforementioned freedom, nothing could be further from the truth. Structure and Order in the Montessori classroom accurately reflect the sense of structure and order in the universe. By using the Montessori classroom environment as a microcosm of the universe, the child begins to internalize the order surrounding him, thus making sense of the world in which he lives.

Beauty: Montessori environments should be beautiful. The environment should suggest a simple harmony. Uncluttered and well maintained, the environment should reflect peace and tranquillity. The environment should invite the learner to come in and work. This atmosphere is easily seen through the attitude of those working there, both child and adult.

Nature and Reality: Montessori had a deep respect and reverence for nature. She believed that we should use nature to inspire children. She continually suggested that Montessori teachers take the children out into nature, rather than keeping them confined in the classroom. This is why natural materials are preferred in the prepared environment. Real wood, reeds, bamboo, metal, cotton, and glass are preferred to synthetics or plastics.

Social Environment: Where there is freedom to interact, children learn to encourage and develop a sense of compassion and empathy for others. As children develop, they become more socially aware, preparing to work and play in groups. This social interaction is supported throughout the environment and is encouraged by the multi-age classroom settings.

Intellectual Environment: If the above aspects are not recognized, the intellectual environment will not reach its purpose. The purpose of the Montessori environment is to develop the whole personality of the child, not merely his intellect. By guiding the child through the five areas of the Montessori curriculum (Practical Life, Sensorial, Language, Mathematics, and Cultural subjects), the child has the structure, which is at the forefront of the creative work in a Montessori classroom.

Montessori Materials: Each classroom at the Montessori School of Shanghai is equipped with the full range of Montessori materials. These unique and specialized materials are often imported from Europe or the United States to ensure authenticity and quality. In addition MSS classrooms are rich with colourful extensions and individualized teacher-made materials that complement and enhance the Montessori materials.

15.8 TEACHERS' ROLE

In Montessori education we believe in the importance of three things, that all work together: the child, teacher, and materials, where each part is important. We believe that each child has many gifts and talents to be discovered, and not that a child is an empty container waiting to be filled up by the teacher. The teacher is an observer, follower, and guide bringing wisdom, thoughtfulness, and experience to the child's academic, social, and intellectual exploration. The Montessori approach demands special professionals who are confident and skilled enough to allow children to be active participants in their learning. It also means that all school decisions are driven by what is best for the child. The authentic and beautiful Montessori materials provide activities that are cherished by the children and that help them learn with joy and understanding.

The teacher establishes guidelines for work and behaviour, showing children how to be successful within the structure of the curriculum and the community. As a result, a pattern of good work habits and a sense of responsibility and cooperation are established in the classroom.

15.9 SENSITIVE PERIODS OF LEARNING

Maria Montessori believed in children having "sensitive periods" for learning. From birth to 6, the child shows a strong interest on particular things he wants to master. This leads to the child doing a task repeatedly, with great interest, until the child has reached his goal of mastery.

The purpose of each sensitive period, which is actually an inner sensibility possessed by children, is to help them acquire a certain skill or characteristic necessary for their growth. As they acquire the skill or characteristic, their sensitivity for it decreases and another sensitivity increases.

15.10 ABSORBENT MIND

Dr. Montessori observed that the first six years of children's lives are directed by their absorbent minds. She divided this six- year time span into two three-year periods. The first three years she calls "unconscious learning" and the second three years, "conscious learning".

During the first three years of life children absorb and take in all that is around them in their environment. They absorb impressions from the environment, "creating themselves". Dr. Montessori said, "The child takes in his whole environment, not with his mind but with his life". The task of adults around the child in this stage of development is not to intervene but to provide a safe, rich environment for the child.

15.11 THE CHILD

According to Maria Montessori, "Children *are human beings to whom* respect *is due, superior to us by reason of their innocence and of the greater possibilities of their future.*" In a Montessori environment, the individual child is regarded with profound respect and we understand that each child learn at his/her own pace and style. Young children, in particular, experience sensitive periods for learning, times when they are especially receptive to certain knowledge or skills. Since the classroom environment provides a rich array of learning materials and activities, children are encouraged to choose appropriate work and to operate independently within the class. As they experience the satisfaction of mastering a task or skill, children are inspired to further challenge themselves.

15.12 MONTESSORI CLASSROOMS

Montessori classrooms are beautifully crafted environments designed to meet the needs of children in a specific age range. Dr. Maria Montessori discovered that experiential learning in this type of classroom led to a deeper understanding of language, mathematics, science, music, social interactions and much more. Most Montessori classrooms are secular in nature, although the Montessori educational method can be integrated successfully into a faith-based program. Every material in a Montessori classroom supports an aspect of child development, creating a match between the child's natural interests and the available activities. Children can learn through their own experience and at their own pace. They can respond at any moment to the natural curiosities that exist in all humans and build a solid foundation for life-long learning.

15.13 MONTESSORI INFANT, TODDLER AND PRE-SCHOOL PROGRAMMES

The Montessori Infant Programme — Ages 12 to 18 months

Children between 12 and 18 months are introduced to our school through the Infant program. A 1:3 ratio is maintained, with the Head Teacher having Montessori Infant and Toddler qualifications. Our teachers and assistants are patient, kind and caring individuals who will help your child develop a routine, provide stimulating activities and care for all your child's needs. Gross motor and fine motor activities are part of the daily routine. Age appropriate materials are provided to enhance the child's language, cognitive and motor skill development.

In addition to the Infant curriculum, Infant children will receive weekly visits to the gym. Music is enhanced through the Kindermusik Program. Outdoor Education and School Visits also enrich their experience.

The Montessori Toddler Programme: Ages 18 Months to 30 Months

At around 18 months, your child is ready to be introduced to the Montessori Toddler program. The class ratio is 1:5 and the Head Teacher has Montessori Infant and Toddler qualifications. The Toddler staff assists your child in developing a routine, making good social choices and provide stimulating age-appropriate activities. This programme has 4 main curriculum areas: Practical Life (self-help skills), Sensorial, Language and Culture. The curriculum can include toilet training, if the child is ready.

In addition to the Toddler curriculum, Toddler *children* will receive French instruction, as well as, weekly visits to the gym. Music is enhanced through the Kindermusik Programme. Outdoor Education and School Visits also enrich their experience.

The Montessori Pre-school Programme: 30 Months to 4 Years Old

At around 30 months, your child is ready to be introduced to the Montessori Pre-School program. The class ratio is 1:8 and the Head Teacher has Montessori Infant and Toddler qualifications, as well as Montessori Casa (3 to 6 year old) qualifications. The Pre-school staff assists your child in developing routines, practicing good social choices and will provide stimulating, age-appropriate activities. This programme has 5 main curriculum areas: Practical Life (self-help skills), Sensorial, Language, Math and Culture. The curriculum also includes toilet training.

In addition to the Pre-School curriculum, Pre-school children will receive French instruction, as well as, weekly library and gym visits. Music is enhanced through the Kindermusik Programme. Outdoor Education and School Visits also enrich their experience.

The outcomes of the Infant, Toddler and Pre-School programs are as follows:

- Trust in people through a warm school environment
- Social Adaptation
- Memory Development
- Spoken Language Development
- Sense of security and safety at school
- Feelings of adequacy, autonomy, independence and confidence
- Independence achieved through walking, talking, eating table food and using the toilet

Montessori Elementary Programme

The Elementary Programme: Ages 6 to 12 years

At this level, children become intellectual thinkers. Academic standards are high and while children are still progressing at their own pace, there are clearly defined expectations for each level. The Ministry of Education guidelines are used as a minimum for achievement but our own curriculum is defined in the 3 year age groupings that are integral to the Montessori philosophy. Specific components of the Ministry curriculum may not be covered in the same year; but rather over the 3 years of each level. As such, parents are encouraged to commit to the full 3 years when entering their child into both Lower and Upper Elementary.

A solid understanding of each concept is first ensured through concrete experiences with the hands-on materials. The children then move on to work with more abstracted materials for these concepts, eventually leading to solid conceptual understanding. The Montessori materials are supplemented with the use of carefully selected workbooks, textbooks, reading and spelling programs and computer software. The result is a broad, integrated and comprehensive curriculum which gives the children an academic advantage and prepares them extremely well for the Middle School experience.

While there is a strong expectation to complete an appropriate amount of class work responsibly and thoroughly, the emphasis is still on the total development of the child. Children have the opportunity for self-expression to pursue their own interests and develop new ones through a rich and varied curriculum.

Most lessons are given to small groups or individuals so that diverse needs, interests and ability levels are easily accommodated. At the same time, daily evaluation and extensive record keeping on the child's progress enables the teacher to assess when a child is ready to move on to the next level of challenge. Thus, there is no limit to the child's accomplishments.

The 1:20 ratio ensures that all students receive the individual attention they require. The classroom teacher holds an undergraduate degree and a TMI/AMI/MACTE accredited Montessori Teaching Diploma. Specialist teachers provide instruction in French, Physical Education, Music, Art and Library.

The educational programme is designed to maximize each student's academic success while, at the same time, teaching the student effective study and research skills and to adapt and learn from mistakes. The children learn to make responsible choices for themselves and discover how to contribute positively to the world and those around them. Their morals and values are nurtured, in part by *The Virtues Project*, with an emphasis on self-discipline and responsibility. The classroom community allows for the strengthening and refinement of social interactions as children learn to consider their own actions, to resolve their own conflicts peacefully and to use the group process for planning and problem solving.

The outcomes of the Elementary Programme are as follows:

- Academic Preparation; mastering one level of academic skills at a time, students apply themselves to increasingly challenging materials across various academic disciplines
- Gain further autonomy and develop self-direction skills
- Gain an intrinsic motivation, an internal desire to engage in an activity for enjoyment and satisfaction
- Increased awareness of social responsibility
- Develop further creativity and originality of thought
- Growth in confidence and competence

Montessori Middle School Programme

Our Middle School programme will accelerate opportunities for Grade 7 and 8 students to learn and develop the skills required to be successful in Secondary School and beyond.

Students in the Middle School will also receive instruction from the Specialist staff at the Montessori Country School, including our French, Music, Art, Physical Education and Library teachers. Access to technology will be a feature of our Middle School program, as students learn to integrate their independent skills with the rigors of disciplined research, study and presentation.

Each Middle School student will be assigned a staff member at MCS to be their personal mentor. Students may go to their mentor for advice on their studies, help with planning, social or personal concerns. The Mentor is a person the student may approach about any topic and anything shared between the mentor and the student is completely confidential. Adolescents must have this foundation of trust in order for the mentorship programme to have value for them.

It is critical that students in a successful adolescent programme have a variety of opportunities to go out of the school, in some cases for a short time during the day and in others for several days at a time. All off-site activities are curricular in nature and will be conducted with adult supervision.

Following the Ontario Curriculum standards, the Middle School programme is delivered in a manner that enhances cooperative learning, discussion, self and group reflection, individual and group problem solving, analysis and critical thinking.

Other key outcomes of the Middle School Programme include:

- Connection of concepts and skills to real life applications
- Learning what it means to make a contribution to society
- Balancing individual initiative in relations to community goals
- Respect for others and their roles
- Growth in confidence

15.14 MERITS OF MONTESSORI METHOD

Reverence/Respect for Small Children: To Madam Montessori, the child was God and her school was the temple. She stated that today there stands forth one urgent need – the reform of methods in education and instruction and he who struggles towards this end is struggling for the regeneration of man. The method as suggested by Montessori gives an important place to the child.

Scientific Basis of the Method: The method is based upon scientific grounds. Madam Montessori was a scientist and she applied scientific principles based on experience and observation and not upon prejudices.

Individual Teaching: Individualism is the keynote of the educators who wanted to give education in a complete atmosphere of freedom. In her method, discipline is that of self control and self directed activity.

Sense Training: The Montessori Method aims at educating the children through the sense training. It is based upon the maxims that proceed from concrete to abstract, from general to abstract.

Unique Method of Reading and Writing: Special importance to the learning of writing has provided in the method. She takes to consideration the muscular movement in the process of writing. Properly graded and co related exercise for reading and writing are provided.

Learning through Living: She has provided practical exercises in her school which enable children to learn good habits and cleanliness. The children learn the lessons of dignity of labour. They are not ashamed of manual work and self help by attending to their needs themselves. Many practical lessons are provided.

15.15 LIMITATIONS OF MONTESSORI METHOD

Mechanical and Artificial Nature of Didactic Apparatus: Too much importance has been given to the didactic apparatus. The critics argue that the apparatus handcuffs both the teacher and the pupil. The child is expected to do different types of exercises with the help of the apparatus and the teacher also has to teach through the didactic apparatus with the result that the free expression of the children is limited and so is the work of the teacher. The apparatus is unreal and unnatural.

More Emphasis on Biological Aspects and Less on Psychological Aspects: The teacher in this system takes special efforts in keeping records of the height, skull and limbs of each individual child. He does not observe temperament and other emotional traits.

Belief in Transfer of Training: The idea of sense training in the Montessori Method is based on the old theory of formal training of the sense. She feels that by training particular faculties through particular sense, it will be possible to get advantage of that training in other life situations through transfer of training to the desired field. Modern psychology disapproves of this idea.

Neglect of the Training of Imagination: There is no place for fairy tales in the Montessori system. Fairy tales used in a proper way form part of the literacy training of children and help in the development of imagination.

Lack of Suitable Teachers: The successful working of the Montessori system depends upon teachers who possess extensive knowledge of child psychology and acquisition of laboratory procedure. It is not possible to find such teachers in sufficient numbers.

Little Scope for Projects and Correlation: The present tendency is to teach all subjects together in the form of projects. Learning by doing is the key note of the present methods of teaching. In the Montessori Method, the children have to depend upon the mechanical apparatus.

Very Expensive: It requires a lot of money to set up a school on the lines as suggested by Dr. Montessori. It is very doubtful, if we could spare huge sums on such schools.

16

Frobel (1782-1852)

A German philosopher, educator and founder of the kindergarten, championed the cause of infant education in response to the inspiration that he derived from the great educationist Pestalozzi. He ushered in a new era in child education. Today, his kindergarten system is highly acclaimed all over the world by both educators and parents alike. It is recognised as an effective way to deal with a highly "teachable moment "in the life of the young child.

16.1 LIFE PROFILE

Frobel was born on April 21st, 1782 in the village of Oberweisback in the south Germany. He lost his mother when he was only of nine months. His father got remarried. His father was not very affectionate to him. The unfair treatment of his stepmother made his childhood all the more miserable. His life presents one of history's strange paradoxes that the man whose own childhood was full of tears should bring smiles for the children of the world. Since Frobel's own child hood was neglected he developed an intensive sympathy for children and spent his life promoting their life. In fact, Frobel had to go through a long and tough struggle before he could make his mark and garner life's richest harvest. Being unable to do well at a village school, he started doing odd jobs when he was only 14 years of age.

His wandering spirit was set at peace when he went to Frankfurt where he came in contact with the director of a model school. He discovered the real genius of his young man and persuaded him to join his school as a teacher. Frobel gladly accepted the offer. But he felt the need of some professional training and he was attracted to Pestalozzi's school at "yverdum". There he stayed for 4 years and later on studied natural science at Gottingen and Berlin universities.

In 1816 he founded a small school which became a successful institution after 10 years. Now the road to success stretched before him. He achieved world wide fame when in 1817 in 1817 he founded his first kindergarten, an institution for the children of age 4 to 6 at Blacken burg. Frobel served the cause of education for the remaining period of his life. He died on 21st June 1852, yet he lives for the children and as it were, continues to pour a silent whisper in the ears of education," come let us live for our children". Frobel died in 1852, in poverty, misery and agony.

16.2 PUBLISHED WORKS OF FROBEL

- The Education of Man
- Pedagogues of Kindergarten
- Mother Play and Nursery Songs
- Education and Development

16.3 FROBEL'S PHILOSOPHY OF EDUCATION

The main ideas of Frobel's philosophy of education are given below:

Creativeness of Childhood: Frobel derives a new conception of childhood. Childhood is not merely preparation for adulthood; it has a value in itself and possesses its own creativeness.

Inner Relatedness of All Education: This means that the educator ought to lead the child through such situations as will help him to relate his experiences originally one with another. Only thus can the child realize his own personal unity inherent in the diversity of life.

Totality of Educational Endeavour: In order to realize the divine character of the universe and his part in it, man needs senses and emotions as well as reasons. They are all windows of the soul.

Concept of Play: It is the most important phase in the spontaneous development of the child, because it allows him to exercise harmoniously all his physical, emotional and intellectual qualities. Play combines attention with relaxation, purpose with independence and rule with freedom.

Education of the Pre-school Child: Frobel reveals an astounding insight into the importance of the early experiences of childhood for the future development of the personality. This anticipation of modern analytical psychology, which he shares with Pestalozzi and Herbert, led him naturally to emphasize the importance of preschool education.

Aims and Targets of Frobel's Education

1. Give children enjoyment in agreement with their nature.
2. Strengthen the bodies of children a healthy mind in healthy body. A child must grow to his maximum physical potential.
3. Exercises their senses for their optimal sensitivity and perceptions.
4. Awaken their minds.
5. Acquaint them with nature and their fellows.
6. Lead them to unity.

16.4 EDUCATIONAL PRINCIPLES

The Law of Unity: According to Frobel there is one eternal law – law of unity – that governs all things, men and nature. All things, an animate or inanimate, originate from god. Man and nature are one. There is unity in diversity and diversity in unity. Each of these has individuality and also a unity. Frobel considers that the aim of education is that man only may well understand the idea of unity in diversity. He said that the essential business of school is not so much to communicate a variety and multiplicity of facts as to give prominence to the ever living unity that is in all things.

The Principle of Development: By development, he meant an increase in bulk or quantity, increase in complexity or structure, an improvement in power, skill and variety in the performance of natural functions. Educations unfold the innate powers of the child in order to enable him to have a spiritual union with god. Education should lead to moral, religious and spiritual development.

The Principle of Self Activity: It is only through self activity that real growth and development is possible. Forced activity is artificial and unnatural. Education should develop the innate qualities of the child. Child's own activities are the best medium of education. Play reflected in the mind of the child and it is considered the free and unfettered natural source of development.

Developments through Social Institutions: According to Frobel school is a miniature society. He remarked, "No community can progress while the individual remains behind". He believed that the individual is not apart from the life of the society. The child should develop his individuality through social atmosphere. All the social institutions like home, school, church are the agencies of education.

16.5 KINDERGARTEN

In the form of kindergarten, Frobel has made an important contribution to the theory and practice of education. He realized the paramount importance of childhood and opened the first kindergarten, an institution of children of age 4 to 6, at Blacken burg in 1837. Kindergarten or KG is a German word meaning, "garden of children". Frobel had a special love and concern for the children and wanted to introduce system which could benefit the small children in learning. He was the first to give the call, "come, let us live for our children".

To Frobel school is like a garden, where children play and dance like flowers and teacher protects them like a gardener. Child like a little tender plant grows and teacher makes his efforts to beautify the garden with the proper growth, care and looking after the plants.

Practice of Kindergarten

Frobel's is a miniature state for children where the watch words are freedom, play, and joyful living. Here no books are prescribed. The learning is activity oriented. Education is imparted through songs, movements and construction. Whatever is narrated in a song is followed by its dramatization in movements and construction. Whatever is narrated in a song is followed by its dramatization in movements and gestures. The same is afterwards represented with the help of construction work in blocks, paper clay, drawing or other materials. This three fold procedures stimulates thought, vivifies imagination, trains and coordinates physical muscle of hands, eyes etc. And ultimately strengthens the moral nature of child. For convenience sake, we may divide the teaching procedure in two parts, i.e. teaching through songs, teaching through gifts and occupations.

Teaching through Songs

The various songs which Froebel employed for the purpose of teaching are included in Mother Play and Nursery songs [1843]. Froebel regarded these songs as the best means to familiarise the child with surroundings and to exercise his senses, limbs and muscles.

Froebel Gifts and Occupations

These gifts are in the form of educational toys. Those gifts are carefully graded and are to be presented to the child in the definite order. Spenser comes first, followed by crystal, cube, cylinder etc. The activities connected with these gifts are called occupations. The purpose of these gifts is to train child's senses of touch and sight and to give him an idea of sizes surface and number. Froebel designed about 20 such gifts but only seven are now usually called by this name.

Seven Gifts of Frobel

The Froebel Gifts are educational materials developed for Friedrich Froebel's original Kindergarten. Perhaps the world's most intricately conceived playthings, these materials appear deceptively simple, but represent a sophisticated approach to child development. The Gifts are arguably the first educational toys.

First Gift: Yarn Balls: It consists of six balls of difference colours, contained in a box. Three balls are of primary colours –red, blue and green and three are secondary colour-orange, green and purple. The occupation consists in rolling them about in play accompanied by little rhymes.

Second Gift: Sphere, Cylinder and Cube: It consists of three objects a sphere, a cube, and a cylinder made of hardwood. While playing with them child notices the difference between their stability and mobility

Third Gift: The Divided Cube: It is a big wooden cube, subdivided into eight wooden cubes. The children have an elementary idea of addition and subtraction through these.

Fourth Gift: Rectangular Prisms: In Gift 4, the two-inch cube is now divided into 8 oblong blocks which are 2 inches by 1 inch by 1/2 inch.

Froebel's Gift 4 is only a slight variation on Gift 3, but the rectangular prisms open up many more possibilities. Children may view them as bricks or tiles and they will seem a familiar shape. The two inch cube is again divided into eight pieces, but the pieces have a proportion of 1 to 2 to 4 (1/2" by 1" by 2"). This feature will aid in creating modular constructions and designs, and proportion can be discussed as part of the Forms of Knowledge.

Fifth Gift: Cubes and Triangular Prisms: Froebel's Gift 5 consists of a three-inch cube divided twice in each direction, with some cubes divided diagonally into triangular prisms (half-cubes and quarter-cubes) yielding 21 one-inch cubes, 6 half-cubes, and 12 quarter-cubes. Gift 5 now represents a larger, three inch cube and incorporates more pieces and variety. The half-cubes and quarter-cubes introduce a triangular shape. This Gift is best used with children 5 years old and older.

Sixth Gift: Classic Building Blocks: Froebel's Gift 6 again divides the three-inch cube into more varieties of rectangular prisms, including 18 oblong blocks, 12 flat square blocks (caps), and 6 narrow columns. Gift 6 continues from the form of the three inch cube introduced in Gift 5. As Gift 4 introduced new proportions to Gift 3's cubes, so does Gift 6 introduce new proportions to the three inch cube. This is a return to concepts of size and modularity introduced in Gift 4. The arrival of the classic construction components of the cap and the column brings a real architectural feel to this Gift.

Seventh Gift 7: Parquetry Tablets: Seventh in the series of Froebel Gifts, this set of parquetry tablets contains a variety of geometric shapes, made from either wood, plastic or paper.

Essentials of Kindergarten

Self Activity: Self activity or self expression is imparted in three ways – through songs, through movements and through construction.

Creativeness: When the child is given certain material, he tried to create always new things and satisfies his urge for construction.

Social Participation: School is a miniature society. What we learn in school influences our behaviour in our later life. The best education of child is possible in the school where he participates in the maximum number of social activities.

Discipline: Children are always free to work, play, sing, or dance in a kindergarten school. A teacher has important responsibilities to perform. He has to inculcate sympathetically values like love, sympathy, humility cooperation and obedience to elders. He has to avoid external restraint and bodily punishment. The child should be made to realize that discipline depends upon his love for order, goodwill and mutual understanding.

Curriculum: The divisions of the curriculum are:

- Manual work
- Religion and religious instruction

- Natural science and mathematics
- Language
- Arts and Objects of Arts

The Place of Teacher: The teacher is not remaining passive. The teacher has to suggest the idea of occupation when the gifts are offered to children. He is also required to demonstrate certain activities to them. He also sings a song with a view to help the child to form appropriate ideas.

16.6 FROBEL'S INFLUENCE ON MODERN EDUCATION

Frobel invited us to live for our children and to love them. The schools for young children are no more jails and the children are no more passive learners. He helped him to make the society conscious of education for very young children. The chief field in which he influenced the modern education are as under:

Emphasis on Pre-Basic or Pre-Primary Education: The present educator fully recognizes the importance of the education in the early ears. Today we find a large number of schools catering to the needs of such children. Frobel had also realised that until the education was reformed nothing solid and worthy could be achieved.

New Conception of School: His school was a society in miniature. The present tendency in education is to regard school as a society in miniature. Dewey also regarded school as social institution. The present school is being regarded as a cooperative institution.

Respect for the Child's Individuality: Frobel lived for children, worked for children and died for children. He had profound love and sympathy for children.

Stress on the Study of the Child: Frobel stressed the need for the study of the nature of the child, his instincts and impulses. Modern education is very careful to see that adequate scope is provided for the free play of the impulses and instincts of children.

Education through Play: Froebel believed that play is the highest phase of self development. He introduced play way in the activities of the school. Today we find that the principle of play way has been accepted by every educator. We teach children through songs, movements, gestures, dramatization, handwork etc.

Sense Training: Frobel introduced gifts for the training of the senses of the children, with the help of these gifts he wanted to give the idea of shape, form, colour, size, and number. Audio-visual aids form and integral part of the present system of education.

Activity in Education: Frobel was the first educator to make self activity as the basis of education. "Learning by doing "is the slogan of today. We provide activities to students so that they may satisfy their instincts of construction, manipulation, curiosity and acquisition.

Nature Study in Education: For Frobel nature study was a means of bringing the child nearer god. He advocated a syllabus of nature study to enable the child to understand the world in which he lived and to develop habits of careful observation.

Women Teachers at the Nursery Stage

It will not be wrong to say that it is due to the influence of Frobel that we find a trend to entrust the education at the pre primary or pre basic stage to women teachers who are considered to be more suited for this task of instruction at this stage.

16.7 LIMITATIONS OF FROBEL'S PHILOSOPHY

1. Frobel's philosophy was a complicated philosophy because Frobel expects too much of the child. it is not possible for the child to understand abstract ideas of organic unity while playing with gifts.
2. In kindergarten, too much stress has been laid on the development from within. The importance of environment has not been fully recognised.
3. Songs as given by him are out of date.
4. The gifts of Frobel formal in nature. The order of presentation of gifts is arbitrary. They do not serve much purpose of sense training.
5. The kindergarten of Frobel does not provide for the study of individual child.
6. There is little of correlation in the teaching of various subjects.
7. The scheme is not applicable to grown up children.
8. Too much emphasis on social aspect.

In the words of Frobel the objectives of kindergarten is to give the children enjoyment in agreement with their whole nature, to strengthen their bodies, to exercise their senses, to engage their awakening mind and through their senses to make them acquainted with nature and their fellow creatures. Frobel is no doubt one of the greatest exponents of child education. He regarded education more as a process working from within. The 19th century came to be known as the century of the child, only because of Frobel.

17

Meaning, Concept and Importance of Sociology

17.1 MEANING AND CONCEPT OF SOCIOLOGY

'Sociology' which had once been treated as social philosophy, or the philosophy of the history, emerged as an independent social science in 19th century. Auguste Comte, a Frenchman, is traditionally considered to be the father of sociology. Comte is accredited with the coining of the term sociology (in 1839). "Sociology" is composed of two words: 'socius', meaning companion or associate; and 'logos', meaning science or study. The etymological meaning of "sociology" is thus the science of society. John Stuart Mill, another social thinker and philosopher of the 19th century, proposed the word 'ethology' for this new science. Herbert Spencer developed his systematic study of society and adopted the word "sociology" in his works. With the contributions of Spencer and others, it (sociology) became the permanent name of the new science.

In the family of social sciences, Sociology is comparatively a new entrant. But because of its dealing with social problems, social relationships and social interactions the importance of the study of this subject has considerably increased. It has considerably developed in methodology, scope and approach. Attempts are now being made to study every social problem scientifically and objectively, eliminating subjectivity to the extent possible a distinctive way of examining human interactions. Sociology is the systematic study of social behaviour and human groups. It focusses primarily on the influence of social relationships upon people's attitudes and behaviour and on how societies are established and changed. As a field of study sociology has a very broad scope. It deals with families, gangs, business firms, computer networks, political parties, schools, religions, and labour unions. It is concerned with love, poverty, conformity, technology, discrimination, illness, alienation, overpopulation and community

17.2 DEFINITIONS OF SOCIOLOGY

Sociology has been defined in a number of ways by different sociologists. No single definition has yet been accepted as completely satisfactory. In fact, there are lots of definitions of sociology as there are sociologists. Some definitions of sociology are:

According to Ward "*Sociology is science of society*".

George Simmel opines that "*It is a subject which studies human inter-relationship*".

Giddins is of the view that "*Sociology is scientific study of society*".

Sorokin is of the opinion that "*Sociology is a study first of all the relationship and correlations between various classes...second between the social and non-social aspects of life and third it studies general characteristics common to all classes of society*".

Ogburn has said that, "*Sociology is concerned with the study of social life and its relations to the factors of culture, natural environment, heredity and group*".

Durkheim while defining sociology has said that, "*It is the science of collective representation*".

Auguste Comete, the founding father of sociology, defines sociology as the science of social phenomena "*subject to natural and invariable laws, the discovery of which is the object of investigation*".

Kingsley Davis says that "*Sociology is a general science of society*".

Harry M. Johnson opines that "*Sociology is the science that deals with social groups*".

Park regards sociology as "*the science of collective behaviour*".

Small defines sociology as "*the science of social relationships*".

Marshal Jones defines sociology as "*the study of man-in-relationship-to-men*".

Ogburn and Nimkoff "Sociology is the scientific study of social life".

Franklin Henry Giddings defines sociology as "the science of social phenomena".

Max Weber defines sociology as "*the science which attempts the interpretative understanding of social action in order thereby to arrive at a casual explanation of its course and effects*".

Alex Inkeles says, "*Sociology is the study of systems of social action and of their inter-relations*".

Kimball Young and Raymond W. Mack say, "*Sociology is the scientific study of social aspects of human life*".

Morris Ginsberg: Of the various definitions of sociology the one given by Morris Ginsberg seems to be more satisfactory and comprehensive. He defines sociology in the following way: "*In the broadest sense, sociology is the study of human interactions and inter-relations, their conditions and consequences*".

We may thus conclude these definitions with the definition of E.S. Bogardus when he says that, "Sociology may be defined as the study of the ways in which social experiences function in developing, maturing and repressing human beings through inter-personal stimulations."

From all these definitions it becomes clear that sociology is concerned with social relationships and studies society, human interactions, interpersonal and intra-personal relations. It tries to study scientifically social institutions, organisations and systems. These definitions also make it amply clear that sociologists view the subject differently and that there is no unanimity in this regard.

17.3 NATURE OF SOCIOLOGY

What is real nature of sociology about this controversy is likely to continue. According to Robert Stead, Sociology is a social science and not a natural science, because it deals with human beings and social phenomena. It is positive and not normative science because it studies social phenomena as it is and not as it ought to be. It is pure and not applied science because it studies underlying factors of a social phenomenon. Sociology is an abstract and not a concrete science because it studies society in general. It deals with society, which in itself is abstract and as such the subject cannot be concrete. It is a science of generalisation and not that of particularisation because it studies a social problem in general, and not in particular way. It does not study a social phenomenon from a particular angle. It is an empirical or rational science because it tries to follow logical method of data collection.

17.4 IMPORTANCE OF SOCIOLOGY

Sociology is becoming quite popular subject of study because it has some obvious advantages. These may briefly be discussed as under:

- Sociology attempts to study how and why people are organised as a society. It allows for a scientific study of society as an organisation, which is of help in the formulation and implementation of policies that benefit society.
- It analyses the structure of society and studies the factors that contribute to the creation of social groups.
- Sociology includes the study of behavioural patterns, interactions, and relationships among the individuals of society, as well as their ethical and moral values.
- It tries to examine the organisational structure of society and the influence it has on the social, political, and religious ideas of its members.
- It attempts to analyse the creation and management of social groups as well as the factors which lead to their breakdown.
- It is a subject which helps us in assessing available human resources and extent of human resources needed for solving our social problems. In this way sociology helps in human planning process which contributes significantly in economic problem.
- It provides us basic and fundamental knowledge about human society, which includes strong and weak points of society, including

human relationships. In this way it saves us from duping in the dark.

- Each society is faced with social problems, which in turn create economic and political problems. Some of the social evils are deep rooted and it is essential that these should be rooted out. Sociology helps us both in identifying those problems and finding out their solution. Without proper understanding magnitude of the problems, these cannot be appropriately tackled.
- It is sociology which helps us in conciliation and adjustment. Each society has diverse elements. These, if not properly reconciled, can result in disorganisation and de-stabilisation of the society. It is sociology which helps us in understanding the extent of diversity and the way in which this diversity can be converted into homogeneity.
- Sociology helps us in social reconstruction.
- Each society has its cultural heritage and wants to preserve that. It is sociology which high-lights and researches past culture heritages, and also helps in the development and growth of cosmopolitan culture, so that there are no cultural clashes.
- It helps in bringing family stability. It is sociology which helps us in identifying the causes of family instability and family disorganisation. It is again sociology which tells us how emerging de-stabilising trends in the family should be checked, so that strong family system continues.
- It is sociology which helps us in understanding social problems. Many social problems remain unidentified and many with the passage of time become maladies. It is essential that these should be timely checked before their tackling becomes difficult. It is sociology which helps us in timely identifying social problems.
- It helps us in properly understanding the needs of social relationship and the way in which this relationship should be maintained.
- It is sociology which makes us tolerant by telling us good points and healthy customs, traditions, norms and value of other societies. It enables us to appreciate what is the best in them which needs to be adjusted in our life style. Thus, sociology helps us in tolerating others and appreciating their view point.
- Sociology studies the role that social institutions play in the development of an individual. These institutions are those through which the society functions. Examples include family, school, church, and the government.
- Sociology helps us understand how people influence the government and law, and how the legal system and political structure influence society and social norms. It gives us an understanding of our rights and duties as parts of society and thus makes us better citizens.

- The study of sociology helps bring social reforms, as it involves an analysis of the social problems and their solutions. Studying sociology builds our understanding of social concerns and the measures needed to address them.
- Studying sociology can give us a different perspective of looking at people and the society at large. It can broaden our outlook towards different elements of society, removing our bias against a particular gender, race, or sections of people.

17.5 RELATIONSHIP BETWEEN SOCIOLOGY AND EDUCATION

The relation between sociology and education has always been a subject of debate. Education and sociology are mutually interrelated and interdependent disciplines. They are so closely intertwined and interconnected that their subject matter and method of study are often overlapped to a great extent. The following are the arguments to highlight the relationship between education and sociology:

- Sociology is the science of society and education in an implicit aspect of any social system.
- Sociology studies the structure and functions of social systems, while education is one of the important functions of any social system.
- The prime concern of sociology is socialised individuals while education is the process of socialising individuals.
- Education is the means for achieving the goals of sociology.
- Education is the laboratory and workshop of sociology.
- Sociology develops methods and techniques to be utilised by educational system to attain its goals.
- Sociology contributes greatly to the planning, execution, monitoring and evaluation of educational process.
- Sociology attempts to ascertain the functions performed by the educational system while education adopts the principles of sociology to improve its functioning.
- In the modern society, sociology generates the data base which is consumed by educational system to realise the goal of social life.
- Sociology develops laws and principles which are adopted by the educational system for its improvement.
- The ever cherishing social values are those attained through education.
- Sociology provides the principles and education practices them.
- Sociology put forth the ideals and values which education is to achieve.
- Education preserves the social and cultural heritage which is owned by sociology.
- Education brings about reforms and changes in the field of sociology.

18

Socialisation and Education

18.1 MEANING OF SOCIALISATION

Socialisation means the development of social behaviour. This social behaviour is developed through the process of social interaction among individuals. Social interaction must take place in a suitable social environment and this environment for the child is provided basically by the school.

Socialisation is a process through which society develops an individual according to its ideas, beliefs and traditions and bestows recognition as social being. The basis of socialisation is interaction. In other words, socialisation means that process through which an individual interacts with other individuals and learns social ideas, attitudes and patterns of behaviour. The individual, inspired by the ideals of social service and social welfare through interaction, makes himself well-adjusted with his family, neighbours and other social groups so that he himself becomes a true social being in the real sense of the term. One is compelled by his biological and social requirements to live in a society or a group. Each one of us is largely a social product.

18.2 DEFINITIONS OF SOCIALISATION

Following definitions of prominent thinkers help us to understand the various dimensions of socialisation:

1. Drever thinks that "Socialisation is a process by which the individual is adopted to his social environment and becomes a recognised, co-operating and efficient member of it."
2. Bogardus defines socialisation as the "process whereby persons learn to behave dependently together for human welfare."
3. Gandhiji observe, "I value individual freedom but you must not forget than man is essentially a social being and socialisation is the process of making a social being."
4. According to Guskin and Guskin, "Socialisation is the process by which an individual learns the behaviour, the values and the expectation of others that enable him to take on particular roles in society."

5. Havighurst and Newgarton are of the view that "Socialisation is the process by which children learn the ways of their society and make those ways part of their personality."
6. Mac Iver writes, "Socialisation and Individualisation are the two sides of a single process."
7. Ross observes, "Socialisation is the development of we-feeling in associates and the growth in their capacity and will to act together."
8. According to Dewey, socialisation is a process by which the individual becomes a 'socially efficient individual'.
9. Cook regards socialisation as a process as a result of which individuals take on themselves the various social learnings, social roles and developmental tasks.
10. Moore and Cole point out that it is through group relations that an individual is socialised and he becomes aware of what it means to work with a purpose and he identifies himself with the group.
11. Margaret Mead and several other scholars regard socialisation 'as a process of acculturation'. Acculturation implies acquiring the culture of the society. Culture refers to the total way of life of people. Thus culture includes attitudes, beliefs, customs, folkways, habits, morals, traditions, knowledge, arts, law etc. of a group or a society.

In simple words, it may be stated that socialisation is a process in which an individual identifies himself with the society. An individual learns social attitudes, social skills and social knowledge which lead to his social maturity and social adjustment.

18.3 PROCESS OF SOCIALISATION

The following points are helpful to understand the process of socialisation:

Acculturation: In the words of Marting and Stendiar, "Culture refers to the total way of life of the people and that complex whole which includes knowledge, belief, art, morals, law, customs and any other capabilities and habits, acquired by man as a member of society". This means that for the adoption of a culture, one must participate in the activities of the society. One must mix up with others to learn the habits of the society to which he belongs. So, in order to socialise oneself, one must learn the culture of the society. Brubacher has observed, "We cannot teach the coming generation to be good simply by teaching them to be wise. They must have plenty of opportunity to habituate themselves to moral ideals. Instead of learning lessons in school apart from life, school must incorporate into itself a social content of shops, laboratories, and play-grounds. Not only that but moral learning in school and college must be continued with moral training outside, through field trips, community activities and the like. If school fulfils this larger function, we may be assured that anything learned in an enterprise having an aim and in cooperation with others will be inescapable and moral."

Child Rearing: The up-bringing of a child plays a significant role in the socialization of a child. The improper upbringing of a child leads to the growth of antisocial tendencies in him because of social maladjustment. For wholesome socialisation, healthy and proper upbringing is essential.

Sympathy: Sympathy also plays an important role in the socialisation of a child. He begins to love those persons who behave with him sympathetically.

Co-operation: Society makes the child social. In other words, the co-operation of society plays an important role to socialise the child. This strengthens his social tendencies.

Suggestion: Social suggestions powerfully influence the socialisation of a child. Suggestions given by his well-wishers determine the direction of social behaviour.

Identification: Sympathy, love and suggestion of parents, relations and well-wishers develop in the child a feeling of identification with others. Those who behave with the child sympathetically, he considers them as his well-wishers. He begins to act according to their ideals, language and standard of living.

Imitation: The child imitates the behaviour, impulses and feeling of his family members. In this way, learning by imitation is the most powerful means of socialising a child.

Social Teaching: Social teaching takes place in the family, among friends and relations etc. who guide the child in one way or the other.

Incentives: Reward and punishment have a great influence on socialisation of a child. When a child behaves according to the ideals and beliefs of society, people appreciate and approve of his behaviour. For antisocial acts, he is criticised and condemned by society. This type of punishment weans the child away from unsocial activities and leads him towards proper socialisation.

18.4 STAGES IN SOCIALISATION

The Development of the Self continues throughout our lives which helps the individual to grow into an adult person and be an accepted member of the society. Values, norms, beliefs are taught to the individual so that the person follows the norms of the society.

An important aspect in the process of socialisation is the development of the self. The development of the self-concept takes place through the child's interaction with the social world and is the heart of socialisation. The self is essentially an individual's awareness of his or her physical and social identity. The self may be divided into two – the physical or existential self and the social or categorical. The first stage in the development of the self-concept is the development of the existential self. For the infant, the first step in developing a self-concept is to understand that he is separate and distinct entity. Once this process is over, the process of defining the social self begins, process that continues over one's entire life span. This is sometimes referred to as categorical self because the definition takes form of placing oneself in a wide range of categories.

Two theorists who have made considerable contribution to the understanding of self are C.H. Cooley and G.H. Mead.

C.H Cooley—'Looking Glass Self'

C.H. Cooley stressed the role of primary groups and social interaction in the development of self. According to him the self develops within the context of social relationships "there is no sense of 'I'....... without its correlative sense of 'you', 'he' or 'they'..." According to Cooley one discovers oneself through reactions of others to him. The self-concept is gained from the reactions of parents and later modified by the reactions of other individuals. Murphy explains self as any individual who is known to have his own identity and self-image. The self of a person is what s/he consciously or unconsciously conceives her/himself to be.

This concept of self is the combination of one's attitude and the feelings of others. Cooley introduced the concept of 'Looking glass self'- there are three elements in the process of development of self:

- The imagination of our appearance to another person
- The imagination of his/her judgment of that appearance
- Some sort of self-feeling such as pride or shame.

Explaining theses points, we can understand that the way we look not only appeals to us but also provokes others to react. The reactions can have a positive or negative reaction on our behaviour. Therefore, this theory 'Looking Glass Self' is considered to be important in the life of an individual.

G.H. Mead—'Development of Self'

Development of Self, according to G.H. Mead has described as the passing of the individual through distinct stages and the self emerges. He expressed the 'double centre of gravity' in his concept of the self, which he divided into 'I' and 'Me'. 'I' is the creative, spontaneous, instinctive part of the self that has ideas and imagination, while 'Me' is the social self with its capacity to take the role of the other takes into account the reactions of others. Both 'I' and 'Me' pulls one to behave in a particular way. Consciousness is a form of a conversation between the 'I' and 'Me'.

According to Mead the development of self takes place in 3 stages:

The stage of developing self-consciousness: In the first stage, the stage of developing self-consciousness is apparent in most children at the early childhood. It is the product of language learning and the social interactions that necessarily accompany it. In this stage he begins to become conscious of him in the same way that others are conscious of him. He becomes self-conscious through the use of language.

The play stage: The play stage begins around the age of 3-5.During this stage the child's verbal ability increases and he or she engages in a great deal of role playing. Children from 5-8 years of age spend much of their free time in imagination role playing of one kind or another. Mother and father, teacher, soldier, policeman etc. are all common roles assumed by children in play. Children learn to do things from this kind of activity – they learn to play the roles of adults around them and they learn who they are by being who they are not. Play is a significant preparation for the later life.

The game stage: In the next stage, game stage, the roles are related to each other by rules that define how they are to be played. In the most simple and universal of all games- hide and seek- there are only 2 related roles: hider and seeker. There is no meaning in hiding if no one seeks or in seeking if no one hides. Thus, in the games the meaning of one role lies solely in its relation to the other roles; it has no meaning outside that relation. Sociologically, therefore, play is characterised by role playing, while games are characterised by position enactment since the rules are the social norms of the game. In this stage, the player in order to do his part, must know all the roles of all other players and adjust his behaviour to the others.

18.5 IMPORTANCE AND OBJECTIVE OF SOCIALISATION

Man becomes a human being only as a member of society. By nature, he cannot live alone or in isolation. He is compelled by his biological and social requirements to live in a group or society. Even a '*Sanayasi*' living in a cave or a very isolated place needs some company at least for some time to survive. Each of us is a social product. Therefore, the main objective of socialisation is to enable the individual to conform to the norms of the group or the society to which he belongs.

18.6 MAIN CHARACTERISTICS OF THE PROCESS OF SOCIALISATION

1. Socialisation is a continuous process.
2. Socialisation is a visible as well as non-visible process.
3. Socialisation is a deliberate and also an unconscious process.
4. A democratic approach to socialisation is the appropriate approach. Autocratic approach leads to regimentation.
5. The process of socialisation aims at enabling the individual to become a self-realised socially useful member of the society.
6. Socialisation improves the individual as well as the society.
7. There are several agencies and groups which are engaged in the

process of socialisation of the individual—the family, the peer group, the club, the media and the school. But the school is the most important agency of socialisation.

18.7 AGENCIES OR FACTORS LEADING TO THE SOCIALISATION OF CHILD

The socialisation of the child is a continuing process and goes on throughout the life. Individuals acquire the culture of their society through participation in a variety of groups and institutions. From their family the child learns the first words of language, religion and several other roles. But the family cannot teach everything; at every stage of life we learn rules and behavioural patterns as we interact with others. The primary agents of socialisation are the family, peer group, school and mass media.

The main agencies or factors that help to lead to the socialisation of child are given below:

Family: Family plays a pivotal role in the socialisation of a child. As he grows older, he learns a number of socially desirable qualities like love, sympathy, tolerance, cooperation etc. By living in his family, he gradually learns the ideals, values, beliefs, customs and traditions of the family directly as well as indirectly. The process of socialisation of the child, through wholesome interaction with the members of his family, goes on continually and effectively.

The family is a permanent, the most complete and primary institution that looks after the needs of an individual. It is the family where the child comes in contact with human beings, specially, the mother and the child has physical and social contact. It is the group into which the child is born. Being the first group which has influence over the individual, the child learns his first lessons in socialisation from the family. From his parents s/he learns her/his speech and language. S/He learns respect for persons in authority. The child gets his first lessons in co-operation, tolerance, love and affection in the family. The family has tremendous influence on the character and morality of the person.

The self-concept of an individual depends to a large extend on one's family. The child develops his sense of self through observing the reactions of his parents. He learns to define himself as his parents define him. The family acts as a mediator between the individual and the other agencies of socialisation. Even though there are other agencies like school, work place, media etc.; it is the family that determines how the individual comes to be influenced by these agencies. For example, which school the child goes to; which friends he has contacts with, etc.

Neighbourhood: Neighbourhood also is like a wider and enlarged family. If the neighbourhood is wholesome, constructive and conductive, socialisation will be desirable. On the contrary bad neighbourhood is likely to spoil the desirable development and socialisation of children. That is why people belonging to noble families prefer to live with good neighbours.

School: In school, children belonging to different families learn together, interact in various patterns and imbibe various traditions of the society. Participation in educational and social functions of the school also inculcates in children social qualities, attitudes, habits and pattern of behaviour which brings about their socialisation.

The school is considered to be an important formal setting where the child spends many hours together with friends and teachers. The school is the first formal agency which exposes the child to the rules of the larger society. Here the child learns to recognise and obey rules, practice skills, and relate to people in positions of authority. Children learn to behave in group settings, sit quietly and listen to teachers, participate in social events, and accept responsibilities. The school plays the most important role in the development of social and intellectual skills and the reception of society's cultural heritage. It is not only responsible for reading, writing, and arithmetic, but for the transmission of the accumulated social heritage of the community. Education refines social skills, and frequent interaction with peers and teachers helps in the formation of a healthy social identity. The school also teaches civic sense, patriotism, and pride in the nation's shared heritage. Above all, education is supposed to foster critical thinking so that individuals can think for themselves and become creative and productive members of the society.

Workplace: As the individual grows into an adult person, work becomes part of life. Occupation brings about reality in front of the person as the individual earns for survival to fulfill his ambition. Occupational socialisation deals with the people as well as with the field. Personal goals and basic needs are fulfilled. The individual learns to cooperate, adjust with others at the work place. Discipline continues and if s/he violates the rules it may cost the loss of job.

Games and Sports: While playing, various social qualities i.e. sympathy, co-operation, fellow-felling, selfless service, sacrifice, team spirit and many other socially desirable values, develop in children to make their socialisation more effective and purposeful. In fact, games and sports have more effective role to play, even than class room teaching.

Scouting, Girl Guiding and National Service Scheme: These schemes motivate and inspire children to launch and pursue social service projects and programmes through co-operative efforts, sacrifice, sympathy, fellow-feeling, selfless service of others and many other human qualities, so essential to be effective in socialisation.

Caste: Each caste tries to socialise its children according to its specific ideals, attitudes, customs, tradition and culture. This is the reason why socialisation of children belonging to different castes is different and apparently visible.

Community or Society: Various social functions and community programmes such as festivals, functions, ceremonies etc. provide ample opportunities to children to participate in them whole heartedly and thus to develop socially describe qualities.

Organisation of Festivals: While participating in festivals, children of different cultural groups participate indifferent activities, which help the process of socialisation.

Religion: Religion is another scintillating agent of socialisation; values about morality, truth and just living are both taught in religious gatherings. There are values about what is holy treated with awe and reference and what is profane which might be handled with laxity. In its entirety religion provides the child with a code of conduct. Most of the acts the society prohibits or prescribes in terms of dressing, friendship, food, sex and sexuality, and alcohol derive from the religion practiced by a people.

Religion has important contribution with regard to the socialisation of child. As the child interacts with children belonging to his own religion and people having faith in other religions, it inculcates in him sympathy, cooperation, respect for the sentiments of others, fellow feeling and attitude of adjustment leading to socialisation in the true sense of the term.

Peer Groups: Peer group refers to people of almost the same who share similar interests. They also help in the development of personality. The first peer group is the neighbourhood play group; children who hang out together in the neighbourhood and play different games. They begin to spend more time together than in their own families. They play games like cricket together, or just hang out. Participation in such groups gives the child important social identity such as a team player, leader, or shy person etc. The first neighbourhood playgroups are breeding grounds for leaders. Children also learn the rules of the game here, their first exposure to rules of the society.

Later in life, peer groups become more influential in school and the workplace. Unlike the neighbourhood playgroups, in the school the child gets to choose his own friends. Friends may be chosen on the basis of physical attraction, common interests, or shared backgrounds. They share similar interests in sports, music, movies, fashion, and even ideologies. The first taste of alcohol or the first act of smoking may be peer-induced. Young adults who grow up in crime-ridden localities are drawn into deviant subcultures.

The influence of the peer group continues in the workplace. The office norm, or the unwritten rules of behaviour, is a product of peer socialisation. For example, in an industry or in a government office, there is often this shared understanding that an honest day's work is not necessary, and the peers frown upon people who are eager to complete the task in a timely fashion. At the same time, friends in the workplace can help individuals tide over many life crises such as domestic problems, divorce, accidents, and death.

Mass Media: In the present-day society, mass media play a significant, although subtle role in the socialisation process. Media imparts information through audio visual and print. Mass media refers to all instruments of communication such as television, radio, newspapers, magazines, movies, and records. Television has become by far the most influential medium in recent years. India has come a long way from the days of the government controlled single-channel television. With the growth of the cable industry and numerous private television channels, people have a choice. Not only is there a wide range of programmes available, but there is also an instant transmission of images, events, styles and fashions from around the world. Young people are now able to enjoy Western music, dance, fashion and fast food, and adopt types of behaviour patterns. There are also educational channels such as Discovery, National Geographic, and History, which inform, entertain and truly instruct. However, there is considerable controversy over what some people call 'cultural pollution', which is the result of the 'pernicious' influence of the West. Much of the controversy is the result of stereotypes and the comparison of our 'ideal' culture with West's 'real' culture.

It is possible that many people watch too much television and that they devote too little to reading. Once upon a time, good books were the only form of entertainment. Now, we can watch television any time of the day or night. Studies show that preschoolers and young children spend almost one-third of the day in front of the television. Studies have also shown that exposure to violence in the media can contribute to aggressive behaviour and insensitivity to violence. In India, parents are more likely to regulate children's viewing of television and violent movies. However, it will be worthwhile to undertake some extensive research on the impact of certain television programmes on young children.

We also depend on other agents of mass media such as newspapers and journals to transmit enormous amounts of information. There are magazines that cater to every conceivable interest – women, young adults, fashion, film industry, sports, health and fitness, news stories, politics, occupations and professions, music and religion. Then there are, of course, the books – fiction, biographies, and social commentaries – which convey a host of ideas. In a sense, every book is a powerful instrument of socialisation.

Once the individual completes his teenage, he enters the long phase of adulthood. The young adult is physically mature and socially responsible. His personality is integrated. He is independent and is able to make decisions for himself. He has the knowledge and skills necessary for social living and environmental mastery. Early adulthood is characterised by maximum physical and mental capacity. Speed of response and work capacity is at their best during this period. Training for a job usually occurs during this period. The young adult usually concentrates his attention on job success and advancement. There is a strong emphasis on work achievements in these years.

Old age, age of retirement, is accompanied by physical mental and social changes. There are important changes in the social roles of an individual. It is at this age period that we find signs of gradual withdrawal from active social involvements.

18.8 FACTORS RESISTING SOCIALISATION OF THE CHILD

According to Maslow, the factors that hinder the smooth working of socialisation are:

Childhood Situations: Unhealthy childhood situations i.e. lack of parental affection, favouritism, undue punishment, insecurity, conflicts and widowed mother etc. stand in the way of proper socialisation.

Cultural Conditions: Conditions of caste distinctions, social disparities, prejudices of religion and social status, snobberies, feeling of inferiority among different sections of society, untouchability, caste prejudice and religious tensions hinder socialisation process of the child.

Current Situations: Experiences of physical hardships, poverty, failure, lack of education, lack of self-reliance, courage and fortitude, occupation, poor family back-ground, stand in the process of socialisation.

Unfavourable Circumstances: Poverty, lack of education, physical hardship, unfavourable family background etc. also stand in the path of smooth socialisation.

Co-education: Mixing up of the students of different sexes creates hindrance in the process of socialisation in traditional cultures.

Languages: Due to industrialisation many people from different provinces migrate to other states for employment. The primary education is imparted in mother language. This creates some hindrances in socialisation as groups on the basis of language form different sub-groups.

18.9 EDUCATION AND SOCIALISATION

A noted French educational sociologist Emile Durkheim has explained the role of education in the socialisation of the child in these words, "Education is the influence exercised by adult generation on those that are not yet ready for social life. Its object is to arouse and to develop in the child a certain number of physical, intellectual and moral traits that are demanded of him by the society. More briefly, education is a socialisation of the young generation." He further explains that education is the means by which every society prepares, within children, the essential conditions of its very existence. The schools, colleges and other educational institutions have the responsibility of socialising the child by inculcating in him appropriate behaviour patterns, knowledge, attitudes and skills so that he adapts himself to a democratic, secular, socialist and modern society.

18.10 DIFFICULT TASK OF SOCIALISATION OF THE CHILD

Earlier, the society was very simple. There were only a few well-established roles for the individual. He did not face much stress and strain. Family was an important agency that enabled the individual to play his role. School was expected to teach knowledge of 3 R's i.e. reading, writing and arithmetic and this was considered adequate for adapting an individual to his environment.

Now, the society has become very complex. An individual is expected to acquire various types of knowledge, skills and attitudes to enable him to adjust himself to the environment.

18.11 ROLE OF THE SCHOOL IN THE SOCIALISATION OF THE CHILD: IMPORTANT PROGRAMMES OF SOCIALISATION

The school is one of the most important social institutions of the society. It has its disposal several means of socialising the child. In fact each aspect of school programme has some potential influencing the child. Through the contents of the curriculum of various subjects, co-curricular programmes, group life in the form of class and the interaction of students with teachers, the school socialises the child.

Following are the important measures of socialising the child:

1. The adoption of the common school system is the most effective way of socialising the child.
2. School curriculum should at every stage lay stress upon the unity of the different sections of the society.
3. Interdependence of States/regions should be brought out clearly so that the students evaluate the values of co-operation.
4. The school programme should be enriched with numerous curricular and co-curricular programmes in which children participate interact, co-operate and learn to live and work together.
5. Children may be taken from time to time to places of cultural, economic, geographical, historical importance,etc. to enable them to understand the contribution of various places to emotional unity and oneness of the country.
6. Exhibitions on 'know your country' may be organised.
7. Children should be acquainted with the work of great men of all regions.
8. Children should be provided opportunities to participate in social events like celebration of birthdays of leaders.
9. Children should be told about the socially accepted institutions and norms of the society.
10. The introduction of common school dress, common lunch etc. in the schools will save children of the lower middle family from suffering the agony due to the inflated ego of the children of the well-to-do families.

11. Communities activities like common meals, camps, social service, etc. should be frequently organised.
12. The mechanism of praise and blame, reward and punishment should be carefully used to socialise the child.
13. The teachers should demonstrate social and democratic outlook.
14. School should become the centre of the community for various purposes.
15. Group singing on national themes should be popularised.
16. Special lectures on socialisation should be arranged.

18.12 ROLE OF THE TEACHER IN THE SOCIALISATION OF THE CHILD

The teachers can exist a great influence on the child in inculcating attitudes and values of socialisation in various ways. The first step is that they should give due respect to the personality of the child. They should encourage the children to mix up in inter-caste rather than intra-caste and inter-regional rather than the intra-regional groups. They should not show any favour to the students belonging to upper class. They should try to understand the limitations of the students of the backward classes. Any impression of discrimination should not be allowed to develop in the minds of the students. They should always impress upon the students that there are no high or low castes. They should encourage the students to develop friendship without any class bias. They should refrain from projecting their class images on the students. The must make all possible efforts to provide a healthy social environment in which students imbibe desirable values of equality, freedom, patriotism etc.

Teachers play a very important role in the socialisation of a child. It is duty of the teacher to activate the process of socialisation by taking the following steps:

Parent-Teacher Association: The association of teachers and parents enriches about needs, interests, attitudes, aptitudes and personality makeup of the child. It smoothens the socialisation process.

Transmission of Culture: Teacher conveys to the children the customs, traditions, ideas, values and patterns of behaviour in a very imperceptible but effective way. It leads to describe socialisation of children.

Social Ideals: Teacher should try to put social ideals before children everywhere – in class rooms, on the playgrounds, during cultural and social functions, in all academic activities and diverse programmes. It will sharpen the socialisation process.

Traditions of School: School traditions exert powerful influence upon the process of socialisation. It is how the students educated in real public schools distinguish themselves from others, who are educated in ordinary schools.

Group Work: The abundance group activities will develop more social qualities which eventually will lead to socialisation.

Development of Inter-Cultural Feeling: Teacher should try to develop inter-cultural feeling in children by their freely mixing up so that they learn to respect their own culture along with other cultures.

Healthy Competition: Teacher should try to develop in children a feeling of healthy competition leading to praiseworthy socialisation. It will lead to healthy socialisation.

Healthy Human Relations: Teachers should build up healthy human relations with children of the school for effective socialisation.

Summing up. Essential conditions for making the process of socialisation most effective in the school are:

1. A democratic social climate in the school.
2. Effective inter-personal relationships.
3. Motivating teaching-learning situations.
4. Harmonious school-community inter-relationships.
5. Student involvement and participation in school management.
6. Rich programme of co-curricular and group activities.

18.13 SUGGESTION FOR PROPER SOCIALISATION OF THE STUDENTS

- Children may be taken from time-to-time to public places like museums, places of historical importance etc.
- People engaged in different economic activities or vocations, may be invited to school for giving a fruitful description of what they do and how useful their work is to the community and nation. This will also develop vocational socialisation in children.
- Socially useful productive work should be introduced in schools. This will enable the children to have firsthand experiences of the activities pursued in farms and factories.
- Children should be acquainted with the social events like the celebration of the birthdays of national leaders, saints and heroes.
- Co-curricular activities should be enriched.
- Children should be told about the socially accepted institutions in their society.
- Teachers and parents may encourage the children to mix up with inter-caste and inter-regional groups.
- The teachers and the parents should respect the personality of child.
- The mechanism of praise and blame, reward and punishment should be carefully used to socialise the children.
- Proper social education may be provided to parents so that they understand the significance of the socialisation of the children.
- The teachers should demonstrate democratic outlook, and encourage such activities amongst students.
- Teacher-parent association should be encouraged and activated.

- Community activities like camps, community meals, social service etc. should be frequently organised and students should be actively involved in them.
- Adequate stress may be laid on group activities.
- Exhibitions on 'Know Your Country' may be organised from time to time.
- Stories depicting self-sacrifices made by the great men for the cause of general good, may be told to children so that they are motivated to rise above petty gains and work for the betterment of the humanity.
- The students' council can be used up to a sense of shared responsibility among children.
- Teachers should ensure safe and healthy social environment for cultivation of freedom, equality, integrity, honesty, patriotism etc.
- Teachers should imbibe the concept of modernisation and globalisation in order to sharpen the process of international understanding.

19

Contemporary Society and Child Rearing Practices

19.1 CONTEMPORARY SOCIETY AND CHILD REARING PRACTICES

Parents use different practices to make their children familiar with the world. They treat their children according to their age, gender, beliefs, religion and culture. All those practices which are performed by the family to protect and socialise a person since his/her birth and even before birth are included in child rearing practices.

19.2 MEANING OF CHILD REARING PRACTICES

A parenting practice is a specific behaviour that a parent uses in raising a child. Parenting practices reflect the cultural understanding of children. Child rearing practices are a form of socialisation process through which the new members of society are being trained to learn about society, cope up with social issues and to behave in a specific manner with the members of society in order to become a useful member of society.

Child rearing practices is a generalised term used to refer to characteristic ways of handling or dealing with one's children. How parents bring up their children and how parental characteristics are infused into child personality are questions that continue to inspire research. The goals, values, and life styles of parents have a great effect on the growing child. As the earliest and most durable source of socialisation, a child's parents are the first people with whom he identifies, and they remain the strongest influence in his development. This overwhelming importance of parenting has led developmental psychologists to take an intense interest in parent-child interactions.

19.3 WHAT IS A FAMILY?

The family may be defined as a basic fundamental and the smallest social grouping, the members of which are united by bonds of kinship. In its simplest form, the primary or elementary family, it consists of two matured adults of opposite sex who live together in a union (marriage) recognised by the society, along with their children. The kinship ties which unite the individuals of family are basically three that exists between the married pair (husband-wife relationship); that exists between the married pair and their children (Parent-children relationship); and that exists between the children of the married pair (sibling relationship).

The family as a social unit is universal; there is not a single society in this universe where family and marriage are absent. The members of a family accept the co-operative division of labour, and they share a common shelter, a common purse, and a common hearth. The conjugal family discharges the following four basic functions, such as:

- The institutionalisation of mating with its attendant's controls over the sexual outlet,
- Co-operative division of labour between male and female,
- Nurture of the young in an atmosphere of intimacy, and
- Basic enculturation of the on-coming generation.

Types of Families in India

Families are different, and the role of the family is changing. According to Smart and Smart (1980), "*Each family is unique in the expectations of the people in various roles, in its patterns of interaction, its history of development, and its relationship with other systems*".

Families in India may be viewed from different view-points and the classifications obtained thereby are indeed varied in nature. From the point of structure, we can divide family into three basic types:

Single Parent Family: Single-parent families are families with children under age 18 headed by a parent who is widowed or divorced and not remarried, or by a parent who has never married. The most common type of single-parent family is one that consists of a mother and her biological children.

Single-parent families can be defined as families where a parent lives with dependent children, either alone or in a larger household, without a spouse or partner. There was a rapid and drastic increase in the number of single-parent families in the latter half of the twentieth century. This change has been used by some to argue that we are witnessing the breakdown of the family (defined as a married couple residing with their dependent offspring) with negative effects for children, families, and society. Others suggest that single-parent families have been present in all societies over time and should not be viewed as deviant or problematic, but rather as an alternative family form. Regardless of how family diversity is viewed, the increase in and prevalence of families headed by one parent has a major influence on the social, economic and political context of family life. Single-parent families are generally categorised by the sex of the custodial parent (mother-only or father-only families).

Working Parent Family

Nuclear Family: The nuclear family consists of a mother, father, and offspring living together. It is composed of the following members: a man, his wife and unmarried children. It is most conspicuous in the modern European and Indian societies as well among the tribal societies.

Joint Family: If two or more nuclear families live together under a common shelter, and share a common hearth, and a common purse, then this type of family is known as joint family. The Hindu joint family is the best example of such type of family in which several uterine brothers live together. Joint family may split up into simple families at any moment as in the case of urban societies.

A joint family is a large undivided family where more than one generation lives together at a common house. It is a form of family where the grand-parents, father, mother and children live unitedly at one home. They share common rights in the household property and their daily-expenses are met from the common fund.

Extended Family: When two or more families live together, this is known as an *extended family*. Within this group are grandparents, uncles, aunts or other relatives. When the nuclear family is found to be extended on all sides by certain adhesions in the form of relatives of both sides i.e. husband's and wife's sides, then it can be declared as an extended family. In most of the matrilineal societies of India, we do find such type of family in which the parents of the old age, his widowed sister with her children and even the old widowed father's sister may live. These persons are originally of some other nuclear families but due to some adverse circumstances; they forced to live in the ego's family. It is interesting to note that these adhesions cannot leave this family so easily. In modern and tribal societies, such a type of family is seldom met with.

19.4 CHILD REARING PRACTICES IN SINGLE-PARENT FAMILY

Single-parent families face special challenges. Single-parent families are challenged in other ways. Social scientists have found that children growing up in single-parent families are disadvantaged in other ways when compared to two-biological-parent families. Many of these problems are directly related to the poor economic condition of single-parent families, not just to parenting style. These children are at risk for the following:

- lower levels of educational achievement
- twice as likely to drop out of school
- more likely to become teen parents
- more conflict with their parent(s)
- less supervised by adults
- more likely to become truants
- more frequently abuse drugs and alcohol

- more high-risk sexual behaviour
- more likely to join a gang
- twice as likely to go to jail
- four times as likely to need help for emotional and behavioural problems
- more likely to participate in violent crime
- more likely to commit suicide
- twice as likely to get divorced in adulthood

It is important to remember that every single-parent family is different. Children who are living with a widowed mother will have a home life that is different from children with divorced parents or those whose parents were never married. Children of divorced parents will have a wide range of relationships with their parents and parents' partners depending on custody arrangements and the commitment of the non-custodial parent to maintaining a relationship with the child. Despite the fact that children from single-parent families often face a tougher time economically and emotionally than children from two-biological-parent families, children from single-parent families can grow up doing well in school and maintaining healthy behaviours and relationships.

Being a single parent can be hard and lonely. There is often no other adult with whom to share decision-making and financial responsibilities. The full burden of finding responsible childcare, earning a living and parenting falls on one individual. However, the lack of a second parent often has a less negative impact on children than family instability, lack of structure and inconsistent enforcement of parental standards. Single parents may want to follow these steps in order to create positive experiences for their children:

- Find stable, safe child care.
- Establish a home routine and stick to it.
- Apply rules and discipline clearly and consistently.
- Allow the child to be a child and not ask him or her to solve adult problems.
- Get to know the important people (teachers, coaches, friends) in the child's life.
- Answer questions about the other parent calmly and honestly.
- Avoid behaviour that causes the child to feel pressed to choose between divorced parents.
- Explain financial limitations honestly.

Advantages of Child Rearing Practices in Single Parent Family

Children with two parents in the home—earning two incomes—tend to have better financial and educational advantages. The effects of a single-parent home on a child's behaviour can be far-reaching and impact several areas of life given below:

- Most single-parent households are run by mothers and the absence of a father—coupled with lower household income—can increase the risk of children performing poorly in school.
- The lack of financial support from a father often results in single mothers working more, which can in turn affect children because they receive less attention and guidance with their homework.
- Children with single mothers who have contact and emotional support from their fathers tend to do better in school than children who have no contact with their fathers.
- Having only one income earner in the home puts single parent households at risk for poverty. Living in poverty is stressful and can have many emotional effects on children including low self-esteem, increased anger and frustration, and an increased risk for violent behaviour. Besides financial constraints, other emotional effects of growing up in a single parent household may include feelings of abandonment, sadness, loneliness and difficulty socialising and connecting with others. Effects vary from child to child, however, and the individual parenting style of the single parent is also a big influence on the child's development.
- Single parenting can have positive effects on children as well, depending on other factors such as personality types and parenting techniques.
- Children in single-parent families may exhibit strong responsibility skills, as they are often called upon to help out more with family chores and tasks.
- Children in single-parent families often form close bonds with their parent, as they are closely dependent on each other throughout the child's life.
- Children from single-parent families may also form closer bonds with extended family members or family friends, as these people often help raise them.

Disadvantages of Child Rearing Practices in Single Parent Family

With the increase of divorce rates in the world, single-parent homes are a major segment of all households with children. Accordingly, it's a point of intense interest to educators and parents how a single-parent environment affects children's learning. The main disadvantages of child rearing practices in single parent families are:

- Typically, single parents have to manage far more tasks than the mothers or fathers in two-parent households, simply because of practical limitations on the division of labour.
- At least until children are old enough to take on household chores,

all the housekeeping responsibilities fall on one person, as well as wage earning and parenting. As a result, it's possible for single parents to have less time or energy to encourage their children's learning by reading together, overseeing homework or planning educational, entertainment and fitness activities, and outings for the family.

- Apart from the direct influence of household structure on academic achievement and learning, a single-family home environment may influence a child's behavioural performance in school, which can indirectly affect learning and interest in school.
- When single parents are working full time and therefore have less available time for their children, the situation may lead to either behavioural issues or lower academic achievement.

19.5 CHILD REARING PRACTICES IN WORKING-PARENTS FAMILY

A working parent is a father or a mother who engages in a work life, aside from their duties as a childcare provider. There are many structures within families including single, working mothers or single, working fathers. There are also married parents who are dual-earners, in which both parents provide income. Within these family structures, there is much concern about gender inequalities. Within the institution of gender, there are expected gender roles that society pins on both mothers and fathers that reflect in the home and at work.

When both parents are occupied with their jobs for eight or more hours per day, there are obvious effects on the family. On the positive side, the family has an increased income and thus fewer financial stresses. Also, when both parents work, there is a potential for greater equality in the roles of husband and wife. Depending on the nature of the parents' work, as well as the family's values, fathers may assume more responsibility for child care and housework than has traditionally been the case. With their wives out in the workplace, men find it easier to define a greater role for themselves in child-raising. This is, particularly, evident when parents have staggered work schedules – for instance, if the father works daytime hours and is home after school and in the evening, while the mother works a shift such as 4:00 p.m. to midnight. Dad may then be in charge of preparing dinner, cleaning up the kitchen and helping the children with their homework.

Advantages of Child Rearing Practices in Working-Parents Family

Since women began entering the workforce in increasing numbers in the late 20th century, psychologists and child development experts have questioned the effects of working parents on a child's overall development. Many families must rely on financial support from both parents, thus necessitating the dual-income family, but healthy social and emotional development depends on more than just the amount of time spent with children. The main advantages of child rearing practices in working-parents families are:

- Many factors, such as parenting styles, parental availability, the presence or lack of siblings, socioeconomic status and the child's individual temperament, influence a child's social and emotional development. One of the most important factors in normal social and emotional development, however, is the ability of a child to bond with her parents, starting from the moment she leaves the womb.
- Parental bonding helps a child feel safe, secure, nurtured and loved. The parent-child bond is one of the strongest predictors of mental, social, physical and emotional health.
- The quality of the time spent with your child may be more important than the quantity. Parents who provide round-the-clock child care and try to follow all of the conventional rules of parenting may still be unable to form a secure bond with their children.
- Working parents who make family time a priority and are committed to their child's development are just as capable of establishing a healthy bond with their child as non-working parents.
- Creating a secure, healthy attachment with your child requires more than a certain amount of time spent together—it requires love, nurturing, commitment, attending to your child's physical needs and developing a sense of connection to your child.
- Children with working parents may view the world as a less threatening place. They may feel a sense of pride knowing that their parents have careers – girls, in particular, may feel motivated and sense that they have more career options if they have a mother who works—and participation in quality day care or after-school child-care settings has been linked to positive developmental traits in children in the areas of cognitive, social and emotional development

Disadvantages of Child Rearing Practices in Working-Parents Family

The main disadvantages of child rearing practices in working-parents families are:

- Certain factors may negatively impact a child's social and emotional development and affect his ability to bond with working parents. Factors such as non-standard work schedules and financial stress may have a negative impact on a child's social, emotional and behavioural development, resulting in issues like behavioural problems and poor academic performance.
- The quality and quantity of time spent in child-care settings may also impact development. Teens who spent the most time in child-

care settings as young children were more likely to exhibit impulsiveness and risk-taking behaviours than peers who had spent less time in child care.

19.6 CHILD REARING PRACTICES IN NUCLEAR FAMILY

A typical nuclear family consists of a husband, a wife, a couple of children. The number of members are very few in a nuclear family. The responsibility of a nuclear family rests on the couple. Compared to nuclear family, there is higher bond of unity and affection among different family members and relations in a joint family. The subsistence of a nuclear family is dependent upon either husband or wife, or both. In a nuclear family, the young couple gets more freedom. They can freely do the things that they like. They can also take risk with their money and display their enterprising nature.

Advantages of Child Rearing Practices in Nuclear Family

The main advantages of child rearing practices in nuclear-parents families are given below:

- The nuclear family is generally believed to be the ideal arrangement to raise a family, although it is not without its problems.
- Two parent families, whether married or not, tend to be more stable than a single parent or multi-generational family.
- Spouses or partners can role model a loving, caring and supportive relationship for their children. This will translate into future success by teaching children how to seek out positive relationships and interact well with others.
- Children will also benefit from watching partners work together to solve problems, delegate household responsibilities and support one another through positive and negative issues.
- Many nuclear families have enough economic stability to provide children with luxuries and opportunities in life.
- Children may be able to attend dance, gymnastics, music or other types of classes, especially both partners work outside the home. Children who are provided with these types of opportunities are more likely do better academically and socially, as well as develop confidence and time management skills.
- The nuclear family can provide children with consistency, in addition to stability.
- Children who have both stability and consistency in their lives are more likely to behave positively, do better in school and become more involved in community and extracurricular activities.
- The nuclear family may eat dinner together on a regular basis, go to church and take family vacations, further strengthening relationships and building a solid foundation for future life goals.

Disadvantages of Child Rearing Practices in Nuclear Family

The main disadvantages of child rearing practices in nuclear-parents families' are given below:

- The nuclear family unit does provide a closeness that many single parent or multi-generational families cannot.
- The smaller family size allows for individualised attention towards partners and children, creating lifelong bonds. However, the nuclear family unit can also isolate people from other relatives and relationships. This can break down the extended family unit, which can be beneficial in hard times.
- Grandparents, aunts and uncles should have a place within a family, but the nuclear family does not always create one for them.
- Family members, particularly mothers, may have a tendency to burn out from attempting to meet every person's needs alone. Mom is the cook, maid, babysitter and sometimes, moneymaker. That leaves little time for pampering and nurturing herself and her relationships with others. Without help, she may need to take off work to care for sick children.
- Mothers may struggle to balance the demands of work, family and friendships without any outside assistance. Stress, depression, anxiety or other problems can all be a result of nuclear family burnout.
- While the idea of less conflict and stress could certainly be considered an advantage to the nuclear family, it also puts the family at a disadvantage. Conflict is a part of life, and conflict resolution skills are beneficial in school, in the community and in the workplace.
- Nuclear families can begin to develop like-minded thinking, which will lead to fewer arguments within the family unit. However, it can increase the disagreements with extended family members. Extended family, with differing opinions and ideas, can help families see alternate viewpoints and learn to effectively deal with conflicts and opinions other than their own.

19.7 CHILD REARING PRACTICES IN JOINT FAMILY

A family when lives together with all family members up to 2nd generation like grandparents, parents, uncle, aunts and their children is called a joint family. The importance of Joint family is understood by the Indians since time immemorial. But, while young people are going advanced with their lifestyles, they are shy away from living jointly with their parents and grandparents. These people usually miss a lot of fun, caring, elder guidance from time to time which causes a lot of problems in the future like loneliness, frustrations, etc.

In a joint family system, the number of dependents living under the roof is much larger. Those living with a joint family may include, in addition to the above, grandparents, married brothers, sisters, wives of sons, grandsons, granddaughters, other dependents and relatives. The joint-family system lays down a responsibility on the head of the family. The elders trains the younger ones for different occupations, marries them, gives them a start in life, and takes care of the infirm and the old. In a joint family, the prosperity and adversity of the family are shared equally. A joint family systemensures a minimum of subsistence to all the members of the family. In a joint family, the individuals get less freedom. The family members have joint rights in family property and wealth. There is less scope for the development of individuality.

Advantages of Child Rearing Practices in Joint Family

The advantages and value of child rearing practices in joint family are described below:

- In the joint family, all members are equally sharing all expenses, works and other things with the other members of the family so the burden of work will not be felt by any single person.
- All children get equal share of love, care, guidance and education by the elder grandparents so that they never miss anything in their whole life. Similarly, they can also easily get help from their parents.
- Small children will get teaching guidance from their uncle, aunts, and other family members. The sharing resources with the cousins and sisters help parents to minimise the expenses on their child.
- On the eve of big occasions like marriage, birthdays, engagements, anniversaries etc., the whole work can easily be shared with all members so that the event will be successful. This will bring down the burden from the parents.
- It is the best pattern of living that is most conducive to the growth.
- It is based on a principle of equitable economy. It holds it as a rule of creation that all men are not equal. Naturally, it imposes a kind of unwritten discipline that those who are more able economically shall share some of the burden of those who are not.
- The joint mess, naturally, runs on an understanding of mutual adjustment. Naturally, those who are benefited by the generosity of others remain obliged and grateful.
- Similarly, in a big joint family the study groups of boys are formed according to their age matching. Naturally the cousins study together, play together, quarrel together and are even punished together. As a result there grows in them a feeling of camaraderie that is free from any discrimination of one being a full brother or a cousin.

- In marriages also, the grooms for marriageable girls become a concern for all the elders in the family. Even if a daughter of a junior brother is selected by someone because of her beauty or brilliance, he would not agree to her marriage until her senior cousin sister is married.
- The basic necessities of all the family members are taken care of. Each member is guaranteed the minimum subsistence for living.
- It supports all the members of the family. Old and elderly people are respected. Proper care is taken for old, widowed, physically weak and disabled family members.
- As such the disciplines in a joint family are self-imposed on its members. The head of the big family becomes virtually its patriarch and the family prospers squarely if the patriarch and the other constituents observe the norms soundly and healthily.
- Finally, the spirit of oneness prevails in a Joint family system.

Disadvantages of Child Rearing Practices in Joint Family

The disadvantages and value of child rearing practices in joint family are described below:

- It often creates parasites who love to feed on other's income. They exploit the goodness and principled behaviour of its partners.
- Sometimes some crooked member of the family plot to torture and exploit another innocent member of the family.
- High earning members often insults the low earning members.
- The cost of education has gone up high. The high earning members often want their children to study in costly schools but they don't want to share the burden of the children of the other members of the family.
- In large families, most of important decisions are made by the head of the family. Since, all the individuals within the family doesn't get the opportunity to participate in major decisions of the family, they often feel lost or develop a feeling of inferiority complex.
- The separation of families was evident in the joint families themselves. It happens when feelings of generosity, charity and fellow-feeling are not balanced by strong moral line, character and farsightedness.

19.8 CHILDREN REARING IN ORPHANAGES

A number of children separated from their parents are forced to get shelter in orphanages when:

- help from relatives are not available
- when they are saved from 'The clutches of the kidnappers' and bad guys

- when they are deliberately abandoned by relatives and single parents in the orphanages (many children are left in temples, lonely places and the premises of orphanages by the unmarried mothers, widows, illegitimate relationship couples etc.)

In such an uncongenial environment it is quite natural for the children rearing in orphanages to suffer from one or the other deprivation or disadvantages such as:

- Deprivation suffered in terms of the satisfaction of their physical needs like availability of enough food for satisfying their hunger, lack of nutritious elements in their food stuff, clean water, clothes and other material for living.
- Deprivation suffered in terms of satisfying their socio-cultural needs such as little or no opportunities for having company and interaction with the social and cultural life of the outside world.
- Deprivation suffered in terms of satisfying their educational needs as no serious attempts are made for their proper education and schooling.
- Deprivation suffered in terms of the satisfaction of their psychological needs such as need to get love and affection, empathy and cooperation etc.

19.9 TYPE OF FAMILY AND QUALITY OF PARENTING

Regardless of family structure, the quality of parenting is one of the best predictors of children's emotional and social well-being. Many single parents, however, find it difficult to function effectively as parents. Compared with continuously married parents, they are less emotionally supportive of their children, have fewer rules, dispense harsher discipline, are more inconsistent in dispensing discipline, provide less supervision, and engage in more conflict with their children. Many of these deficits in parenting presumably result from struggling to make ends meet with limited financial resources and trying to raise children without the help of the other biological parent. Many studies link inept parenting by resident single parents with a variety of negative outcomes among children, including poor academic achievement, emotional problems, conduct problems, low self-esteem, and problems forming and maintaining social relationships. Other studies show that depression among custodial mothers, which usually detracts from effective parenting, is related to poor adjustment among offspring.

Although the role of the resident parent (usually the mother) in promoting children's well-being is clear, the non-resident parent (usually the father) can also play an important role. Children had higher academic achievement and fewer emotional and conduct problems when non-resident fathers were closely involved in their lives.

Children also thrive when their parents have a cooperative co-parental relationship. When parents agree on the rules and support one another's decisions, children learn that parental authority is not arbitrary. Parental agreement also means that children are not subjected to inconsistent discipline when they misbehave. Consistency between parents helps children to learn and internalise social norms and moral values. Another benefit of a positive co-parental relationship is the modelling of interpersonal skills, such as showing respect, communicating clearly, and resolving disputes through negotiation and compromise. Children who learn these skills by observing their parents have positive relationships with peers and, later, with intimate partners. When children's parents live in separate households, however, cooperative co-parenting is not the norm. Although some parents remain locked in conflict for many years, especially if a divorce is involved, most gradually disengage and communicate little with one another. At best, most children living with single parents experience "parallel" parenting rather than cooperative co-parenting.

19.10 SOCIALISATION AND CHILD REARING

Socialisation is the process by which children are prepared to become successful members of society. This requires the learning of skills, behaviour patterns, ideas and values needed for competent functioning in the society in which a child is growing up. More broadly, socialisation is a process by which culture is transmitted or reproduced in each new generation. Parents hope to instill cultural continuity and competence in their children. Socialisation also includes inadvertent outcomes, such as when harsh parental practices and poor home environments send children on negative trajectories of poor achievement and antisocial behaviour.

The traditional concept of socialisation guiding research and parent education was unidirectional and deterministic. In this view, children are assumed to enter a social world that contains pre-existing meanings, rules and expectations, with the role of parents being to teach or transmit this knowledge to children. Despite competition with other sources of influence on children, parents—including all primary caregivers acting in the role of parents—are regarded as the most important agents of children's socialisation, and they lay the foundations for later changes as the child interacts with the wider world outside the family.

Socialisation is a lifelong process that encompasses the different stages of childhood and continues throughout adulthood. Socialisation and child rearing have been topics of sustained interest for almost one hundred years and the groundwork for contemporary ideas can be found in thousands of years of philosophical and religious discourses.

20

Social Diversity and Socialisation

Caste, Class, Social Mobility, Literacy, Poverty, Region, Language

20.1 MEANING OF DIVERSITY

In precise, diversity means differences. However in social context, it means collective differences among people, i.e. the differences which mark off one group from another group of people. These differences can be biological, religious, linguistic etc. On the basis of biological differences, there are racial diversity. And, on the basis of religious differences, there are have religious diversity. The point to note is that diversity refers to collective differences.

20.2 MEANING OF SOCIAL DIVERSITY

Social diversity is a feature of a society which is determined by caste, class, religion, literacy, language occupational pattern in a given territory. This is very different from social hierarchy where society is divided into several layers of superiority and inferiority. In case of social diversity, social hierarchy may be present but at the same time society may be egalitarian i.e. hierarchy-less. All the determinants given are not necessarily present at the same time together.

Social diversity means people with different opinions, backgrounds (degrees and social experience), religious beliefs, political beliefs, sexual orientations, heritage and life experience. Diversification is a principle that maintains how individual develop into quite different people so that they can peacefully occupy different niches within the environment. Humans have evolved adaptations or solutions to threats to survival. Just as different plant species will coexist alongside one another in different areas of creek-bed ecosystem, individual diversify by developing different traits, abilities and preferences, thereby occupying different identities and sometimes mingled identities in order to survive and exist productively at intrapersonal as well as at interpersonal level. Social diversity means variety or the opposite of homogeneity. In social organizations, the term usually refers to the range of personnel who more accurately represent minority populations and people from varied backgrounds, cultures, ethnicities and viewpoints.

A broad definition of diversity ranges from personality and work style to all of the visible dimensions of diversity such as race, age, ethnicity or gender, to secondary influences such as religion, socio-economics and education, to work diversities such as management and union, functional level and classification or proximity/distance to headquarters. The greater this individual diversity the greater must be the allowed social diversity in our societies. This implies an increase in the number of variables applicable to our natures. To define a unique social being requires a very large array of different values (impossible to quantify accurately), thus the same must be true of the society that contains them all.

20.3 MEANING OF SOCIALIZATION

Socialization is a term used by sociologists, social psychologists, anthropologists, political scientists and educationalists to refer to the lifelong process of inheriting and disseminating norms, customs, values and ideologies, providing an individual with the skills and habits necessary for participating within their own society. Socialization is thus "*the means by which social and cultural continuity are attained*".

Socialization describes a process which may lead to desirable outcomes—sometimes labeled "moral"—as regards the society where it occurs. Individual views on certain issues, for instance race or economics, are influenced by the society's consensus and usually tend toward what that society finds acceptable or "normal". Many socio-political theories postulate that socialization provides only a partial explanation for human beliefs and behaviours, maintaining that agents are not blank slates predetermined by their environment; scientific research provides evidence that people are shaped by both social influences and genes. Genetic studies have shown that a person's environment interacts with his or her genotype to influence behavioural outcomes.

20.4 SOCIAL DIVERSITY AND SOCIALIZATION

Socialization is the process by which human infants begin to acquire the skills necessary to perform as a functioning member of their society, and is the most influential learning process one can experience. Unlike many other living species, whose behaviour is biologically set, humans need social experiences to learn their culture and to survive. Although cultural variability manifests in the actions, customs, and behaviours of whole social groups (societies), the most fundamental expression of culture is found at the individual level. This expression can only occur after an individual has been socialized by his or her parents, family, extended family, and extended social networks. This reflexive process of both learning and teaching is how cultural and social characteristics attain continuity. Many scientists say socialization essentially represents the whole process of learning throughout the life course and is a central influence on the behaviour, beliefs, and actions of adults as well as of children.

20.5 SOCIAL DIVERSITY AND SOCIALISATION — CASTE, CLASS, SOCIAL MOBILITY, LITERACY, POVERTY, RELIGION, REGION, LANGUAGE

The child is socialized by several agencies and institutions, in which he or she participates, viz. his or her family, school, peer group, the neighbourhood., and the social class. The position of the family in the social structure is determined by the social class, caste, region, language, religion, etc. Some other factors which are important in the socialization process are—whether one is rich or poor, whether one is tribal or non-tribal, whether one is a boy or a girl or whether one is a child or an adult. The differentiation in socialization may also be reflected through music, rituals, language, art and literature, which form part of one's culture consisting of complex set of variables.

These are the factors and agencies which introduce differentiation in the socialization process within different societies. These are very crucial and should be taken into account to dispel the impression that socialization is uniform across all societies or within a particular society.

20.6 FACTORS RESPONSIBLE FOR THE VARIATION IN THE SOCIALIZATION PROCESS

A city-born person when comes across a person from the semi-urban village or village is likely to notice him or her because of the differences in their dress, dialect and their deportment. The villager is recognizable not only by the outward symbols mentioned but also by his or her values norms and behaviour patterns he/she upholds and considers appropriate. On the other hand, a person living in a village will be struck by the difference in dress, dialect and deportment of those belonging to the city. One may have often heard that a person hailing from a village or a small town feels that people in the city are too involved in their own affairs to be bothered about their guests or the elders in the family. These differential responses are the outcome of differential socialization processes in the rural and urban areas. Some of the factors responsible for the variation in the socialization process are discusses below:

Caste and Socialization

If one is living in a village or in a small town, one may be aware of the behaviour that is expected from one as a member of a small town. Thus, there are certain value norms and behaviour patterns that are common to most villages. Certain rituals and ceremonies may also be common to all the members of a village. However, a village community is also divided into small groups called castes. The castes are divided on the basis of birth because people are born into them. One may be able to distinguish between a Brahmin and Kshatriya; a goldsmith or a washerman. Therefore, within a village, there are likely to be sub-cultures while the culture of a village itself may have something in common which is shared by all its members and bind all the members together. The language or the dialect also tends to vary. The upper castes speak better form of the language than spoken by the other. Similarly, there are differences in the dress that is considered appropriate or inappropriate for a particular caste. Again, the behaviour that is considered proper by one caste may not be so considered so by the other. For example, vegetarianism may be more popular among the Brahmins than among other castes.

Each caste tries to socialise its children according to its specific ideals, attitudes, customs, tradition and culture. This is the reason why socialisation of children belonging to different castes is different and apparently visible.

Family, Social Class and Socialization

These two dimensions are being taken together because 'family' here includes not only the size, the composition and the type but the social position. Class is an "open" system. Under this system vertical mobility is absolutely free. Movement from one status to another has no barrier. Status is based on achievement. It is determined by the talents, wealth, money, intelligence, power, education, income, etc. of a person. There is no inheritance of parental status. Impact of stratification due to class: divides society into haves and have not's, could lead to crime, poor health, illiteracy, class struggle, benefits of progress limited to few, low Gross Domestic Products (GDP). Obviously class also affects socialization process of the children.

The social position of a family is determined by caste, race and social class, etc. A key agency of socialization in all human societies is the family which transforms the young infant into a member of a human community. Each child is more or less uniquely prepared for the cultural reality that his or her family has experienced or wishes to experience.

Social Mobility and Socialization

Mobility stands for shift, change and movement. The change may be of a place or from one position to another. Further, change is value free i.e. it cannot be said that change is for good or bad. When we prefix 'social' along with mobility, it would imply that people or individual occupying a social position, move to another position or status.

Social mobility is the movement of individuals, families or other categories of people within or between social strata in a society. It is a change in social status relative to others' social location within a given society. Social mobility may refer to classes, ethnic groups or entire nations and may measure health status, literacy or education; however, more commonly it refers to the change in income, wealth and social status of individuals or families. However, it may also refer to changes in health status, literacy rate, education or other variables among groups such as classes, ethnic groups or countries.

Movement up or down the social hierarchy is called vertical social mobility. Movement between two equally ranked social positions is called horizontal mobility. Social mobility typically refers to vertical mobility, which is the movement of individuals or groups up or down from one socioeconomic level to another, often by changing jobs or through marriage.

Literacy and Socialization

According to Akinnaso, literacy,...should be regarded as a way of preparing man for a social, civic and economic role that goes beyond the limits of rudimentary literacy training, consisting merely in teaching of reading and writing. The very process of learning....should lead to... training for work, increased productivity, and should ultimately open the way to basic human knowledge.

Literacy is a basic human need and human right to knowledge. It has meaning only when it leads to participation in cultural and social activities. It leads to make decisions and control affairs of one's own life, economically, socially and politically. It is the foundation of all skills and pre-requisite for economic development. Literacy makes the pupil more consistent in their actions, more polite and civilized in dealings, more accurate and perfect in decisions. Moreover, literacy helps in building confidence by providing the necessary knowledge and skills to face the problems and difficulties. Finally, literacy occupies an essential place in the life of the community.

People today have to be able to realize that they can use education to seek vocational skills to improve the quality of life so as to reach happiness which is based on each individual's personal experiences, complete happiness can be achieved when there is no physical or emotional conflict between man and his environment physically or mentally. Thus education or literacy today plays the important role as the tools that will enable individual to create his own harmony between himself and the surroundings.

The most important aspect of education is that without it all learning comes to a stop. Literacy is important because it makes us who we are. It makes us individual, and distinct. Literacy is the key to all learning and the path to the future.

Poverty and Socialization

The poverty can be defined as '*the lack of ability to attain a minimum standard of living*'. Later, the World Bank (2000) defines poverty as lack of control over commodities, or as a severe limitation of the choice set over commodities, leading to pronounced deprivation in well being or welfare. Socialization help people, find out to function effectively in their social worlds.

Poverty damages the overall picture of the society. Its curse hinders the ways to success and prosperity. The children socialization particularly influence by this evil of poverty. The major loss is that a large population of children remains deprived from the education due to poverty.

Poverty badly affects child's early life in five ways — (1) child health and nutrition, (2) parent mental health and effective interactions, (3) provision of a stimulating home environment, (4) school and child care quality and (5) neighbourhood conditions (Nancy E et al, 1993).

Family income directly influences the material resources available to children in their homes. Higher income children benefit from higher levels of cognitively stimulating materials available in their homes compared to low-income children. Children from poor families are getting to lower quality school and child care settings compared to their non-poor counterparts. The neighbourhoods in which poor families reside may negatively affect children's educational outcomes because of high levels of crime and unemployment, low levels of resources and a lack of collective efficacy among the residents. Poverty is key indicator for children's poor socialization and limited education. Government should provide equal educational opportunities to alleviate poverty.

Religion and Socialization

Agents of socialization differ in effects across religious traditions. Religion may be like an ethnic or cultural category, making it less likely for the individuals to break from religious affiliations and be more socialized in this setting. Parental religious participation is the most influential part of religious socialization—more so than religious peers or religious beliefs.

Difference in the socialization processes and practices is noticeable among certain religious communities. As for example, the rites and ceremonies, customs, dress, sometimes language and beliefs, attitudes and values and the behaviour patterns of Christians, Hindus, Sikhs or Muslims are different. These may be at variance with one another although some of the external symbols such as dress, speech, slang and deportment have become uniform for all religious groups in the big cities during the last few years, so that it has become difficult to distinguish members of one religious community from another on the basis of dress, etc. In the semi-urban villages or villages, a significant section of people still wear their traditional dresses and are distinguished on the basis of these outward symbols. In addition and more importantly, the emphasis on what constitutes a good Hindu or a good Muslim or a good Sikh or a good Christian, also creates differences in the values and behaviour of members of a larger society. For example, a good— Muslim is to perform prayers five times a day, — Christian is to attend church on Sundays, — Sikh should do service at a Gurdwara, and — Hindu should give charity in the temples.

Similarly, further subdivisions can be drawn on the basis of Shaivite and Vaishnavite Brahmins of southern India. So, also the marriage ceremony and rites differ among those who follow the Arya Samaj and Sanatana Dharma, the two Hindu sects. Thus, the differences are not confined to religious ideology but are reflected in the socialization process through the beliefs, attitudes, norms and behaviour patterns of the people belonging to these sects and sub-sects.

Region/Geographical Environment and Socialization

Region/geographical environment are also responsible for the variation in the socialization process of children and their education. Socialization in urban, sub-urban and rural environments has somewhat different dynamics. Each type of geographical location provides strengths and challenges based on the topography of the region. People and children are also socialized to accept different political values, ideologies, and parties based on the region of the country in which they grew up or currently live.

Language and Socialization

People learn to socialize differently depending on a particular language and culture in which they live. A specific example of this is code switching. This is where immigrant children learn to behave in accordance with the languages used in their lives: separate languages at home and in peer groups (mainly in educational settings). Depending on the language and situation at any given time, people will socialize differently.

21

Role of Education to Promote Inclusion in Schools and Society

Exclusion from meaningful participation in the economic, social, political and cultural life of communities is one of the greatest problems facing individuals in our society today. Such societies are neither efficient nor desirable.

The purpose of education is to ensure that all students gain access to knowledge, skills and information that will prepare them to contribute to their nations and workplaces. The central purpose becomes more challenging as schools accommodate students with increasingly diverse backgrounds and abilities. As we strive to meet these challenges, the involvement and cooperation of educators, parents, and community leaders is vital for the creation of better and more inclusive schools.

21.1 WHAT IS INCLUSION?

UNESCO views inclusion as "a dynamic approach of responding positively to pupil diversity and of seeing individual differences not as problems, but as opportunities for enriching learning." Inclusion is seen as a process of addressing and responding to the diversity of needs of all learners through increasing participation in learning, cultures and communities, and reducing exclusion within and from education. It involves changes and modifications in content, approaches, structures and strategies, with a common vision which covers all children of the appropriate age range and a conviction that it is the responsibility of the regular system to educate all children.

Inclusion is an educational approach and philosophy that provides all students with community membership and greater opportunities for academic and social achievement. Inclusion is about making sure that each and every student feels welcome and that their unique needs and learning styles are attended to and valued.

21.2 WHY INCLUSION?

Because the world is changing, because moral values are being re-examined as stereotypical thinking is increasingly exposed, because national and international guidance advocates inclusion and, quite simply, because any alternative seems unacceptable, if not morally flawed:

1. Valuing some people more than others is unethical.
2. Maintaining barriers to some students' participation in the cultures, curricula and communities of local schools is unacceptable.
3. Preserving school cultures, policies and practices that are non-responsive to the diversity of learners perpetuates inequalities.
4. Thinking that inclusion mostly concerns disabled learners is misleading.
5. Thinking that school changes made for some will not benefit others is short-sighted.
6. Viewing differences between students as problems to be overcome is disrespectful and limits learning opportunities.
7. Segregated schooling for disabled learners violates their basic human right to education without discrimination.
8. Improving schools only for students is disrespectful to all other stakeholders.
9. Identifying academic achievement as the main aim of schooling detracts from the importance of personal and moral development.
10. Isolating schools and local communities from one another deprives everyone of enriching experiences.
11. Perceiving inclusion in education as a separate issue from inclusion in society is illogical.

21.3 INCLUSION IN EDUCATION

Inclusion in education involves:

1. Putting inclusive values into action.
2. Viewing every life and every death as of equal worth.
3. Supporting everyone to feel that they belong.
4. Increasing participation for children and adults in learning and teaching activities, relationships and communities of local schools.
5. Reducing exclusion, discrimination, barriers to learning and participation.
6. Restructuring cultures, policies and practices to respond to diversity in ways that value everyone equally.
7. Linking education to local and global realities.
8. Learning from the reduction of barriers for some children to benefit children more widely.
9. Viewing differences between children and between adults as resources for learning.
10. Acknowledging the right of children to an education of high quality in their locality.
11. Improving schools for staff and parents/carers as well as children.

12. Emphasizing the development of school communities and values, as well as achievements.
13. Fostering mutually sustaining relationships between schools and surrounding communities.
14. Recognizing that inclusion in education is one aspect of inclusion in society.

21.4 INCLUSIVE EDUCATION

Inclusive education happens when children with and without disabilities or marginalised children participate and learn together in the same classes. When a child with disabilities attends classes alongside peers with no disabilities, good things happen. For a long time, children with disabilities were educated in separate classes or schools. But, when children are educated together, positive academic and social outcomes occur for all the children involved. Inclusive education occurs when there is ongoing advocacy, planning, support and commitment.

These are the principles that guide quality inclusive education:

All Children Valued Equally: Inclusive education is based on that every child is valued equally and deserves the same opportunities. Inclusive education is about marginalised and children with disabilities whether the disability is mild or severe. It's about building friendships, membership and having opportunities just like everyone else.

Children Learn in Different Ways: It is about providing the help children need to learn and participate in meaningful ways. Sometimes, help from friends or teachers works best and sometimes, specially designed materials or technology can help. The objective is to give only as much help as needed.

Every Child has Right to be Included: Inclusive education is a child's right. The Individuals with Disabilities Education Act clearly states that all children with disabilities should be educated with non-disabled children their own age and have access to the general education curriculum.

21.5 DEFINITION OF INCLUSIVE EDUCATION

Inclusive education is a philosophy that promotes:

- the right of all students to attend school with their peers and to receive appropriate and quality programming;
- a continuum of supports and services in the most appropriate setting (large group, small group, individualized) respecting the dignity of the child;
- a welcoming school culture where all members of the school community feel they belong, realize their potential, and contribute to the life of the school;

- an atmosphere which respects and values the participation of all members of the school community;
- a school community which celebrates diversity; and
- a safe and caring school environment

21.6 THE BENEFITS OF INCLUSIVE EDUCATION

Here are key findings about the benefits of inclusion for children and families:

Families' Dream can Come True: All parents want their children to be accepted by their peers, have friends and lead "regular" lives. Inclusive settings can make this vision a reality for many children with disabilities or marginalised children (from minorities/refugees/OBC etc. families).

Positive Understanding: When children attend classes that reflect the similarities and differences of people in the real world, they learn to appreciate diversity. Respect and understanding grow when children of differing abilities and cultures play and learn together.

Friendships Develop: Schools are important places for children to develop friendships and learn social skills. Children learn with and from each other in inclusive classes.

Learning Important Academic Skills: In inclusive classrooms, all children are expected to learn to read, write and do math. With higher expectations and good instruction children with disabilities learn academic skills.

Children Learn by being Together: Because the philosophy of inclusive education is aimed at helping all children learn, everyone in the class benefits. Children learn at their own pace and style within a nurturing learning environment.

21.7 COMMON PRACTICES IN INCLUSIVE CLASSROOMS

Students in an inclusive classroom are generally placed with their chronological age-mates, regardless of whether the students are working above or below the typical academic level for their age. Also, to encourage a sense of belonging, emphasis is placed on the value of friendships. Teachers often nurture a relationship between a student with special needs and a same-age student without a special educational need.

Teachers can use a number of techniques to help build classroom communities:

1. Using games designed to build community
2. Involving students in solving problems
3. Sharing songs and books that teach community
4. Openly dealing with individual differences by discussion
5. Assigning classroom jobs that build community
6. Teaching students to look for ways to help each other
7. Utilizing physical therapy equipment such as standing frames, so

students who typically use wheelchairs can stand when the other students are standing and more actively participate in activities

8. Encouraging students to take the role of teacher and deliver instruction (e.g. read a portion of a book to a student with severe disabilities)
9. Focusing on the strength of a student with special needs
10. Create classroom checklists
11. Take breaks when necessary
12. Create an area for children to calm down
13. Organize student desk in groups
14. Create a self and welcoming environment
15. Set ground rules and stick with them
16. Help establish short-term goals
17. Design a multi-faced curriculum
18. Communicate regular with parents and/or caregivers
19. Seek support from other special education teachers

22

Education and Culture

In the words of Golda Meyer, "*The purpose of education is to civilise the thousands of barbarians that are born in to this world every hour*". If education fails to bring change in the learner, then it is worthless. Education is considered the most powerful tool in bringing change in man. On one hand, education acculturates an individual; on the other hand, it preserves, transmits and develops the culture of a society. In short, education and culture are mutually interdependent, complementary and supplementary in all their aspects and activities. Thus, the relation between education and culture is inseparable.

Culture plays a vital role in man's life. Education of various elements of culture can help man in the adaptation to the natural and social environment, development of individual's personality, socialisation of the individual, proper use of leisure, and understanding other cultures and proper meaning of liberality. Education in culture is imparted mainly by the family, society and the school. Considering the importance of culture in man's life and the role played by education in the socialisation and acculturation of an individual, it is worthwhile to analyse the changes that have taken shape in our culture. Before embarking on the discussion on the impact of education on culture, let us briefly understand the concept of culture itself.

22.1 CONCEPT AND MEANING OF CULTURE

Culture is a unique possession of man. Every man is born into a society is the same as saying that "every man is born into a culture". Every man can be regarded as a representative of this culture. Culture is the unique quality of man which separates him from the lower animals. As used by sociologist and cultural anthropologists, culture has a different meaning.

To a sociologist, a culture is a system of ideas, values, beliefs, knowledge, norm, customs and technology shared by almost everyone in a particular society.

Culture can be said to include all the human phenomena in a society. Culture includes all learned behaviour. Culture is a very broad term that includes in itself all our walks of life, our modes of behaviour, our philosophers and ethics, our morals and manners, our customs and tradition, our religious, political, economic and other types of activities.

22.2 MEANING AND DEFINITIONS OF CULTURE

All the human societies have complex ways of life that differ greatly from one to another. These ways have come to be known as culture in 1871. Edward Tylor gave us the first definition of this concept. Culture as defined by Edward "*is that complex whole which includes knowledge belief, art, law, morals custom and other capabilities and habit acquired by man as a member of society*". Robert Bierstadt Simplified Tylor's definition by stating "*culture is the complex whole that consists of all the ways we think and do and everything we have as member of society*".

In the word of MacIver and Page, culture is "*the realm of styles of values of emotional attachments of intellectual adventures*".

B. Malinowski has defined culture as the "*cumulative creation of man*". He also regarded culture as a handiwork of man and the medium, through which he achieves his ends.

Culture is often referred as a "*Sum total of behaviour traits which a person, comes to acquire through instruction and learning. It shapes an individual's reaction to external environment it provides the individual a structure of socially approved ideas and beliefs, norms and values.*"

22.3 KINDS OF CULTURE

According to the subject there are four types of culture:

Individual Culture: Each individual has some personal traits and qualities which guide his habits of thinking and behaving in all fields of human activities. These personal likes and dislikes, interests, modes of thinking and patterns social behaviour constitute his personal culture.

Communal Culture: As in the case of individual culture, different communities exhibit their distinct traits of life styles comprising specific modes of community beliefs and life styles. All the members of different communities show different traits known as community culture.

National Culture: Similarly, each nation has some distinct national traits and attributes of character which condition its national patterns of ideals, values, modes of thought and behaviour. Such national traits are known as national culture.

World Culture: Due to the rapid rise in the means of transport and communication, the world has shrunk into a small unit with the result that different nations of the world live together as members of a world community having common values, namely co-operation, sympathy, social service, social awakening and social sensitiveness etc. there by constituting a world culture.

22.4 FUNCTIONS OF CULTURE

Man is not only a social animal but also a cultural being. Man's social life has been made possible because of culture. Culture is something that has elevated him from the level of animal to other superior animal. Man cannot survive without culture. It represents the entire achievements of mankind.

Culture has been fulfilling a number of functions among which the following may be noted:

Culture Defines Situation: Culture defines social situation for us. It not only defines but also conditions and determines what we eat and drink, what we wear, where to laugh, weep and sleep, to make friends with, what work we do, what to worship etc.

Culture is the Treasury of Knowledge: Culture provides knowledge which is important for the physical, social and intellectual existence of man. Birds and animals behave instinctively with the help of instincts they try to adapt themselves with the environment. But man has greater intelligence and learning capacity, with the help of these he has been able to adapt himself with the environment or modify it to suit his convenience. Culture has made such an adaptation and modification possible and easier by providing man the necessary skills and knowledge. Culture preserves knowledge and helps its transmission from generation to generation through its element that is language. Language helps in not only the transmission of knowledge but also in its preservation, accumulation and diffusion. On the contrary, animals do not have this advantage because culture does not exist at sub-human level.

Culture Provides Behaviour Patterns: Culture directs and confines the behaviour of an individual. Culture assigns goals and provides means for achieving them. It rewards his noble walk and punishes the immoral ones. It assigns him status and roles. We see, dream, aspire, work, strive, enjoy, according to the cultural expectation. Culture not only controls but also liberates human energy and activities. Man, indeed, follows his culture in every path of his life.

Culture Defines Attitudes, Values and Goals: Attitudes refer to the tendency to feel and act in certain ways, values are the measure of goodness or desirability. Goals refer to the attainment which our values define as worthy. It is the culture which conditions our attitudes towards various issues such as religion, morality, science, family planning, prostitution, and so on. Our values concerning private property, fundamental rights representative governments etc. are influenced by our culture. Our goals of winning the target, understanding others, attaining salvation, being respectful and obedient to elders and teachers, being patriotic, loyal etc. are set forth by our culture. We are being socialised on these models.

Culture Models Personality: Culture exercises a great influence on the development of personality. No child can develop human qualities in the absence of a cultural environment. Culture prepares man for group life and provides him the design of living. It is culture that provides opportunities for the development of personality and sets limits on its growth.

Culture Decides Our Career: What career, we are likely to pursue is largely decided by our culture. Whether we should become a politician, a social worker, a doctor, an engineer, a solider, a farmer, a professor, an industrialist, a religious leader and so on, is decided by our culture. Culture sets limitations on our choice to select different careers. Individuals may develop, modify or oppose the trends of their culture but they always live within its framework. Only a few can find outlet in the culture.

Thus, the individual is exposed to and moulded by the culture of the group into which he is born. But the culture provides not only for "universals" but also for "alternatives". There is not only conformity in cultural learning but also variations. Every individual is unique in any culture. The uniqueness may be based on individual differences in ability, aptitude and learning. The impact of culture on the individual is not always identical in every case. Every individual is sooner on later exposed to influences which are not completely determined by culture. Travelling, books, radio, cinema, television, newspaper, exposes an individual to many influences outside the culture. Various biological and social factors bring about uniqueness of the individuals in any culture.

22.5 TYPES OF CULTURE

According to contents there are two types of culture in each society:

Material Culture: Material culture includes all those man-made things and objects which human society has created for its physical welfare in times of peace and war. Items such as clothes, utensils, homes, roads, ornaments, T.V., radio, various machines, gadgets and various means of transport and communication are some examples of material culture.

Non-material Culture: Non-material culture includes all those ideals, attitudes and values which modify the behaviour of man, language, literature, art, music, religion, customs, traditions etc.

22.6 EDUCATION AND CULTURE

Education and culture are intimately and integrally connected. The cultural pattern of a society conditions its educational pattern. For example, if a society has a spiritual pattern of culture, then its educational procedures will emphasise the achievement of moral and eternal values of life. On the other hand, if the cultural pattern of a society is materialistic, then naturally its educational pattern will be shaped for the attainment of material values which promote pleasures of senses and material comforts. A society devoid of any culture will have no definite educational organisation. Hence the culture of a country has a very powerful impact on its educational pattern.

The ultimate relationship between culture and education is evident from the fact that one of the major aims of education is to impart to the child his cultural heritage. In any human group, the various elements and parts of culture evolve after thousands of years of the experience, and these are handed down as a whole to the succeeding generations. Hence every individual is born into a particular culture which provide him definite patterns of behaviour and values which guide his conduct in different walks of life. He has, thereby, saved the necessity of making fresh experiments every time. Obviously, then, culture plays an important part in man's life in the adaptation to the natural environment, in the adaptation to the social environment, in the development of personality and socialisation.

Every society has a culture or a method of operating which is unique to it. To live harmoniously in a given culture, its members must be aware of the various modes of conduct which are acceptable to that culture. It is through the process of education that children and new members are apprised of these facts. Also, in order to survive, the individual must become acquainted with the nature of these things in his environment with which he may have to cope. In very general terms then, it may be said that universally, the purpose of education is to inform the individual about the nature of his culture and the acceptable methods of coping with that culture. The implication, clearly, is that education should teach the students of a particular country how to look at the world and doing things according to the way of doing things of his own country.

22.7 IMPACT OF CULTURE ON EDUCATION

As mentioned above, culture and education have a give and take relationship. Both compliment and supplement each other in various aspects. The following are some of the influences of culture on education:

- *The aims and ideals* of education are mostly determined by the values and patterns of society.
- *Curriculum* is conditioned according to the culture of society. It is framed according to the ideals and needs of the society to realise the cultural values.
- *Methods of teaching* and culture are intimately connected. The changing cultural patterns of a society exert powerful influence upon the methods of teaching also. The shift from the old teacher centred teaching to child centred education is an example. Socialised methods like project method, seminar, symposium, discussion, etc. are widely used in the teaching learning process because of the influence of culture.
- *Discipline* is also influenced by the cultural values. The present cultural patterns of thinking and living are directly linked to our concept of discipline. The concept of repressive discipline of ancient and Middle Ages has been replaced by the modern values of life.
- *Text books* which are written according to the formulated curriculum and promote and foster cultural ideals and values are welcomed.
- *Teacher* who has imbibed the cultural ideals and values of the society only can achieve his mission successfully. Only such teacher is able to infuse higher ideals and moral values in children.
- *School* is a miniature of society. The total activities and programmes of the school are organised according to the cultural ideals and values

of society. Hence, school is the centre of promoting, moulding, reforming and developing the cultural patterns of the society.

22.8 INFLUENCE OF EDUCATION ON CULTURE

Wherever there are human groups there is culture i.e. a man-made part of environment and learned patterns of behaviour. Wherever there is culture, it is diffused and transmitted to succeeding generations by education. Since human beings live in groups, we might say that wherever there are human beings there is culture and education in various forms. School education is limited mainly to literate cultures. The role of education is much smaller in non-literate groups.

Just as culture influences education, much is the same way education also exerts a powerful influence upon the culture of a country. Following are the various ways by which education influences the culture of country.

Preservation of Culture: Each country believes and flaunts the superiority of its own culture over the rest. Hence it tries to preserve its culture in its original form. Education is the only means to complete this task. Thus, education preserves the culture of the society.

Transmission of Culture: The process of preservation includes the process of transmission as well. Transmission of culture from one generation to another is the best guarantee of its preservation. In the words of Ottaway, the famous sociologist, "*The function of education is to transmit the social values and ideals to the young and capable members of the society*".

Development of Culture: The function of education is to bring about the needed and desirable changes in the cultural ideals and values for the progress and continued development of society, without which social progress will stratify and come to a naught. Education encultures individuals, modifies cultural processes by research and deeper investigations into all areas of human requirements.

Continuity of Culture: Culture is the life blood of society. Without culture a society is bound to decay and die sooner or later. Education upholds the continuity of culture through its diverse activities and programmes. A society establishes schools to preserve and transmit its culture from generation to generation. It is found that some schools try to develop undesirable cultural chauvinism and superiority complexes among its children. Children should be motivated to learn more and more from cultural interaction among various cultures. Ideally, education should help them to develop the qualities of tolerance and adjustment along with mutual give and take attitude. This cultural integration and cultural synthesis is the dire need of the world society in modern times. Dr. S. Radhakrishnan says that one of the important aspects of Indian culture is its perennial nature. He observed "*the more Indian culture changes, the more it remains the same. The power of Indian spirit has sustained us through difficult times. It is the intangibles that give a nation its character and vitality*".

Development of Personality: Education employs diverse cultural patterns of thinking, behaviour and items of cultural values so that children are physically, mentally, socially and emotionally developed to the maximum extent. Thus education aims at developing the personality of the child.

Removing Cultural Lag: Material culture develops at a fast pace due to scientific researches and innovations, whereas non-material culture consisting of ideals, values and norms' lags behind creating a gulf between the two. Education is the only means to bridge this cultural lag by its activities and programmes of development.

Attaining Unity: For the unity of mankind, there should be diffusion of culture of various groups in the world. The cultural isolation should go, and there should be no iron curtain between one culture and another. Dr. Zakir Hussain observes, "*The characteristic mark of an educated man should be a positive attitude towards the goals of culture, that is, towards the ultimate objective values. The attitude should be the cherished product of educational and institutional activity*".

Correction of Cultural Ills: Education is corrective for the cultural ills. By explaining the dimensions of culture, education corrects egoism and false individuation. Educational enlightenment does not imply only aesthetic appreciation of art and beauty, it also means having kind and generous heart and soul. Culture liberates the mind. Literacy and moral education and education in arts constitutes real techniques for realisation of the cultural values.

22.9 EDUCATION AND RACIAL PREJUDICES AND ANTAGONISM

Education reduces racial prejudices and antagonism, which result from ideas about other cultures. Imbibing of one's own culture, taking pride in it and preserving the same is a patriotic act. But resisting any change in it; shutting doors to the entry of other cultural patterns; and maintaining a strong iron curtain to preserve one's culture shows jingoism. It is not conducive to the cultural growth. Cultural diffusion is good for the individual cultural group, and for the humanity as a whole.

22.10 HUMAN CULTURE AS A WHOLE

Too much of emphasis on one's own culture will lead to disunity and lack of international understanding which is one of the tasks of education. This is possible by bringing about diffusion of various cultures. Education should treat human culture as whole, "*like a flower with different petals, and each petal representing one cultural group*". Education should strive for unity in diversity and not over-emphasise diversity.

22.11 FUNCTION OF SCHOOL

A school is the simplified environment to explain the present culture of the society and the school education makes the child imbibe the same and even makes its own contribution. The school (in its broader meaning) determines the quality of culture with a view to play the role of cultural construction-agent. Education, being the absorber and reflector of culture, is the best medium for the initiation of the rising generation into the cultural norms and process of the society.

22.12 INTER-CULTURAL UNDERSTANDING

Education can promote inter-cultural understanding among various cultures. To quote Dr. S. Radhakrishnan, "*the greatness of a nation is to be measured not by its material power and wealth but by the inter-cultural relationships of its people. Inter-cultural understanding refers to the development of that insight and attitude in the individuals who, rising above their own selfish and narrow interest, find out the really valuable items in all other cultures, besides their own. It is now realised by educational planners and educationists alike that we should provide such educational experiences and programmes which develop this understanding of other's culture and that development of such understanding will promote co-operation and through a process of give and take, a cultural synthesis will take place. Education will be able to achieve the goal of national culture so essential to national unity and national integration.*" Klausmeir says – "*Inter-cultural education is concerned with helping students to understand the differences and likeness of individuals who comprise our society and the world*".

22.13 EDUCATION OF CULTURE AND FOR CULTURE

Culture enables a person to appreciate good ideas and art. It enlivens human interests and social efficiency. A cultured person is neither too assertive nor too dogmatic and aggressive. He does not manifest extremes of passions or violence of feelings or extravagance of language. Education plays a crucial role in the making of such persons.

22.14 FLUX IN THE TRADITIONAL CULTURE

Culture is in constant flux. It changes as society changes. No nation has had constant cultural traditions. India is no exception to it. Every generation adds something new and modifies something old. The family bond in India is considered to be one of the strongest in the world. The joint family system is gradually disappearing giving way to nuclear family, bringing freedom, although at the same time accentuating loneliness and insecurity. We can see that the pattern of nuclear family and its culture is being accepted among the educated rapidly, among the semi-educated progressively, and among the illiterate gradually. Due to education, and coming to contact with other cultures, our food habits are changing, our dress pattern is changing, our appreciation of art has new criteria time to time, and our religious beliefs are undergoing change. Majority of people have come to welcome these changes without much resistance even though there is a sort of resistance from certain quarters due to vested interest or pressure from certain religious sects etc.

22.15 REALISATION OF COMMON CULTURE BY HUMAN BEINGS

Education is intimately bonded with the intellectual, emotional, cultural and social life of the human race. On the one hand, it enables the individual to realise the qualities with which he is endowed and on the other hand, it gives him the realisation that all human beings share a common culture, which contributes to the common good. In the words of Addison, – Education, when it works on a noble mind, draws out to view every latent virtue and perfection. Education derives its meaning and strength from the surrounding environment of things and men. So, it cannot ignore the cultural values which give meaning to the environment. Man learns from the circumstances in which he lives, the people he meets, the ideas he receives and the geographical situations and times of history. Education is the vital configuration of the societal system, shaping the personality of younger generation and their culture raising them for life and preparing them for the kind of society they live in and they should live in.

22.16 MEANING OF CULTURAL DIFFERENCES

Cultural differences are the variations in the way of life, beliefs, traditions and laws between different countries, religions, societies and people. Many people see culture as an all-encompassing overview of large groups of people. However, the word culture can be used to describe the way of life of much smaller groups.

The most common meaning of culture is that of large groups of people and how their lifestyles and beliefs differ; this is where cultural differences come in. Where we live and what we believe has a great impact on all aspects of our life whether we realise it or not. Some of the differences between cultures are enforced by internal rules (such as legal age of marriage) whereas others just happen through many years of development towards a certain way over another.

Some examples of cultural differences include:

- *Clothing:* Many cultures can be identified by their clothing. For example, Sikh men who wear turbans.
- *Food:* Some cultures are not allowed to eat some dishes. Most cultures have traditional dishes.
- *Language:* Different countries tend to have their own language and methods of communication. However, there are also sub cultural differences, such as regional accents or sign language.
- *Rules/Laws:* Cultures can often be recognised by the regulations they have to live by. However, lesser known rules can prove

problematic. For example, tourists unaware of local custom may be arrested for inappropriate behaviour.

Cultural differences are important to identity and to provide us with a sense of belonging. A person's culture is often very important to them and will have usually been a part of them since birth.

22.17 CULTURAL DIFFERENCES AND ITS INFLUENCE ON EDUCATION

Cultural differences/diversity is the quality of diverse or different cultures, as opposed to monoculture, as in the global monoculture, or a homogenisation of cultures, akin to cultural decay. The phrase cultural diversity can also refer to having different cultures respect each other's differences. The phrase "cultural diversity" is also sometimes used to mean the variety of human societies or cultures in a specific region, or in the world as a whole. The culturally destructive action of globalisation is often said to have a negative effect on the world's cultural diversity.

Cultural tendencies impact the way children participate in education. The table below describes different expectations about "normal" school behaviour for students from individualist and collectivist cultures. As you review this information, take a moment to think about how teachers who lack knowledge about culture might interpret the behaviour of a child from a collectivist culture. These differences may cause educators to inaccurately judge students from some cultures as poorly behaved or disrespectful. In addition, because cultural differences are hard to perceive, students may find themselves reprimanded by teachers but fail to understand what they did that caused concern.

Table: Individualist and Collectivist Cultural Perspectives on Education

Individualist Perspective	*Collectivist Perspective*
Students work independently; helping others may be cheating.	Students work with peers and provide assistance when needed.
Students engage in discussion and argument to learn to think critically.	Students are quiet and respectful in class in order to learn more efficiently.
Property belongs to individuals, and others must ask to borrow it.	Property is communal.
Teacher manages the school environment indirectly and encourages student self-control.	Teacher is the primary authority, but peers guide each other's behaviour.
Parents are integral to child's academic progress and participate actively.	Parents yield to teacher's expertise to provide academic instruction and guidance.

23
Composite Culture, Multiculturalism and Education

23.1 COMPOSITE CULTURE

Meaning and Concept of Composite Culture

In simple terms, 'culture' is the arts, customs, institutions of a nation, people or group. Culture is a sense of ultimate values possessed by a particular society as expressed in its collective institutions, by its individual members in their dispositions, feelings, attitudes and manners as well as in significant forms which they give to material objects.

'Composite' means 'made up of various parts'. Composite culture has been the mainstay of our society for ages. Indian culture has earned a lot of dignity and respect worldwide. Our culture is a diversified one; still we have unity in our presentation and outlook. India is a place where we find every religion, culture and dialect has equal respect and prestige.

Importance of Indian Culture

Indian culture has a special significance. It's presence in the country increases the pride and prestige of the nation throughout the world. Not just within India, but Indian culture has its spell spread all over the world. Many of the foreigners get attracted to our culture and prefer getting settled in our nation. This is another uniqueness of our culture and tradition that we have a welcoming heart. Our gates are open for anyone and everyone who wants to get incorporated into our living and lifestyle. The compositeness of our culture gives a variety of choice for the outsiders to start on with a research work. Our culture is so vast that it could hardly be explained into words.

Importance of the Composite Culture of India

The composite culture of India has a captive nature. It has a magnetic property which attracts lot many people. The inquisitiveness increases the more the person tries to get into the knowledge of India culture and traditions. Our country has immense diversity in lifestyle, traditions, customs, outlook, religion, region, caste and much more. People across the world are in a great surprise to understand the unity in our thinking and affection for the motherland with such a vivid and varied lifestyle among the citizens. This is what, is the beauty of the composite culture of India.

Religion: India is said to be country of unity in diversity, where people of several religions like–Hindu, Muslim, Sikh, Christian, Parsi etc. live together. Each religion preaches its followers to live a peaceful and fruitful life, to pray to god, to have a clean heart, to not harm anyone, to do charity, to contribute to the society. They are a part of Indian value system; they provide direction to the way of living.

Marriage and Family Structure: It is one of the few countries where marriages are arranged by parents rather than the more popular western culture of live-in relationships, co-habiting, and love marriages. There is still vast existence of joint families where new generation takes care of the old generation and the elders spend time with their grand-children helping them grow with knowledge of the value and ethics of past.

Clothing: While western culture is corrupting and finding its way in to the modern Indians, our traditional way of dressing is still prevalent and most people post their university age knowingly or unknowingly follow it. It is not surprising that many westerners adore Indian way of dressing and you may be surprised that some of them can wear a saree orsuit as good as an Indian. In short, the Indian way of clothing is to cover your body sufficient to not show off what is not required or not considered decent in public. It does have a charm to it.

Indian Cuisine: As in case of religion India have several regions (states) and each state has a different flavour which is delightful in its own way. There are too many to mention or count but the same dish has a different taste in different state and different dishes obviously have a difference. Indian Cuisine has both taste and nutrition and one can spend a decade trying to taste all of them, but the list will not exhaust. There are countless spices which are used uniquely with each dish which will turn on your taste buds.

Dialect: There are as many or more languages than the number of states in the nation, and each language is unique in its own way. Hindi is the national language, but each individual has affinity to his/ her mother tongue. Though having so many dialects, still our people respect and reciprocate the same humbleness to each other even without the knowledge of other's languages.

Music and Arts: Indian music and dance forms also have a great charm. Indian states have their own dance patterns which is unique to the state viz. kuchipudi, bhangra, bharatnatyam etc. Similarly we have taste for all sorts of music forms ranging from Hindustani, classical, soft light music, high beats to the western music forms. People have a liking and respect for all forms of music forms. The art doesn't limit itself to the paintings, but the sculptures, the various sorts of paintings, the craftsmen and many more. Our people have a sound knowledge of the art and craft work and an appreciable delivering hand and potential.

Heritage: Our heritage across the nation is the evidence of our culture and civilization even prior to the era of kings. The heritage of India is well maintained and government takes every possible step to preserve this as a National Treasure. The Indian Heritage attracts many tourists even from abroad.

Festivals and Celebrations: A country with several religions and regions, India has the advantage of celebrating all the different festivals for each of these. Mostly these festivals are celebrated by all irrespective of religion like Holi – a festival of colour, Dipawali – festival of lights, Id, Ramzan, Christmas, Easter, Budh Poornima, Guru Purab and many more. Each festival is celebrated with same delight, pomp and show. The happiness is not limited to people of a single religion, but all other take equal part in the delight and merry. We can hardly find any other country where people of different religion enjoying the festive mood for the festivals of other religions as well.

23.2 MULTICULTURALISM

Cultural diversity has been present in societies for a very long time. In Ancient Greece, there were various small regions with different costumes, traditions, dialects and identities. In the 21st century, societies remain culturally diverse, with most countries having a mixture of individuals from different races, linguistic backgrounds, religious affiliations and so forth. Contemporary political theorists have labeled this phenomenon of the coexistence of different cultures in the same geographical space multiculturalism. That is, one of the meanings of multiculturalism is the coexistence of different cultures.

The term 'multiculturalism', however, has not been used only to describe a culturally diverse society, but also to refer to a kind of policy that aims at protecting cultural diversity. Although multiculturalism is a phenomenon with a long history and there have been countries historically that did adopt multicultural policies.

Meaning and Concept of Multiculturalism

Multiculturalism is the view that cultural differences should be respected or even encouraged. Sociologists use the concept of multiculturalism to describe one way of approaching cultural diversity within a society. Underlying multiculturalism is the belief that members of different cultures can live peacefully alongside each other; assimilation is not necessary, nor perhaps even desirable. Contrasted with multiculturalism is the "melting pot" perspective, according to which cultural differences — such as differences in religion, language, and other customs — blend into another to form a new whole. Proponents of multiculturalism favour people keeping at least some features of their traditional culture.

In general terms, within contemporary political philosophy, the concept of multiculturalism has been defined in two different ways. Sometimes the term 'multiculturalism' is used as a descriptive concept; other times it is defined as a kind of policy for responding to cultural diversity.

Multiculturalism as a Describing Concept for Society: The term 'multiculturalism' is sometimes used to describe a condition of society; more precisely, it is used to describe a society where a variety of different cultures coexist. Many countries in the world are culturally diverse. There are a variety of ways whereby societies can be diverse, for example, culture can come in many forms. Perhaps the chief ways in which a country can be culturally diverse is by having different religious groups, different linguistic groups, groups that define themselves by their territorial identity and variant racial groups.

Religious diversity is a widespread phenomenon in many countries. India can be given as an example of a country which is religiously diverse, including citizens who are Sikhs, Hindus, Buddhists, among other religious groups. Linguistic diversity is also widespread. In the 21st century, there are more than 200 countries in the world and around 6000 spoken languages.

A third kind of group diversity can results from distinct territory location. This territory location does not necessary mean that members of distinct cultures are, in fact, different. That is, it is not necessary that habits, traditions, customs, and so forth are significantly different. The fourth kind of group diversity is race. Races are groups whose physical characteristics are imbued with social significance. In other words, race is a socially constructed concept in the sense that it is the result of individuals giving social significance to a set of characteristics they consider that stand out in a person's physical appearance, such as skin colour, eye colour, hair colour, bone/jaw structure and so forth.

Multiculturalism as a Policy: The term 'multiculturalism' can also be used to refer to a kind of policy. This kind of policy has two main characteristics. First, it aims at addressing the different demands of cultural groups. That is, it is a kind of policy that refers to the different normative challenges (ethnic conflict, internal liberalism, federal autonomy, and so forth) that arise as a result of cultural diversity. Second, multicultural policies are policies that aim at providing groups the means by which individuals can pursue their cultural differences. Put differently, multicultural policies have as their objectives, the preservation, allowance or celebration of differences between different groups.

Definitions of Multiculturalism

'Multiculturalism' is the co-existence of diverse cultures, where culture includes racial, religious, or cultural groups and is manifested in customary behaviours, cultural assumptions and values, patterns of thinking and communicative styles.

Multiculturalism means that we all have needs and desires; we have likes and dislikes. We are different but there is nothing wrong or threatening in that difference. We are all seeking a better life for ourselves and future generations and there is no place for an '*us and them*' mentality in our society, today or in the future.

Multiculturalism is the policy or practice of giving overt recognition to the cultural needs and contributions of all the groups in a society, esp. of those minority groups regarded as having been neglected in the past.

Multiculturalism describes the existence, acceptance or promotion of multiple cultural traditions within a single jurisdiction, usually considered in terms of the culture associated with an ethnic group. This can happen when a jurisdiction is created or expanded by amalgamating areas with two or more different cultures or through immigration from different jurisdictions around the world. Multicultural ideologies and policies vary widely, ranging from the advocacy of equal respect to the various cultures in a society, to a policy of promoting the maintenance of cultural diversity, to policies in which people of various ethnic and religious groups are addressed by the authorities as defined by the group to which they belong.

Implications of Multiculturalism for Education

Education that is multicultural provides an environment that values diversity and portrays it positively. Students' educational and vocational options are not limited by gender, age, ethnicity, native language, religion, class or disability. Teachers have the responsibility to help students contribute to and benefit from our democratic society. Diversity is used to develop effective instructional strategies for students in the classroom. The integration of multicultural education throughout the curriculum should help students and teachers think critically about institutionalized racism, classism, sexism, ageism, and homophobia. Ideally, teachers will begin to develop individual and group strategies for overcoming the debilitating effects of these societal scourges.

Multicultural Education

Multicultural education is a field of study based on the idea that students from diverse backgrounds should have equal opportunities to education. It draws on insights from a number of different fields, including ethnic studies and women studies but also reinterprets content from related academic disciplines.

Multicultural education, also viewed as a way of teaching, promotes principles such as inclusion, diversity, democracy, skill acquisition, inquiry, critical thought, value of perspectives and self-reflection. It encourages students to bring aspects of their cultures into the classroom and thus, allows teachers to support the child's intellectual and social/emotional growth.

Multicultural education is also attributed to the reform movement behind the transformation of schools. Transformation in this context requires all variables of the school to be changed, including policies, teachers' attitudes, instructional materials, assessment methods, counseling, and teaching styles. Multicultural education is also concerned with the contribution of students towards effective social action. It therefore necessitates students from all backgrounds to acquire "democratic skills and knowledge" in order to become effective citizens in a democratic society.

Aims and Objectives of Multicultural Education

The aims and objectives of multicultural education are:

- Promote civic good

- Right the historical record
- Increase self-esteem of non-mainstream students
- Increase diversified student exposure
- Preserve minority group culture
- Foster children's autonomy
- Promote social justice and equity
- Enable students to succeed economically in an integrated, multicultural world
- Creating a safe, accepting and successful learning environment for all
- Increasing awareness of global issues
- Strengthening cultural consciousness
- Strengthening intercultural awareness
- Teaching students that there are multiple historical perspectives
- Encouraging critical thinking
- Preventing prejudice and discrimination

Advantages of Multicultural Education

- Helps students develop positive self-image.
- Offers students an equitable educational opportunity.
- Allows multiple perspectives and ways of thinking.
- Combats stereotypes and prejudicial behaviour.
- Teaches students to critique society in the interest of social justice.

Implementation of Multicultural Education in the Classroom

Multicultural education encompasses many important dimensions. Practicing teachers can use the dimensions as a way to incorporate culture in their classrooms. The five dimensions listed below are:

Content Integration: Content integration deals with the extent to which teachers use examples and content from a variety of cultures in their teaching.

Knowledge Construction: Teachers need to help students understand, investigate, and determine how the implicit cultural assumptions, frames of reference, perspectives, and biases within a discipline influence the ways in which knowledge is constructed.

Prejudice Reduction: This dimension focuses on the characteristics of students' racial attitudes and how they can be modified by teaching methods and materials.

Empowering School Culture: Grouping and labeling practices, sports participation, disproportionality in achievement, and the interaction of the staff and the students across ethnic and racial lines must be examined to create a school culture that empowers students from diverse racial, ethnic, and gender groups.

Equity Pedagogy: An equity pedagogy exists when teachers modify their teaching in ways that will facilitate the academic achievement of students from diverse racial, cultural, gender, and social-class groups.

24

Role of Education in the Preservation of Cultural Heritage of India

24.1 RICH CULTURAL HERITAGE OF INDIA

Sir James, an English thinker has paid the following glowing tribute to the cultural heritage of India:

"At a time when our ancestors were thinking of killing animals or one another, India, perhaps had philosophy which was very nature, also in art, poetry, literature and in fact everything."

About the richness of ancient Indian education (a vital element of culture), Dr. F.W. Thomas, one of the most distinguished indologist has written, "Education is no exotic in India. There is no country where the love of learning had so early an origin or has exercised so lasting and powerful an influence."

Regarding India's cultural contribution to world culture, Swami Vivekananda has remarked, "Even as the gentle dew of the morning blossoms forth the fairest of flowers, the Indian culture has contributed to the thought and culture of the world."

24.2 MEANING OF CULTURAL HERITAGE

With a view to understand the meaning of cultural heritage, we may first consider the meaning of the term culture. Culture has been seen and defined differently by scholars. Here only some important definitions of culture are given.

According to Brown, culture cannot be defined. It is better to describe it. He describes culture as:

(i) Culture is a way of life of people.
(ii) Culture is the things they value.
(iii) Culture is their habits.
(iv) Culture is their works of art.
(v) Culture is their music.
(vi) Culture is their history.

In brief Brown regards culture as "What they are, what they do and what they like". This definition is very comprehensive but at the same time very vague.

In the words of Brown, "Culture is composed of integrated customs, traditions and current behaviour patterns of human groups."

Ellwood describes culture as, "Culture includes all man's material civilisation, tools, weapons, clothing, shelter, machines and even systems of industry." This is a very narrow view of culture. It excludes non-material elements of culture.

Mac Iver states, "Culture is the expression of our nature in modes of living and thinking in everyday intercourse in arts, in literature, in religion and enjoyment."

Mathew Arnold views culture as "the best that man has thought and known."

Taylor defines culture as, "The complex whole which includes knowledge, belief, art, morals, law, customs and any other capabilities and habits, acquired by man as a member of society."

According to T.S. Eliot, "The term culture includes all the characteristic activities and interests of the people."

Swami Dayananda considers culture as "acceptance of truth and abandonment of untruth."

Jawaharlal Nehru points out that "Culture is the widening of the mind and of the spirit."

Gandhiji has described culture in these words, "Culture is the foundation, the primary thing. It should show itself in the smallest details of your conduct and personality behaviour, how you sit, how you walk, how you dress etc. Inner culture must be reflected in your speech, the way in which you treat visitors and guests, and behave towards one another and towards your teacher and elders."

The University Education Commission 1948–49 defines culture as "an attitude of mind, an inclination of the spirit".

In simple words, culture is a system or a way of live consisting of ideals and values of the people of a country. It also consists of material things.

Heritage implies something acquired, inherited, and possessed from the predecessor or predecessors.

Thus, Indian cultural heritage means our ideals and values as expressed in our way of life, art and architecture, history and philosophy.

Indian cultural heritage consists of primarily four elements:

1. Common outlook on life – spiritual element.
2. Intellectual influences of various movements – humanism, liberalism, tolerance and universalism.
3. Cultural objects – achievements in arts and sciences.
4. Common ways of living with minor deviations.

24.3 CHIEF CHARACTERISTICS OF INDIAN CULTURAL HERITAGE

Indian culture is the outcome of thousands of years of interaction. It is the result of mutual give and take. It has assimilated the richness and variety of several cultures. Following are its chief characteristics:

1. Indian culture is very old.
2. Indian culture is very rich.
3. Indian culture is composite.
4. Indian culture denotes unity in diversity.

24.4 COMPOSITE CULTURAL HERITAGE OF INDIA

Some people compare Indian culture with a 'banyan tree' which has a number of aerial roots to support it. The different aerial roots are sub-cultural patterns which give strength to the cultural stems of the Indian culture.

Indian culture has been compared by some people with a 'bouquet of flowers' in which we find that flowers of different colours and fragrance are tied together and they present a unique and colourful appearance. Such is the background of our culture.

1. The composite culture of India is the product of interaction and intermingling among the Aryans, the Dravidians, the Sakas, the Kushans, the Huns, the Afghans, the Pathans, and the Mughals. The Britishers also influenced it.
2. It is the product of the contribution of the Hinduism, Buddhism, Jainism and Sikhism. Islam and Christianity also contributed to it.
3. Composite culture of India includes the influences of
   a) The Vedic vision.
   b) Philosophy of Bhagvad Gita.
   c) Bhakti Marg Saints.
   d) Muslim Sufi Saints.
   e) Indian Nationalist Movement.
   f) Gandhian thought.
4. The most illustrious representatives of the composite culture of India of the medieval period and modern period are: Amir Khushan, Sant Kabir, Guru Nanak (13th, 14th and 15–16th century), Prince Dara Shukoh (17th century), Raja Rammohan Roy (19th century) and Mahatma Gandhi (20th century).

Essence of Indian cultural heritage may be expressed as under.

1. '*Sarva-dharma-Sambhave*' – Equal regard for all religions.
2. *Ekam Bhahma Vipra Bahuda Vadanti* – God is one, wise man call Him by different names.
   This is reflected in:
   (i) Composite nature of culture of India.
   (ii) Unity in Diversity.
   (iii) Tolerance.
   (iv) Equality.
   (v) Humanism.
   (vi) Universalism.
   (vii) Spiritualism.

24.5 CULTURAL HERITAGE AND EDUCATION

1. *Inter-relatedness of Education and Culture:* Education and culture are inter-related. Education is conceived as a systematic effort to maintain a culture. Education is regarded as an effective instrument of social change. Education can impart knowledge, training and skill as well as inculcate new ideas, attitudes and values among the young. It can also preserve past culture and enrich it.

On the other hand, it is the culture in which education germinates and flowers. It is the culture, also upon which education exerts a nourishing influence.

2. *Functions of Education Relating to Cultural Heritage:* The National Policy on Education 1986 and as amended in 1992 has observed that education can and must bring about the fine synthesis between change oriented technologies and country's continuity of cultural heritage. It further observed that de-culturalisation and dehumanisation must be avoided at all costs.

Society is very keen that its education should perform the following functions in relation to its cultural heritage.

1. Education should transmit cultural heritage.
2. Education should improve cultural heritage where needed.
   In short, the students should be taught to get due aspiration from the lofty past heritage, to live amicably in the dynamic and complex present and to face boldly and effectively the challenges of the uncertain future.
3. *Measures through which Education Performs Its Functions Relating to Cultural Heritage.*

The entire process of education must be enriched by cultural content in as many dimensions as possible. Following are the important means in this regard.

1. Contents of school curriculum.
2. Methods of teaching.
3. Co-curricular activities.
4. Textbooks and cultural values.
5. Synthesis of moral and spiritual values with scientific values.
6. Cultural tours.
7. Personality of the teacher.
8. Value education.

25

Social Change: Nature, Process, Causes and Effects

25.1 MEANING OF SOCIAL CHANGE

In simple words, social change implies change in the social structure and functions of the various units which form society. Social structure includes social institutions like the family, the marriage system, caste system, educational institutions, customs, manners, literacy forms, language, dress and food habits etc.

Kingslay Davis defines social change as "only alternations as occur in social organisation, i.e. in the structure and functions of society."

B.B. Mathur explains social change as, "Social change refers to the modifications in the organisation and behaviour of the group as expressed in its laws, customs, modes and beliefs."

According to B. Kuppasmwami, "When we speak of social change we might assert that there is some change in social behaviour and in the social structure."

Henry Johnson would like to include five kinds of charges in social change. These are as under:

1. Change in social values.
2. Institutional changes.
3. Change in distribution of possessions and rewards.
4. Change in personnel.
5. Change in abilities and attitudes of personnel.

According to Mac Iver and Page, "Social change is a process responsive to many types of changes—changes in the man-made conditions of living, changes in the attitude of man and changes that go beyond human control to the biological and physical nature."

Delbert C. Miller observes, "Social change refers to a pattern of social relationship in a given setting."

25.2 NATURE AND CHARACTERISTICS OF SOCIAL CHANGE

Social change is inevitable. Society is dynamic. It is in a constant flux. Whether we want a change, whether we like it or not, times are moving fast. Change is the law of nature.

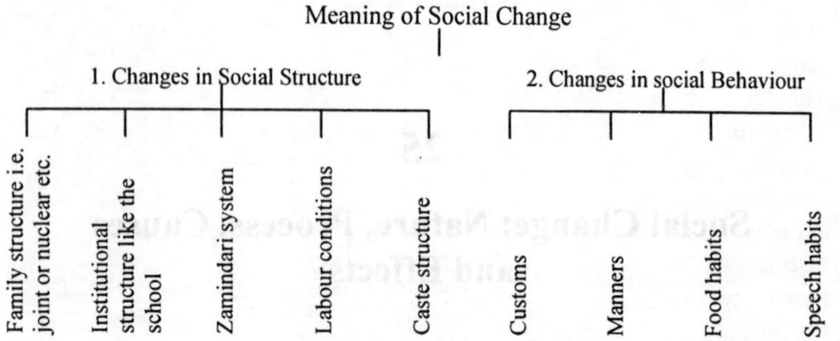

Fig. 25.1: Illustrative Areas of Changes in Social Structure

(*Not* : The list is not exhaustive. Only some examples of various areas of social life are mentioned)

Following characteristics of the change reflect the nature of social change:

1. Social change may be sudden, slow or rapid.
2. All aspects or elements of the social structure may not change.
3. Each aspect of social change may not change with same intensity.
4. Social change may mean discarding some old things or elements.
5. Social change may mean addition of new things or elements.
6. Social change may be brought through non-violent or violent means.
7. Social change may be outcome of only one factor or number of factors.
8. Social change may be for the good of the society or otherwise.

25.3 FACTORS OF SOCIAL CHANGE

For social change, not one cause may be effective. There may be many factors which set the process in motion. Although social causation is always a multiple causation, some sociologists have emphasised on factor over another, we would take into account all the factors, though some consider social and cultural factors to be most predominant.

Physical Factors: Changes in the physical environment are not rapid, but the occasional changes in the environment bring total changes in human social lives. E.g. Earthquake, storms, heavy rainfall. These changes force people to migrate to new areas, hence people have to change themselves according to that society. This brings out change I culture, way of clothing, manners etc.

Biological Factors: Biological factors, too, have some indirect influence upon social change. Among the biological factors is the qualitative aspect of the population related to heredity. The qualitative aspect of population is based upon powerful and great men and their birth is dependent to a large extent upon heredity and mutation. Hence, biological factors play a part in social change to that extent. In addition to this the biological principals of natural selection and struggle for survival are constantly producing alterations in society.

Technological Factors: Human beings are never satisfied. In the process of satisfying his wants, man devised new means and created new needs. To satisfy his new needs man invented new techniques to use natural resources. This technological factor brought out severe changes in the society.

Technological factors have immense influence in social change. Technology changes society by changing our environments to which we in turn adopt. This change is usually in the material environment and the adjustment we make to the changes often modifies customs and social institutions. In this way, the increase in new machines and methods due to new discoveries has had a very great influence upon social institutions. In the modern age, technological factors are among the predominant causes of social change.

Economic Factors: Karl Marx has given economic interpretation of social changes. With the changes in the economic system, the entire society changes in its structure and functioning. Economic conditions in countries do affect the health, mortality, marriages, divorce rate, suicide, crime and emigration etc. It can also bring social unrest and revolution and war. Of course, not all the social changes are necessarily caused by economic conditions. Changes have also occurred due to educational moulding in peoples' attitudes etc.

Cultural Factors: The main cause of social change is the cultural factors. Changes in the culture are accompanied by social change. Changes and variations in culture inevitably influence social relationships. Culture gives speed and direction to social change and determines the limits beyond which social changes cannot occur. Max Weber, has proved this hypothesis by a comparative study of religious and economic institution.

Environmental Factors: The geographists have emphasised the impact of geographical environment upon human society. Huntington has gone so far as to assert that an alteration in the climate is the sole cause of the evolution and devolution of civilisations and cultures. Even if these claims of the geographists are to be discarded, it cannot be denied that floods, earthquakes, excessive rain, drought, change of season etc. have significant effect upon social relationships and these are modified by such natural occurrences.

Psychological Factors: Most sociologists regard psychological factors as important elements in social change. The cause of social change is the psychology of man himself. Man is, by nature, a lover of change. He is always trying to discover new things in every sphere in life and is always anxious for novel experience. As a result of this tendency, the mores, traditions, customs etc. of every human society are perpetually undergoing change. The form of social relationship is constantly changing in the process of integrations between the tendencies of moving towards the new while preserving the old. New customs and methods replace the old traditional customs while old traditions that demand change with time adapts to changing traditions.

Other Factors: In addition to the above mentioned factors, another factor of social change in the appearance of new opinions and thoughts. E.g. Changes in the attitudes towards dowry, caste system, female education etc. have resulted in widespread social variations and modifications. In fact, a majority of the social revolutions take place as a result of the evolution of new ways of thinking. War, thoughts of great thinkers i.e. Mahatma Gandhi, Karl Marx etc. influence the population and has socio-economic impact causing social change.

25.4 PROCESS OF SOCIAL CHANGE

Process of social change may be classified in a number of ways.

Process of social change: Classification I

- **Planned Process of social changes**
- **Unplanned process of social change**

Process of social change: Classification II

- **Non-violent process of social change**
- **Violent process of social change**

Process of social change: Classification III

- **Evolutionary process of social change**
- **Revolutionary Process of social change**

Process of social change: Classification IV

- **Man-made process of social change**
- **Natural or geographical process of social change (The Indus Valley Civilisation vanished perhaps on account of floods or some natural calamity**

Fig. 25.2: Illustration of the Process of Social Change

S.P. Ruhela mentions the most significant processes of social change as under:

1. Westernisation.
2. Industrialisation.
3. Urbanisation.
4. Sanskritisation.
5. Secularisation.
6. Social Mobility.
7. Politicisation.
8. Hinduisation.
9. Indianisation.
10. Modernisation.

A brief analysis of each process of social change is given here.

Westernisation. This is the process of social change in India which has influenced culture, living styles, values etc. of the Indian people as a result of western impact, especially during the British rule.

Industrialisation. Industrialisation is the process of social change which has given rise to crimes, drinking, trade union activities, growth of slums, educational institutions, banks, roads etc.

Urbanisation. This is the process of social change which has led to continuous migration from rural areas to towns. This results in the same social problems as industrialisation.

Sanskritisation. In this process, low caste Hindu or tribe or other group attempts to change its customs, ideologies, rituals and ways of life in the direction of a high caste.

Secularisation. Movements like Arya Samaj and Brahmo Samaj have promoted the process of secularisation. It is a process of change which views events, things and ideals from a rational point of view.

Social Mobility. Social mobility is the process of change in status.

Politicalisation. It is the process of social change through the spread of knowledge about political ideologies, parties and leaders. In this process of social change, people become aware of their rights and responsibilities.

Hinduisation. This process of social changes consists of the attempts of many tribal communities in India to enter the broad field of Hindu social structure. Also attempts are made to popularise Hindu beliefs and customs etc.

Indianisation. This is the process of social change in which several people belonging to difficult faiths, tend to identify themselves with Indian culture. In several catholic churches in South India and elsewhere, it is observed that many nuns wear Indian dresses—Sarees and blouses. Worship is also done in Indian style. Lamps, candles, incense, '*prasad*' etc. are used in the Indian style. Instead of English, regional languages are used in religious songs and prayers.

Modernisation. Modernisation is a process of social change which emphasises rational, secular and scientific approach in one's life.

A persual of above would indicate that processes of social changes cannot be divided into water tight compartments. They are inter-related.

Sometimes it becomes very difficult to make a clear-cut distinction between process, cause and effect of social change. All are inter-related.

25.5 CAUSES/FACTORS OF SOCIAL CHANGE

There are a large number of causes or factors that bring about social changes. Sometimes even one cause may become responsible for social change. At other times, some factors or causes jointly act in such a way that social change becomes inevitable. Again it is stressed that the processes, causes and effects of social change work simultaneously.

Ideas and ideologies of great leaders have played an important role in social change. The influence of prominent personalities like Marx and Lenin in Russia, Mao Tse Tung in China and Gandhiji in India are some of the well-known examples of modern history.

Ideas like 'Liberty', 'Equality' and 'Fraternity' proved great forces in giving birth to French Revolution which in turn immensely changed the French society.

Industrial Revolution resulted in marked social changes.

The American War of Independence was the outcome of the social and economic causes. This brought about revolutionary changes in the social life of the people of America.

Causes of Social Change

1	2	3	4	5	6	7	8	9	10	11	12	13
Climatic and weather causes of social change	Demographic causes of social change	Economic causes of social change	Educational causes of social change	Industrialisation causes of social changes	Legislation as a cause of social change	Natural causes of social change	Philosophical causes of social change	Political causes of social change	Religious causes of social change	Urbanisation causes of social change	Westernisation causes of social change	Scientific and Technological causes of social change

Fig. 25.3: Illustration of Causes of Social Change

25.6 EFFECTS OF SOCIAL CHANGES

Following are some of the examples of marked social changes.

1. Climatic factors led to the disappearance of the Indus Valley. The entire civilisation collapsed and new civilisation came up.
2. The British rulers introduced a new system of education which changed the etiquettes, habits and manners etc. of the several sections of Indian society. New dresses emerged.
3. Lack of occupational opportunities in the villages led to migration of people to towns. Several slums in the towns changed the life style of the people.
4. Natural factors like earth-quakes, droughts and floods etc. make people homeless and force the people to change their life style.
5. Political factors like the rise of Communism, Fascism, and Nazism entirely changed the social structure of several societies.

6. Religious and social reformers become responsible for changes in rites, customs, modes of worship etc.
7. Scientific and technological causes exert far-reaching influence on social changes.
8. Political change like the end of foreign rule in India altogether changed the social outlook of the people. New aspirations, ideals and values like democracy, secularism and socialism became the cornerstones of social life.
9. Religious reformers like Gautama Buddha and Vardhamana Mahavir greatly influenced the social life of the people.
10. Religious and social reformers like Swami Dayanand and Swami Vivekananda of the 19th century made the people of India conscious of their social responsibility.
11. Mahatma Gandhi's work touched almost all dimensions of life including social.

25.7 TEACHER AS AN AGENT OF SOCIAL CHANGE

A teacher is regarded as an effective agent of social change. The teacher knows the needs of the society and the nature and direction of social change. The present democratic society expects that the teacher should really act as an agent of social change. Following are some of the suggestions to increase the teachers' contribution in social change:

Model of Modernity: In the process of social change, important role can be performed successfully by the teacher only when he makes himself a model of modernity i.e. when he himself imbibes modern values and allows them to manifest in his own conduct. In other words, the following qualities should be imbued in behaviour of the teacher: (i) Scientific attitude, (ii) Rational thought, (iii) Empathy, (iv) Mobility, (v) Democratic style, (vi) Sentiment of respect for individual's personality, (vii) Secularism, (viii) Faith in change and transformation, (ix) Democratic, (x) Constituted, and (xi) Production.

Competent and Skilled: The teacher should be competent i.e. fully knowledgeable and skilled to transmit his knowledge to the students because he is to led younger generation and the future citizens of tomorrow.

Psychological Climate: The teacher must prepare the psychological climate favourable to new attitudes and values. He is to be conscious and alive that correct attitudes be developed. The knowledge of small family norms is not to cultivate hatred for brothers and sisters, but to go in for a constructive attitude towards healthy social set up.

Reorientation: Knowledge is increasing at a tremendous speed. It has been well said that the knowledge created in the world during the last 25 years is more than the knowledge generated prior to it in 19th Century A.D. It is hoped that its speed will further go up in the time to come. It is thus essential that teacher should go on getting his knowledge reoriented both in terms of content and methods of teaching and also become alive to the direction of social change to be brought up, so as to pave a way for it.

Suggestions for Change: The teacher is supposed to come forward with his wise suggestions to bring about appropriate social change. For example, he is supposed to create a welcome atmosphere for girls' education. In the field of agriculture, he is supposed to go in for boosting the production so that his income increases, which will raise his standard of living, which in turn is positively connected with social change too.

Boosting Changes: The teacher should welcome the positive changes taking place. He should welcome what science and technology has bestowed upon mankind and inculcate proper attitudes and values in students. He is to encourage non-formal education, technical education, population education, adult education, women education, education of the backward classes and participate actively in these activities in the larger interest of social change.

Formation of Secular Attitude: The teacher should have secular outlook i.e. respect for all religions. He should eschew all caste, community and class considerations in dealing with students and colleagues. He should do it by correlating it with the school subjects in the organisation of co-curricular activities, imparting information for human rights and consumer rights also.

Developing National and International Outlook: The teacher should have national and international outlook. He should try to inculcate emotional integration, national integration and international understanding in the students. He should eschew violence and destruction and develop positive, constructive, realistic and humanitarian outlook amongst the students.

Pupil-centred and Community-centred Education: The teacher should impart pupil-centred education with proper emphasis on quality of life and communal involvement so as to go in for the best development of the pupils through the best possible use of material and human resources of the school and community. By making himself an active member of this process of community, the teacher can impart a powerful momentum to the process of social change operating to community life itself, the cultivation of the knowledge of UNO, UNESCO, World Bank and other international organisations.

Development of Scientific Attitude among Students: The teacher should develop a rational, curious, thoughtful, positive, constructive and scientific attitude in his students by encouraging debate and discussion in the classroom, as well as in co-curricular activities so that they shed all superstitions, blind faiths and prejudices.

Use of Modernised Instructional Technology: The teacher should make effective use of science and technology in the routine activities of the school and in this way habituate students to their use and give them practice in applying science and technology in other situations. Kit-based instruction for teaching of science, language, laboratories for teaching languages, programmed learning for all subjects, wise exploitation of radio and television lessons and educational journals etc. to supplement classroom teaching are essential steps.

It can be concluded that the teacher through his multifarious roles and activities can accelerate the process of social change in a very powerful way. To quote E.W. Gordon, "*It is the task of the teacher to educate for change to educate through change – to educate for orderly planned revolution, and if necessary to educate through revolutionary actions*".

To Create an Atmosphere against Drug Addiction: One of the major problems with our youth is that due to social degradation process and employment, our youth is now taking to drugs, which is sending them away by creating problems for constructive nation building, which is the need of our international environment. It is thus, one of the functions of social change that the teacher should create an atmosphere of hatred for the drug addiction.

To Strengthen the Democratic Causes: It is a very enlightened process to inculcate proper values for democratic atmosphere. In the initial stages, it gets some temporary setbacks due to immature democracy. The need of the hour is to strengthen it in the behaviour of students, who are the citizens of tomorrow. It can be better done by creating an atmosphere of hatred against political corruption so that those who indulge in it are up rooted from the political life.

In gist, it can be said that the teacher has a very constructive and effective role to play by way of spreading hatred for social evils and to prepare the students to go in for a constructive social change. This can to some extent be done if his own knowledge is up to date by becoming a keen reader.

26

Education as a Means and Product of Social Change

26.1 EDUCATION AS A MEANS OF SOCIAL CHANGE

It is not without reason that education has received great attention at the hands of leaders, religious and social reformers. They have strongly advocated the use of education as the most important agent/means or instrument of bringing about changes in the society. Education is not for the sake of learning or knowledge only.

The British rulers in India introduced a system of education in India which would enable the Indians to imbibe British culture, and manners. Lord Macaulay, the architect of the British System of education in India, in a letter to his father in 1836 wrote, "Hindus are much influenced with education. There is no Hindu who may keep faith in his religion after studying English." Earlier in 1835 in his Minute on Education which was accepted by Lord William Bentinck as the basis of the system of education in India, Lord Macaulay had written, "We must at present do our best to form a class of persons, Indian in blood and colour, but English in taste, in opinions, in morals and intellect." This indicates the importance of education as an agent or means of social change. Religious and social reformers Raja Rammohan Roy, Swami Dayananda and Vivekananda considered education as the potent weapon of social reform. Freedom fighters, political leaders and statesmen like Gandhiji laid great stress on education for improving the economic and social conditions of the people.

Gandhiji wanted his scheme of Basic Education to be the main instrument of social change. In his words, "The Basic School should be the spearhead of a non-violent social revolution."

The well-known American philosopher and educationist, John Dewey observes, "Education is the fundamental method of social progress and reform. This it does in two ways: by guiding children towards new values and by assisting the development of intelligence in individual children and increasing society' potential for its own transformation".

J.S. Brubacher has explained the role of education in the process of social change in these words. "If the lamp of reason is not lit or if the light is blown out, it but remains to struggle. When rational processes are put aside, it is only too likely that clubs and machine guns will become the social arbiters. Bullet will replace ballots."

The report of the Education Commission 1964-66 begins with these words, "The destiny of India is being shaped in her classrooms. This we believe is no mere rhetoric." The Commission further observed that if social change is to be achieved on a grand scale, there is one instrument and one instrument only that can be used is 'Education'.

26.2 BROAD AREAS OF SOCIAL CHANGE AND TRANSFORMATION THROUGH EDUCATION

Developing Awareness. Education is considered as an important means of making people aware of their weakness and enabling them to gain necessary knowledge for bringing about social changes in a non-violent, rational and scientific manner.

Developing Appropriate Values. Education is expected to change the attitudes and values of the people to create in them necessary motivation for social change.

Realisation of Important Goals. Education is considered to be of immense help in realising the national goals of social change like democracy, secularism and socialism.

Providing Necessary Skills. It is generally accepted that education will provide necessary training in skills and occupations so as to produce competent personnel needed for manning the different jobs in agricultural, business, commerce, educational, industrial and research establishments etc. in accordance with the requirements of social change.

26.3 FUNCTIONS OF EDUCATION IN SOCIAL CHANGE

According to H.C. Dent, a national system of education has two functions to perform: a traditional preservation function and a growth facilitating function. In a time of social flux both these functions become overwhelmingly important.

Some scholars are of the view that education has to perform the following three functions:

1. Conservation of traditional heritage.
2. Adjustment and growth of the present society.
3. Creation of a suitable base for new order and new ideas which should become an instrument of social change in the future.

For performing the above mentioned social functions, education has to establish the following linkages:

1. Education should link the past with existing realities of the present national identity and the emerging future goals and aspirations of the society.
2. For achieving meaningful national integration, education should

establish proper linkage of the urban elite and the rural people. This task can be performed through providing equal opportunities for education. Programmes of formal and non-formal education through various types of institutions should be organised extensively in the rural areas.

3. There is a need for closer involvement of the students and the community in educational programmes for a developing a 'sense of belonging' and creating necessary enthusiasm for social change.
4. Science and spirituality should be linked together.
5. Formal education should be linked to the world of work and the world of culture to serve the needs of the social change.

26.4 EQUALITY OF OPPORTUNITY IN EDUCATION AND SOCIAL CHANGE

Equality of opportunity in education is very helpful in promoting social change. The National Policy of Education 1986 has observed, "The New Policy will lay special emphasis on the removal of disparities and to equalise educational opportunity by attending to the specific needs of those who have been denied equality so far."

26.5 AGENCIES OF EDUCATION AND SOCIAL CHANGE

There are a large number of agencies of education – formal, informal and non-formal agencies that can be used effectively for bringing about social change in the society. (The details of these agencies are provided in a separate Chapter).

26.6 LIMITATIONS OF EDUCATION IN BRINGING ABOUT CHANGES

1. *Limited Resources*. Adequate funds are needed for providing educational facilities on a large scale. Besides funds are needed for qualitative improvement of education. Ill-equipped individuals cannot bring about social changes in the society.
2. *Attitude of 'No Change'*. People in general and even educated people are reluctant to follow new paths.
3. *Poverty and Ignorance of the Masses*. Percentage of literacy remained very low in India for a number of years. It is only recently that considerable improvement has become visible. Likewise, a substantial percentage of people are still below the poverty line. In such a situation, social reforms cannot take place.
4. *Lack of 'Political Will'*. Revolutionary constructive educational reforms could not be carried out on account of the non-availability of necessary political support. Thus education remained ineffective to a considerable extent in playing its role in social change.

26.7 TEACHER AS AN AGENT OF SOCIAL CHANGE

Prof. Ottaway is convinced that teachers in the schools can exercise a powerful influence on the community if they choose to do so.

Edmund W. Gordon, an American educationist has explained the role of the teacher in social change in these words, "It is the task of the teacher to educate – to educate for change – to educate through change – to educate for orderly planned revolution".

The McNair Report on the Training of Teachers in England states, "It is a truism to say that every teacher, in however humble a capacity he or she may be serving, is directly involved in moulding the shape of things to come."

Prof W.O. Smith of the University of London observed that those who aspire to teach should think about the problems of society and work accordingly.

The role of the teachers in social change in the context of situation in India is questioned by S.P. Ruhela and K.C. Vyas. They advance three important reasons for this (i) Occupation of school teachers has so far not emerged as a profession in the strict sense of the term. (ii) Several teacher's training institutions continue to be disgusting educational slums. (iii) School teacher's professional organisations are not duly committed.

26.8 EDUCATION AS A PRODUCT OF SOCIAL CHANGE

Social reformers advocated several reforms for bringing about social change in the society. They called for the removal of superstition and ignorance. They encouraged the people to develop a sense of equality and self-improvement to improve their lot rather than depending upon destiny. They encouraged them to read scriptures and other books to gain knowledge and insight. They promoted rational and scientific thinking.

Swami Dayananda made the Vedas as the basis of social reforms. He asked people to read them thoroughly. For spreading his message, his followers opened a chain of educational institutions in various parts of India.

Raja Rammohan and Swami Vivekananda urged the people to study western science and literature also so that they could acquaint themselves with the progress made by foreign countries.

Thus on account of the emphasis on various aspects of social reforms, people began to realise that it was not possible to develop self-confidence, self-respect and status without obtaining education. The social reformers themselves started educational institutions at various places to create necessary awareness among the people. Therefore, we say that education is the product of social change.

Under the British rule, the social life of the people and especially of higher sections of society was geared to meet the requirements of the colonial power. Accordingly, education system became subservient to social change. This necessitated far reaching changes in all dimensions of education—aims of education, contents of education, methods of instruction and discipline etc.

26.9 INTERDEPENDENT ROLE OF EDUCATION AND SOCIAL CHANGE

Education is a means as well as a product of social change. This implies that educational changes and social changes are complementary. An educational change leads over time to a social change and social change, in turn, intensifies and strengthens the social change.

The process of change may be in the reverse order. A social change may lead to an educational change. The educational change, in turn, may intensify and strengthen social change.

Let us explain the mutual relationship of educational change and social change by taking an example. The spread of education among the Scheduled Castes helped to improve their socio-economic conditions and this brought about some social changes. They became more aware of the importance of education. They began to avail benefits themselves of the opportunities provided in the formal and non-formal system of education.

The constant emphasis on equality by the political and social reformers developed a desire of social change among the Scheduled Castes. They, therefore, saw in education as the promoter of their status. They began to avail themselves of educational opportunities in a great measure. In this way through education the process of social change was intensified and strengthened.

The spread of education among females led to a new awareness among them. Their social status underwent changes. With the improvement in the social status of women they become more conscious of education and this strengthened the process of educational change among them.

26.10 FACTORS WHICH INFLUENCE SOCIAL CHANGE IN INDIA

In every society, social control is exercised with a view to make individual members conform to its standard. In other words, social values and objectives are laid down by the society. It is through the social process that the individual is made to conform to the ways of social life.

In a society, two opposing forces always operate. They are centripetal and centrifugal. The centripetal force wants to keep the tradition of the society intact. It moves backward. On the other hand, the centrifugal force wants radical changes. Because of these opposing forces there is a necessity to maintain balance between the two.

The factors which influence social change in India are:

Means of Communications: For the last so many years, Indian education suffered a lot for want of communication. Schools were scattered at far of distances. As a result of which many deserving and desirous students could not get the benefit of education. Further difficulties arose because of the fact that some regions were thinly populated and had a population of less than 150 persons to the square mile.

Growth of Cities and Changing Population: Another important factor responsible for social change in India is growth of cities and rate of population. People from rural areas migrating to the urban areas being attracted by new industries

Growth of Mass Media of Propaganda: Another agency of social change in the emerging Indian society is the growth of mass media of propaganda. Because of this development, there is spread of new ideas and beliefs. The sizeable growth of newspapers, periodicals, books and press work as a powerful factor in building and developing social consciousness among the educated people of our country

Social Legislation and Social Awakening: The development of new social awakening is leading the Indian society to a welcome change in the attitude of the people. In the past, the Indian laws and customs had religious sanctions. Two important elements, marriage and child labour have relevance with education.

Philosophy of Humanism: Because of the change in social outlook; the old cultural and caste ridden prejudices are vanishing day by day. Now people proclaim the value of human national character. Thus education helps for the progress of humanism in our country.

Development of Prestige Value of Education: As a result of change, education has developed a prestige value in the society. Educated people are respected everywhere in the country. It encourages the parents to educate their children.

Economic Worth of Education: Till recently, education was considered as a non-productive activity. The doors of the temples of learning were opened for the rich people. For the common people, education was a 'closed shop'. With the dawn of independence, education is considered to be the no. 1 nation-building activity, as it is realised that country's greatness depends on the quality and quantity of education.

26.11 SOCIAL AWARENESS

Social awareness is awareness of the social situation in a group or community in a shared environment, which can be physical, virtual or both: people's role, activities, positions, status, responsibilities, social connections and group processes. Social awareness encompasses awareness of social situation in general, and social situation at a certain moment. The knowledge about the general social situation can be achieved by answering questions about the group structure, relations and interactions between group or community members, their roles and associated (recourses) for example knowledge). The awareness or knowledge of a general social situation is acquired by collecting and analysing awareness information from social situations at a certain moment and answering questions like who is present, who is available and who is doing what and talking to whom at the moment.

Social awareness in real world is often achieved by collecting different cues from the environment, for example, by looking at what other people in the same room are doing, their conversational patterns and emotional state.

Definitions of Social Awareness

1. Social awareness means knowing about your environment, your surroundings, everything that's happening in society.
2. Social awareness means that you should know what is socially acceptable from you in society and you should act in that manner.
3. Social awareness in defined as awareness about the social situation of other people, i.e. what they are doing, whether they are engaged in a conversation and can be disturbed, and of who is around and what is up.
4. Social awareness that is all the general knowledge about the others in a social or conversational context. It can indicate whether a partner is paying attention or being interested.

26.12 HOW TO DEVELOP SOCIAL AWARENESS

Developing social awareness involves learning about the dynamics of social relationships between individuals, groups and communities. A socially aware individual values human rights and acknowledges the importance of harmonious social interaction for the developmental progress of human beings. Social awareness spans a wide spectrum, beginning with social skills development in early childhood and encompassing the level of social consciousness that leads to social activism and societal transformation. Here are some strategies for developing social awareness:

Consider the Needs of Individuals and Groups: People need to feel heard, valued, respected and acknowledged. Develop sensitivity to the needs of others. For children, this means learning how to share toys and play harmoniously on the playground.

Examine Your Role in Conflicts: The use of excessive force, intimidation and aggression are common strategies when dealing with conflict. Some people avoid conflicts at all costs. Others choose the company of passive people or engage in passive aggressive behaviours. Consider the role that you play in perpetuating conflicts and commit to living a more socially harmonious life.

- Focus on commonalities and points of agreement to reduce conflict. An overemphasis on social differences can lead to disharmony. Find the commonalities. For children, this may mean choosing a game that both children enjoy.

- Develop conflict resolution skills. Take a course in conflict resolution or spend time talking to and observing the behaviours of leaders and mentors who are known for their harmonious natures.

Increase your Sensitivity to Social Justice and Harmony: In children and teens this may mean treating others fairly regardless of their level of popularity or style of dress.

Educate Yourself on Social Issues: Racism, and poverty are just a few examples of issues plaguing society. Children can learn about these social issues at school or at home.

Step out of your Comfort Zone to Experience Unfamiliar Groups: Whether you venture out to a different side of town or travel to a different country, exposing yourself to diverse cultures and ways of life will expand your thinking and view of the world. Being exposed to different belief systems, cuisines and lifestyles is useful for expanding your social circle and building tolerance for diverse viewpoints.

Practice Compassion: Social transformation requires a commitment to exploring and understanding divergent viewpoints. Develop empathy by consciously imagining yourself in the position of those in a different or less fortunate situation. Children can be taught to do this when they have hurt another person's feelings.

Commit to a Social Awareness Plan: Slipping into apathy and isolation can be easy given life's sometimes overwhelming demands. Design a plan that keeps you continually aware socially.

- Serve in your community. Explore service opportunities in schools, cultural centers, political organisations, religious communities or neighbourhood activities.
- Engage in a social activity on a daily basis. Choose an activity that requires you to listen to and tend to the needs of another person or group.
- Practice speaking up in defence of others. Commit to voicing your opinion on behalf of marginalised group who are deprived of their basic human rights.

Ask other people to support your efforts to become more socially aware. When friends, family and colleagues realise that you want to become more socially engaged, they are more likely to invite you to volunteer at an event and join them in social activities regularly.

27

Human Rights and Education

Human Rights have become an established reality since the establishment of the United Nations in 1945, which has as its central concern reaffirmed its faith in fundamental human rights, in the dignity and worth the human person, in the equal rights of men and women and of nations large and small.

In other words, human rights being eternal part of the nature of human beings are essential for individuals to develop their personality, their human qualities. Their intelligence, talent and conscience and to enable them to satisfy spiritual and other higher order needs. The purposes of securing human rights as such are to provide protection to these rights against the abuse of power committed by organs of state such as to promote institutions that promote the living conditions of human beings for the development of their personality and to provide effective remedial measures for obtaining redress in the event of these rights being violated.

The history and development of human rights is very fascinating. The origin is traced, by some scholars, back to the times of ancient Greeks. The fact that human rights were recognised as natural rights of man is illustrated in a Greek play *Antigone.* In philosophy, the development of the notion of natural rights of man was contributed by the stoic philosophers. They first developed natural law theory which states that every human being possessed rights by virtue of being human beings. However, this concept of natural rights and natural law went progressively through various changes before the concept of Human Rights finds its mention in the Universal Declaration of Human Rights of 1948, is of course the revival of the eighteenth century concept of 'Rights of Man'.

27.1 MEANING OF HUMAN RIGHTS

Human rights are commonly understood as being those rights which are inherent to the human being. The concept of human rights acknowledges that every single human being is entitled to enjoy his or her human rights without distinction as to race, colour, sex, language, religion, political or other opinion, national or social origin, property, birth or other status. Human rights are legally guaranteed by *human rights law,* protecting individuals and groups against actions that interfere with fundamental freedoms and human dignity. They are expressed in treaties, customary international law, bodies of principles and other sources of law. Human rights law places an obligation on States to act in a particular way and prohibits States from engaging in specified activities. However, the law does not establish human rights. Human rights are inherent entitlements which come to every person as a consequence of being human. Treaties and other sources of law generally serve to *protect* formally the rights of individuals and groups against actions or abandonment of actions by Governments which interfere with the enjoyment of their human rights.

Defining Human Rights

Human: A member of the Homo sapiens species; a man, woman or child; a person.

Rights: Things to which you are entitled or allowed; freedoms that are guaranteed.

Human Rights: The rights you have simply because you are human.

A right is a freedom of some kind. It is something to which you are entitled by virtue of being human. Human rights are based on the principle of respect for the individual. Their fundamental assumption is that each person is a moral and rational being who deserves to be treated with dignity. They are called human rights because they are universal. Whereas nations or specialised groups enjoy specific rights that apply only to them, human rights are the rights to which everyone is entitled—no matter who they are or where they live—simply because they are alive.

27.2 NEED OF HUMAN RIGHTS

Below are three reasons why human rights are necessary:

Moral Vision: We need to set down human rights because they give us a moral vision of human nature and human dignity. They create a vision of what life would look like if everybody's basic humanity was equally respected and protected. If our needs for survival and protection were met, then we could focus on developing our individual and collective potential through educational and cultural activities.

The reality is that war, violence, intolerance and poverty around the world result in daily violations of human dignity. Human rights remind us of what is possible and what is due to people, even in the worst of situations.

Political Vision: Human rights also give us a political vision or an agenda for change. If we evaluate our own schools, communities or countries against the standards set out in the Declaration, we can develop an agenda for social and political change. New policies and procedures, new development projects and new laws can be constructed in order to try to improve the achievement of human rights for all.

Protection: We need human rights for protection when our legal rights are violated by the state, and to encourage justice and fairness within our societies. Ironically, we may be most aware of our human rights when they are being threatened or denied. Human rights can be matters of life and death.

Because of these three widely-accepted reasons, human rights are occasionally protected by raising both national and international awareness of human rights violations. This can help draw attention to and resolve such situations, by creating moral pressure on governments.

27.3 CHARACTERISTICS OF HUMAN RIGHTS

The following are the basic characteristics of human rights:

Universal: All human beings have certain rights, for no other reason than their humanity and the values attached to humanity; this means that human rights precede and trump considerations of national sovereignty and that national sovereignty, therefore, does not provide a means to escape human rights obligations.

Pre-political: They are a moral order that has legitimacy and existence preceding contingent social, legal, political, cultural and historical conditions and that can be used to assess and question those conditions.

Independent from Legal/Social/Cultural/Religious Recognition: Human beings have human rights even if the laws and customs of their country/group do not recognise or perhaps even violate these rights – although people's rights are obviously much more secure when they are translated into law and culture.

Unconditional: People have rights without conditions; respect for rights is not conditional upon fulfilment of duties, status, legal recognition of rights or persons etc.

Inalienable: Since rights are owned by human beings because of their humanity, these rights aren't given and hence can't be taken away; people still have rights when those rights are violated.

Not Forfeitable: People can't give their rights away for the same reason that these rights can't be taken away; however, people can decide that they don't want their rights enforced.

Equal Rights: Rights are equal in two meanings of the word; they are equal between people (because all people are equally human) and they are equal to other human rights (there are no "basic" and "less urgent/important" human rights).

Interdependent: Different rights need each other, violations of one right most likely lead to violations of other rights (which is one reason why there can't be a core of "basic" rights).

Limited: Rights have to be balanced against each other because respect for one right can imply a violation of another right; balancing means imposing limitations on some rights for the benefit of other rights (or of the rights of others); the fact that there are no basic rights makes this balancing more difficult but not impossible. Conflicting rights then have to be balanced by taking into account the nature of the underlying values, or the way in which the two conflicting rights realise the values they are supposed to uphold.

Not Politically Neutral: Not all forms of government can equally respect human rights; there's a close link between human rights and democracy.

Multidimensional: Human rights are not just a matter between citizens and the state; they are addressed at everyone and impose duties on everyone. Corporations and other organisations also have to be mindful of their operations' human rights implications. This means that human rights also function in a trans-national and trans-generational dimension.

Simultaneously Negative (free from x) and Positive (free to do x): They always and everywhere require both self-restraint and tolerance as well as active intervention, according to the circumstances.

Inherent: Human Rights are inherent because they are not granted by any person or authority.

Fundamental: Human Rights are fundamental rights because without them, the life and dignity of man will be meaningless.

Imprescriptible: Human Rights do not prescribe and cannot be lost even if man fails to use or assert them, even by a long passage of time.

Indivisible: Human Rights are not capable of being divided. They cannot be denied even when other rights have already been enjoyed.

Moral Claims: Human rights are moral claims and therefore they are grounded in morality, not just law. They have a very high priority compared to other moral or non-moral claims, such as claims based on honor, disgust, utility etc.

Mandatory Compliance: They require mandatory (as opposed to discretionary) compliance and are, therefore, more than mere aspirations – they are necessary for the protection and realisation of certain fundamental, basic and universal human values and interests.

Instrumental Principles: They are instrumental principles in the sense that we don't want them for their own sake; they are means for the creation of better life quality and not just goals in themselves.

27.4 IMPORTANCE OF HUMAN RIGHTS

- They are essential for every human being. They cannot be

categorised as the preserve of one particular nation but are, in fact, the possession of mankind as a whole.

- Just like that of moral rights the element of their enforcement lies in the individual's conscience.
- They cover legal rights which are safeguarded by the law of the land. They also comprise fundamental rights which are included in the constitution of a particular country. As such, they are accorded special treatment as regards their amendment and forms of rights—social, economic and political—which enable a person to lead a life of dignity and live in peace and security.
- The human rights are universal. They are provided to members of the human society as a whole whether or not some section of them are aware of them or not.
- If human rights are infringed in any part of the world, besides persuasion, even force by alien powers—the votaries of the human rights is permissible, for their enforcement.
- The Human Rights are not unbridled. They are to be restricted in the interest of public peace, political security, morality and social decency. Each state has its own cultural standard and norms of civilisation, in the light of which reasonable restrictions are indispensable. This shows that human rights are not limitless. They have to function within boundary of civilised norms and cultural legacy of a country.

27.5 TYPES OF HUMAN RIGHTS

The following are the types of human rights:

Article 1: All human beings are born free and equal in dignity and rights. They are endowed with reason and conscience and should act towards one another in a spirit of brotherhood.

Article 2: Everyone is entitled to all the rights and freedoms set forth in this Declaration, without distinction of any kind, such as race, colour, sex, language, religion, political or other opinion, national or social origin, property, birth or other status. Furthermore, no distinction shall be made on the basis of the political, jurisdictional or international status of the country or territory to which a person belongs, whether it be independent, trust, non-self-governing or under any other limitation of sovereignty.

Article 3: Everyone has the right to life, liberty and security of person.

Article 4: No one shall be held in slavery or servitude; slavery and the slave trade shall be prohibited in all their forms.

Article 5: No one shall be subjected to torture or to cruel, inhuman or degrading treatment or punishment.

Article 6: Everyone has the right to recognition everywhere as a person before the law.

Article 7: All are equal before the law and are entitled without any discrimination to equal protection of the law. All are entitled to equal protection against any discrimination in violation of this Declaration and against any incitement to such discrimination.

Article 8: Everyone has the right to an effective remedy by the competent national tribunals for acts violating the fundamental rights granted him by the constitution or by law.

Article 9: No one shall be subjected to arbitrary arrest, detention or exile.

Article 10: Everyone is entitled in full equality to a fair and public hearing by an independent and impartial tribunal, in the determination of his rights and obligations and of any criminal charge against him.

Article 11: 1. Everyone charged with a penal offence has the right to be presumed innocent until proved guilty according to law in a public trial at which he has had all the guarantees necessary for his defence. 2. No one shall be held guilty of any penal offence on account of any act or omission which did not constitute a penal offence, under national or international law, at the time when it was committed. Nor shall a heavier penalty be imposed than the one that was applicable at the time the penal offence was committed.

Article 12: No one shall be subjected to arbitrary interference with his privacy, family, home or correspondence, nor to attacks upon his honour and reputation. Everyone has the right to the protection of the law against such interference or attacks.

Article 13: Everyone has the right to freedom of movement and residence within the borders of each State including his own, and to return to his country.

Article 14: 1. Everyone has the right to seek and to enjoy in other countries asylum from persecution. 2. This right may not be invoked in the case of prosecutions genuinely arising from non-political crimes or from acts contrary to the purposes and principles of the United Nations.

Article 15: 1. Everyone has the right to a nationality. 2. No one shall be arbitrarily deprived of his nationality nor denied the right to change his nationality.

Article 16: 1. Men and women of full age, without any limitation due to race, nationality or religion, have the right to marry and to found a family. They are entitled to equal rights as to marriage, during marriage and at its dissolution. 2. Marriage shall be entered into only with the free and full consent of the intending spouses. 3. The family is the natural and fundamental group unit of society and is entitled to protection by society and the State.

Article 17: 1. Everyone has the right to own property alone as well as in association with others. 2. No one shall be arbitrarily deprived of his property.

Article 18: Everyone has the right to freedom of thought, conscience and religion; this right includes freedom to change his religion or belief, and freedom, either alone or in community with others and in public or private, to manifest his religion or belief in teaching, practice, worship and observance.

Article 19: Everyone has the right to freedom of opinion and expression; this right includes freedom to hold opinions without interference and to seek receive and impart information and ideas though any media and regardless of frontiers.

Article 20: 1. Everyone has the right to freedom of peaceful assembly and association. 2. No one may be compelled to belong to an association.

Article 21: 1. Everyone has the right to take part in the government of his country, directly or through freely chosen representatives. 2. Everyone has the right of equal access to public service in his country. 3. The will of the people shall be the basis of the authority of government; this 'will' shall be expressed in periodic and genuine elections which shall be by universal and equal suffrage, and shall be held by secrete vote or by equivalent free voting procedures.

Article 22: Everyone, as a member of society, has the right to social security and is entitled to realisation, through national effort and international cooperation and in accordance with the organisation and resources of each State, of the economic, social and cultural rights indispensable for his dignity and the free development of his personality.

Article 23: 1. Everyone has the right to work, to free choice of employment, to just and favourable condition.

27.6 CATEGORIES OF HUMAN RIGHTS

The Human Rights may be grouped under five categories viz. Civil, Political, Economic, Social and Cultural.

(A) Civil Rights

The Civil Rights as enumerated in the Human Rights are:

- All human beings are born free and equal in dignity and rights. All are equal before the law.
- Everyone has the right to life, liberty and security to persons.
- None is to be held in slavery or servitude. Hence Slave Trade in all its forms is to be prohibited.
- No one is to be subjected to arbitrary arrest, detention or exile.
- Everyone has the right to freedom of thought, conscience and religion.

(B) Political Rights

The following are the political rights:

- Every one possesses the right to take part in the Government of his country, directly or indirectly through freely chosen representatives.

- Everyone has access to public services in the country.
- The 'will of the people' is the basis of authority of government. This 'will' is to be expressed through periodical elections to be held on the basis of Universal and equal suffrage. The election shall be held by secret ballot.
- Everyone is entitled to right to a nationality. No one shall be arbitrarily deprived of it.

(C) Economic Rights

The following economic rights have been included in the Charter on the Human Rights:

- Everyone possesses the right to own property.
- Everyone has the right to social security. Social security system impels a government to pay monthly allowance to the needy, the distressed, the disabled and the old who are devoid of any income or earn a very meagre income not enough for subsistence.
- Everyone is to be assured right to work. In erstwhile Soviet Union and Communist China, work is guaranteed to all able bodied persons. The erstwhile Soviet Union adopted a famous maxim—"He who does not work neither shall he eat". The right includes right to rest and leisure.
- Everyone is to get equal pay for equal work. Discrimination on the basis of sex is not desirable. In India, women labour and child labour are invariably engaged on comparatively less remuneration in the fields or factories which is a violation of human rights and law does not permit it.

(D) Social Rights

The Social Rights enumerated in the Declaration are as follows:

- Men and Women of adult age have the right to marry and set up a family. Marriage is to be arranged with the full consent of would be spouses.
- The family is the natural and fundamental units of society. It is entitled to full protection both by the state and the society.
- Everyone has the right to Education. Education is to be made free at the elementary stage. In case of India, Primary Education up to the age of 14 has been made free and compulsory now, after the passage of Right to Education through an amendment in the Constitution. Previously also, the provision existed in the Directive Principles.

(E) Cultural Rights

Everybody possesses the right to participation in the cultural life of the community. This enables everyone to enjoy the various arts and take part in the scientific advancement and its benefits.

27.7 MEANING OF HUMAN RIGHTS EDUCATION

Human rights education is an integral part of the right to education and is increasingly gaining recognition as a human right in itself. Knowledge of rights and freedoms is considered a fundamental tool to guarantee respect for the rights of all. UNESCO's work in human rights education is guided by the World Programme for Human Rights Education.

Education should encompass values such as peace, non-discrimination, equality, justice, non-violence, tolerance and respect for human dignity. Quality education based on a human rights approach means that rights are implemented throughout the whole education system and in all learning environments.

Human rights are highly inspirational and also highly practical, embodying the hopes and ideals of most human beings and also empowering people to achieve them.Human rights education shares those inspirational and practical aspects. It sets standards but also produces change. Effective human rights education can:

- Produce changes in values and attitude
- Produce changes in behaviour
- Produce empowerment for social justice
- Develop attitudes of solidarity across issues, communities, and nations
- Develop knowledge and analytical skills
- Encourage participatory education.

27.8 NEED TO ENSURE HUMAN RIGHTS EDUCATION

- It promotes social cohesion, integration and stability
- It builds respect for peace and non-violent conflict resolution
- It contributes to positive social transformation
- It is more cost-effective and sustainable
- It produces better outcomes for economic development
- It builds capacity.

27.9 THE UNIVERSAL DECLARATION OF HUMAN RIGHTS (1948)

The *Universal Declaration of Human Rights* is probably the best known list of human rights. The United Nations adopted it in 1948, when the whole world was recovering from the wounds of the Second World War, particularly from the horrors of genocide. After a period that showed some of the worst of human potential, the world community tried to focus on and promote the best of human potential. The Preamble to the Declaration implies that making sure that every person knows about and understands the Declaration will be one of the best ways of ensuring that human rights are respected around the world. The Declaration is a key starting point for understanding human rights – most other human rights conventions expand on specific parts of it. The Universal Declaration of Human Rights are summarised below:

1. *We Are All Born Free & Equal.* We are all born free. We all have our own thoughts and ideas. We should all be treated in the same way.
2. *Don't Discriminate.* These rights belong to everybody, whatever our differences.
3. *The Right to Life.* We all have the right to life, and to live in freedom and safety.
4. *No Slavery.* Nobody has any right to make us a slave. We cannot make anyone our slave.
5. *No Torture.* Nobody has any right to hurt us or to torture us.
6. *You Have Rights No Matter Where You Go.* I am a person just like you!
7. *We're All Equal Before the Law.* The law is the same for everyone. It must treat us all fairly.
8. *Your Human Rights Are Protected by Law.* We can all ask for the law to help us when we are not treated fairly.
9. *No Unfair Detainment.* Nobody has the right to put us in prison without good reason and keep us there, or to send us away from our country.
10. *The Right to Trial.* If we are put on trial this should be in public. The people who try us should not let anyone tell them what to do.
11. *We're Always Innocent Till Proven Guilty.* Nobody should be blamed for doing something until it is proven. When people say we did a bad thing we have the right to show it is not true.
12. *The Right to Privacy.* Nobody should try to harm our good name. Nobody has the right to come into our home, open our letters, or bother us or our family without a good reason.
13. *Freedom to Move.* We all have the right to go where we want in our own country and to travel as we wish.
14. *The Right to Seek a Safe Place to Live.* If we are frightened of being badly treated in our own country, we all have the right to run away to another country to be safe.
15. *Right to a Nationality.* We all have the right to belong to a country.
16. *Marriage and Family.* Every grown-up has the right to marry and have a family if they want to. Men and women have the same rights when they are married, and when they are separated.
17. *The Right to Your Own Things.* Everyone has the right to own things or share them. Nobody should take our things from us without a good reason.
18. *Freedom of Thought.* We all have the right to believe in what we want to believe, to have a religion, or to change it if we want.

19. *Freedom of Expression.* We all have the right to make up our own minds, to think what we like, to say what we think, and to share our ideas with other people.
20. *The Right to Public Assembly.* We all have the right to meet our friends and to work together in peace to defend our rights. Nobody can make us join a group if we don't want to.
21. *The Right to Democracy.* We all have the right to take part in the government of our country. Every grown-up should be allowed to choose their own leaders.
22. *Social Security.* We all have the right to affordable housing, medicine, education, and childcare, enough money to live on and medical help if we are ill or old.
23. *Workers' Rights.* Every grown-up has the right to do a job, to a fair wage for their work, and to join a trade union.
24. *The Right to Play.* We all have the right to rest from work and to relax.
25. *Food and Shelter for All.* We all have the right to a good life. Mothers and children, people who are old, unemployed or disabled, and all people have the right to be cared for.
26. *The Right to Education.* Education is a right. Primary school should be free. We should learn about the United Nations and how to get on with others. Our parents can choose what we learn.
27. *Copyright.* Copyright is a special law that protects one's own artistic creations and writings; others cannot make copies without permission. We all have the right to our own way of life and to enjoy the good things that art, science and learning bring.
28. *A Fair and Free World.* There must be proper order so we can all enjoy rights and freedoms in our own country and all over the world.
29. *Responsibility.* We have a duty to other people, and we should protect their rights and freedoms.
30. *No One Can Take Away Your Human Rights.*

27.10 UN CONVENTION ON THE RIGHTS OF THE CHILD (UNCRC), 1989

According to UNCRC, every child has the right to an education, to be healthy, to grow up safe and to be heard. The United Nations Convention on the Rights of the Child (UNCRC) is a legally-binding international agreement setting out the civil, political, economic, social and cultural rights of every child, regardless of their race, religion or abilities. Since being adopted by the United Nations in November 1989, the CRC has received 194 ratifications with only two countries in the world still to ratify. This means they have agreed to do everything they can to make the rights a reality for children around the world.

All signatories are bound to the UNCRC by international law and its implementation is monitored by the Committee on the Rights of the Child. Under the terms of the convention, states are required to meet the basic needs of children and help them reach their full potential. Central to this is the acknowledgment that every child has basic fundamental rights. These include:

- The right to life
- The right to his or her own name and identity
- The right to be protected from abuse or exploitation
- The right to an education
- The right to having their privacy protected
- To be raised by, or have a relationship with, their parents
- The right to express their opinions and have these listened to and, where appropriate, acted upon
- The right to play and enjoy culture and art in safety

On May 25, 2000, two optional protocols were added to the UNCRC. The first of these ask governments to ensure that children under the age of 18 are not forcibly recruited into their armed forces. It also requires governments to do everything they can to make sure members of their armed forces who are under the age of 18 do not take part in combat.

The second of these protocols call on states to prohibit child prostitution and child pornography and the sale of children into slavery. So far, both protocols have already been ratified by more than 120 states.

27.11 NATIONAL COMMISSION FOR PROTECTION OF CHILD RIGHTS (NCPCR)

The National Commission for Protection of Child Rights (NCPCR) was set up in March 2007 under the Commission for Protection of Child Rights Act, 2005, an Act of Parliament (December 2005). The Commission's Mandate is to ensure that all Laws, Policies, Programmes, and Administrative Mechanisms are in consonance with the Child Rights perspective as enshrined in the Constitution of India and also the UN Convention on the Rights of the Child. The Child is defined as a person in the 0 to 18 years age group.

The Commission visualises a rights-based perspective flowing into National Policies and Programmes, along with nuanced responses at the State, District and Block levels, taking care of specificities and strengths of each region. In order to touch every child, it seeks a deeper penetration to communities and households and expects that the ground experiences inform the support the field receives from all the authorities at the higher level. Thus the Commission sees an indispensable role for the State, sound institution-building processes, respect for decentralisation at the level of the local bodies at the community level and larger societal concern for children and their well-being.

The National Commission for Protection of Child Rights (NCPCR) emphasises the principle of universality and inviolability of child rights and recognises the tone of urgency in all the child related policies of the country. For the Commission, protection of all children in the 0 to 18 years age group is of equal importance. Thus, policies define priority actions for the most vulnerable children. This includes focus on regions that are backward or on communities or children under certain circumstances, and so on. The NCPCR believes that while in addressing only some children, there could be a fallacy of exclusion of many vulnerable children who may not fall under the defined or targeted categories. In its translation into practice, the task of reaching out to all children gets compromised and a societal tolerance of violation of child rights continues. This would, in fact, have an impact on the program for the targeted population as well. Therefore, it considers that it is only in building a larger atmosphere in favour of protection of children's rights, that children who are targeted become visible and gain confidence to access their entitlements.

Functions and Duties of NCPCR

The main function and duties of the NCPCR is to:

- Examine and review the safeguards provided by or under any law for the time being in force for the protection of child rights and recommend measures for their effective implementation.
- Present to the Central Government, annually and at such other intervals, as the Commission may deem fit, reports upon the working of those safeguards.
- Inquire into violation of child rights and recommend initiation of proceedings in such cases.
- Examine all factors that inhibit the enjoyment of rights of children affected by terrorism, communal violence, riots, natural disasters, domestic violence, HIV/AIDS, trafficking, maltreatment, torture and exploitation, pornography, and prostitution and recommend appropriate remedial measures.
- Look into matters relating to children in need of special care and protection, including children in distress, marginalised and disadvantaged children, ,children in conflict with law, juveniles, children without family and children of prisoners; and recommend appropriate remedial measures.
- Study treaties and other international instruments and undertake periodic review of existing policies, programmes, and other activities on child rights and make recommendations for their effective implementation in the best interests of children.
- Undertake and promote research in the field of child rights.
- Spread child rights literacy among various sections of society and

promote awareness of the safeguards available for protection of these rights through publications, media, seminars and other available means.

- Inspect or cause to be inspected any juvenile custodial home or any other place of residence or institution meant for children, under the control of the Central Government or any State Government or any other authority including any institution run by a social organisation, where children are detained or lodged for the purpose of treatment, reformation or protection and take up with these authorities for remedial action, if found necessary.
- Inquire into complaints and take notice of matters related to:
  - Deprivation and violation of child rights.
  - Non-implementation of laws providing for protection and development of children.
  - Non-compliance of policy decisions, guidelines or instructions aimed at mitigating hardships to and ensuring welfare of the children and to provide relief to such children or take up the issues arising out of such matters with appropriate authorities.

Such other functions as it may consider necessary for the promotion of child rights and any other matter incidental to the above functions.

28

Value Education

28.1 MEANING AND CONCEPT OF VALUES

Value literally means something that has a price, something precious, dear and worthwhile. Hence, it is something for which someone is ready to suffer and sacrifice. Values are a set of principles or standards of behaviour. The word "Value" is derived from the Latin word "Valerie" meaning to be strong and vigorous. To be of value is to have certain virtues. From an historical view point a value may be defined as "*a thing which is good*". A widely accepted concept of value in traditional Indian philosophy is, "Truth", "Goodness" and "Beauty" i.e. 'satyam, shivam and sundaram' are considered as eternal values.

Values are principles, fundamental convictions, and ideals, standards of life which act as general guide to behaviour or as a reference point in decision making. Values are beliefs about what is right and what is wrong and what is important in life. Value literally means something that has a price, precious, dear and worthwhile; one is ready to sacrifice for.

It is a set of principles which guide the standard of behaviour. Values are desirable and held in esteem. They give strength to a person's character by occupying a central place in his life. It reflects ones attitudes, choices, decisions, judgments, relationships, dreams and vision.

These are the guiding principle of life which is conducive to all value development. It is like the rails which keep the train on track. Without values, life will be chaotic. Values are virtues, ideals and qualities on which actions and beliefs are based. Values are guiding principles that shape our world outlook, attitudes and conduct. The moral values present a true perspective of the development of any society or nation. They tell us to what extent a society or nation has developed itself.

28.2 DEFINITIONS OF VALUES

According to Perry (1968), "*Value means the relation of an object to a valuing subject.*"

According to Hindzay (1966), "*By values we mean a person's idea of what is desirable, what he actually wants*"

In the words of John Dewey (1966), "*Value education means primarily to prize to esteem to appraise, holding it dear and also the act of passing judgment upon the nature and amount of its value as compared with something else*".

Sigmund Freud (1908) — "*The acquisition of morality meant the installation within the child's personality of an agency, i.e., the super-ego.*"

Geiger (1950) — "*Values are the outcomes of human choices among competing human interests.*"

Allport (1951) — "*A value is a belief upon which a man acts by preferences.*"

Cattle (1965) — "*By Values we mean the social, artistic, moral and other standards which the individual would like others and himself to follow*".

According to Zaleznik and David, "*Values are the ideas in the mind of men comparable to norms in that they specify how people should behave. Values also attach degrees of goodness to activities and relationships*"

I.J. Lehner and NJ Kube, "*Values are the integral part of personal philosophy of life by which we generally mean the system of values by which we live. The philosophy of life includes our aims, ideals and manner of thinking and the principles by which we guide our behaviour*"

T.W. Hipple, "*Values are conscious or unconscious motivators and justifiers of the actions and judgement*"

28.3 MEANING OF VALUE EDUCATION

Values' education is a term used to name several things, and there is much academic controversy surrounding it. Some regard it as all aspects of the process by which teachers (and other adults) transmit values to pupils.

Others see it as an activity that can take place in any organization during which people are assisted by others, who may be older, in a position of authority or are more experienced, to make explicit those values underlying their own behaviour, to assess the effectiveness of these values and associated behaviour for their own and others' long term well-being and to reflect on and acquire other values and behaviour which they recognize as being more effective for long term well-being of self and others.

This means that values education can take place at home, as well as in schools, colleges, universities, offender institutions and voluntary youth organizations. There are two main approaches to values education. Some see it as inculcating or transmitting a set of values which often come from societal or religious rules or cultural ethics.

Others see it as a type of Socratic dialogue where people are gradually brought to their own realization of what is good behaviour for themselves and their community. Value education also leads to success. It has values of hard work, how nobody is useless and loving studies.

Explicit Values Education is associated with those different pedagogies, methods or programmes that teachers or educators use in order to create learning experiences for students when it comes to value questions.

Implicit Values Education on the other hand covers those aspects of the educational experience resulting in value influence learning, which can be related to the concept of hidden curriculum. This discussion on implicit and explicit raises the philosophical problem of whether or not an unintentional action can be called education.

28.4 OBJECTIVES OF VALUE EDUCATION

1. To improve the integral growth of human begins.
2. To create attitudes and improvement towards sustainable lifestyle.
3. To increase awareness about our national history our cultural heritage, constitutional rights, national integration, community development and environment.
4. To create and develop awareness about the values and their significance and role.
5. To know about various living and non-living organisms and their interaction with environment.

28.5 TYPES OF VALUES

There are a number of different categories into which values can be placed.

Personal Values: Personal values are those you take for yourself and which constitute a critical part of your values and are apparent in attitudes, beliefs, and actions. Personal values may be prioritized, such as honesty then responsibility then loyalty and so on.

Social Values: Social values are those which put the rights of wider groups of people first. This may include equality, justice, liberty, freedom, and national pride. These are often instilled into us when we were young.

***Moral Values*:** Moral values impart respecting others and ourselves, respecting the right of others, keeping promises avoiding unnecessary problems with others avoiding cheating and dishonesty, showing gratitude to others and encourage them to work.

Spiritual Values: The ultimate ethical value is called spiritual value. Spiritual values are piety, meditation, yoga, self-discipline, control, purity, and devotion to God etc. Spiritual values highlight the principles of self-restraint. Self-discipline contentment, reduction of wants, freedom from general greed and austerity.

Universal Values: It is universal values that indicate the essence of the human condition. It is through Universal Values that we link ourselves with humanity and the cosmos. Universal Values can be experienced as life, joy, brotherhood, love, compassion, service, bliss, truth and eternity.

Political Values: Political values are ideological beliefs about the best way to govern a country or organization, for example through welfare, democracy and civic responsibility.

Economic Values: Economic values are those around money, and may include beliefs around ownership of property, contributing to the common good (taxes!), the balance of supply and demand and so on.

Religious Values: Religious values are spiritual in nature and include beliefs in how we should live.

Cultural Values: Cultural values are concerned with right and wrong, good and bad, customs and behaviour. Cultural values are reflected in language, ethics, social hierarchy, aesthetics, education, law, economics, philosophy and social institutions of every kind.

28.6 NEED FOR VALUE EDUCATION

1. Moral awareness should be endorsed to orient the progress in science & technology towards the welfare of mankind.
2. Common values should be re-discovered to unite human beings with the general decline of traditional values.
3. Teachers pass values to the students both consciously and unconsciously through their conduct in and out of class rooms. Therefore the need for a consciously planned value education programme is obvious to establish a formal learning.
4. The students might face more complicated decision making situations about issues involving values. They should be helped in developing the ability to make proper choices in such situations through value education.
5. Increase in Juvenile delinquency is a crisis to youth who under goes the process of personal growth. In such situation value education assumes a special significance.
6. Value Education awakens curiosity, development of proper interests, attitudes, values and capacity to think and judge about oneself.
7. Value Education helps in Promoting Social and Natural Integration.

28.7 IMPORTANCE OF VALUE EDUCATION

Value education is rooted in Indian philosophy and culture and ingrained in every tradition of Indian culture. Educational institutions play a significant role in the promotion of value. The Vedas and Upanishads form the source of inspiration for value education. In the Vedic period, In Ashram education, the Guru insists his sishya to follow certain values throughout his life.

Socialist, Secular, Democratic, Justice, Liberty Equality, Fraternity, Dignity of the individuals and integrity of the nation are the ideal conditions in the Constitution. Our values in life must draw their inspiration from these ideals. University education commission 1948-49 mentioned the various aspects of morality as: loyalty, courage, discipline, self-sacrifice and spirituality.

The Secondary Education Commission 1952-53 laid special emphasis on the following values in the formation of character of the students:

- Efficiency
- Good Temper
- Cooperation
- Integrity
- Discipline

28.8 SOURCES OF VALUE EDUCATION

The society is a place of informal learning that guarantees inheritance to its members. It caresses the child with love and sense of possessiveness and the child learns to value the social patterns and its philosophy.

The social tradition carries values of intimacy, language, love, equality, wishes to live, action, conduct, morality, unity, attachment and jealousy. These are the obvious traits, which a child borrows from the members of the society.

The child encounters with many behavioural patterns and makes common causes with the peer groups; learns the value of neighbourhood, unity in diversity, service to man is the service to God, co-operation and virtues comprehensively.

The school is an important receiver to the society. It helps the member in choosing and distinguishing the values for which the nation aspires to achieve—democracy, socialism and secularism. '*As the goals and aims have their own consequential values, lately schools have failed to put its learners on right track*'.

The main sources of value education are discussed below:

Society

The child is initiated into learning in the society to which he/she is a *bona fide* member with all facilities at disposal. The society may be assigned new roles to play effectively and vigorously towards development and inculcation of values of multi-dimension. The society is expected:

- To create homogeneous environment so as the learners may take up valuable lessons on ethics, behaviour, adjustment, living together, sympathy and service
- To reflect simplicity, honesty, kindness, and fairness in their conduct, for development of positive habit, attitude, inner capacity, and feeling and wish to live
- To provide maximum freedom for fuller growth with experiences (Spencer) and with facilitation of desired suggestion and persuasion (Stuart Mill).
- To explain its traditions, rituals, mythological stories, consequences and contribution to the modern order of society
- To take the valuable lesson from Gandhian thoughts, '*do not hear*

ill, do not speak ill and do not see ill of others'

- To narrate the cultural-socio-economic life patterns and the values the society members should continue to give quality lessons taking from the scriptures of *Vedas, Upanishads, Geeta, Koran, Bible* and the preaching of the great men and the saints
- To make the children emotionally integrated for practicing the values of oneness, unity, neighbourhood, code-conduct, love and sympathy for the poor. The values of co-operation, sincerity and commitment can be learnt in the society
- As the children are the working force and asset to the society vis-à-vis the nation, they require learning the '*value of dignity of labour*'

School

The school is a formal learning channel, which begins to formalize, and co-ordinate the experiences received in the society. It has a system to function with curriculum; textbooks, resources and other required infrastructure, teachers, students and the management to develop cumulated value. The schools are required:

1. To function as a true family, community and miniature society
2. To check the cultural, religious, community divides and its eroding values and to develop the sense of responsible citizenship
3. To work on multi-dimensional value education through its courses. Aesthetic education and values should be imparted, as it *is a valuable branch of philosophy, which tries to make clear the laws and principles of beauty*
4. To foster cultural values as it reflects the '*state of advanced development of the body, mind and spirit by training the experiences*'. It also represents '*all the art, belief, social institutions and the characteristics and heritage of community, race, etc.*'
5. To organise the activities for inculcating the practical '*moral*' and '*spiritual*' values
6. To explain and examine the ancient values in terms of emerging trends as the values can never be absolute. '*Values are as unstable as the forms of clouds*' (Dewey). The values and its priority change as per the urges and needs of the learners
7. To impart lessons on truth, reverence, tolerance, love, compassion, endurance, integrity, honesty, sincerity and sacrifice. Hinduism, Islam, Christianity, Sufism, Sikhism and other religions and its synthesis and anti-thesis should be explained with their common purpose and values
8. To organize N.C.C., A.C.C, N.S.S., educational and historical tours, for developing the values of social and national heritage.
9. To foster values related to vocational education, work experience, dignity of labour as reiterated by the various Educational Commissions

Teacher

The teacher is a mentor, facilitator, communicator and manager of the teaching learning activities. He/She is the source of inspiration having full of action, thought, vision and wisdom. A teacher is supposed to discharge the duty as assigned:

1. The teacher is the narrator of the skills to live the life completely and is supposed to act as the friend, philosopher and guide
2. Honesty, morality, truth, non-violence should be the forte as the learners copy the behaviour of their teachers
3. He should have competency, methodology, strategy, technique of teaching and innovative skills at command to organize learning
4. He requires to explain the social and the national heritage, culture, civilization and its useful values to the modern adolescents
5. The values related to the teacher's habits, behaviour, actions and thoughts must reflect the real face before the students

28.9 ROLE OF THE TEACHER IN DEVELOPMENT OF MORAL AND SOCIAL VALUES

It has been stressed again and again that nothing can be more helpful in moulding the child's moral behaviour than the teacher's own conduct. A Teacher has to set a high standard of moral behaviour before the child. The school plays a very important role in the moral values of the child. Through the organization of various curricular and co-curricular activities, teachers can foster among children various moral qualities. In the teaching of different subjects like languages and social studies etc., teacher may stress moral qualities like love, sacrifice, self-control, truthfulness, uprightness, etc., Dramas, games and sports provide many opportunities for an appeal to the moral sense of the students. A suggestive list of some activities for the moral and social values development of children is given below:

1. Appreciating pupil's ideas
2. Giving less directions, commands or orders
3. Asking more questions while guiding the content – oriented part of classroom discussions
4. Adopting creative models of teaching
5. Providing adequate opportunities to pupils to observe, to ask questions and experience things
6. Organizing group projects
7. Organizing group games
8. Organizing school panchayat
9. Conducting daily morning school assembly
10. Through shows, folk songs and dance
11. Role-plays constitute another important model for inculcating values among very young students. Role plays allows students to

place themselves in the position of others. If the role-play is handled appropriately, teachers can develop student's values like co-operation, good manners.

12. Social service programmes are also very helpful to inculcate many values like tolerance, cooperation etc.,
13. Picnics, visits to Zoo etc., are useful for developing values such as co-operation, pity and love for animals.
14. Folklores and riddles can also be used to inculcate values among children.
15. The learning process itself has a great bearing on the value orientation of children. All activities in the school curriculum marking, instructional techniques and evaluation, etc., should be so designed that they lead to spontaneous development of desirable values.
16. There is a need for producing literature especially designed for value – orientation of education.
17. Special teacher – orientation programmes should be taken up at the state level to train teachers in the effective methods of development of values among students and teachers.
18. Celebrating National Days
19. Celebrating Festivals
20. Organizing camps
21. Screening appropriate films
22. Stressing the main teachings of saints and seers
23. Looking after the school garden
24. Organizing girl guiding and scouting
25. Celebrating festivals of difference communities
26. Visiting backward and slum areas and rendering some sort of service to the people living in these areas.
27. Arranging community and school get together

28.10 INCULCATION OF VALUES THROUGH CURRICULAR ACTIVITIES

Every subject can be means of building good character and values. Some examples are given below:

Language: In language through conversation and discussion the teacher educator can enable students to embody higher and noble ideas.

Social Sciences: Through social science in general we can develop values like secularism, socialism, hard work and democracy etc.

Geography: Through geography we can develop values of conservation, preservation, adventure etc.

Economics: Through economics a teacher can lay emphasis on the value of thrift and saving, which lead to the prosperity of a person.

Civics: Through civics we can develop values of cooperation, sense of mutual welfare, obedience of law, concern for environment etc.

Science: Everything in nature has a lesson to teach. For example, we can say while blowing up a balloon, if person blows too much air into it, it will burst. Similarly if we are too greedy and acquire more material wealth sooner or later, we will have problems.

Mathematics: In mathematics there is a wide scope of imparting values like neatness, accuracy, proper planning etc.

Thus, we can say that education and values go hand in hand and values are inherent in every module of learning; even co-curricular activities can serve as a sound base for the inculcation of values among students.

28.11 INCULCATION OF VALUES THROUGH CO-CURRICULAR ACTIVITIES AND COMMUNITY SERVICES

Co-curricular activities values play a very significant role in inculcating different values in the students. For all-round development of personalities of the students, co-curricular activities are considered to be very important now-a-days. Previously the term "extra-curricular activities" was used for outdoor activities and other cultural programmes organized in the school. But, now-a-days this term has been discarded keeping in view the importance of these activities. In many progressive schools there is an allotment of certain periods for these co-curricular activities in their regular time table.

Through these activities, many values can be inculcated profitably. Co-curricular activities form an integral part of the modern school curriculum. They should be made more and more purposive and fruitful as well as value oriented with the democratic base and purposeful pursuit. This can be done, provided children have an opportunity of having living experience of moral life through these activities.

In programmes of outdoor activities, the children are taken out of the school to the areas of adventure, appreciation of art and culture and the places of historical values. They can be brought avenues in the training of initiative, team-work, self-discipline and learn much about our cultural heritage and historical details. Besides games and sports, there are several outdoor activities, namely, NCC, Scouting & Guiding, Mountaineering, Trekking, Excursion, Field trips etc., which may serve the purpose of inculcation of desired values among the students and formation of character.

Co-curricular activities like Meditation and Morning Assembly (prayer) make the body and the mind calm and assist in achieving tangible results such as improvement in memory, concentration, intuitive power and the development of calm and balanced nature. Sports and socially productive works develop qualities of cooperation, goodwill and equality. Celebrating Cultural programmes and days of national importance develop good and refined tastes along with giving knowledge about our culture, national history. These activities imprint the mind of students with positive thoughts and feelings about the wealth in our culture and heritage.

29

Education for Peace

29.1 MEANING OF EDUCATION FOR PEACE

Education for Peace is a conceptual framework from which schools may devise a programme comprising the transmission of universal values and enduring attitudes, and the development of skills which will enable our students to become active global citizens. This framework is guided by the recognition of the following principles:

- Each member of the global society is bound by principles relating to human welfare, such as justice, liberty, responsibility, equality, dignity, security, democracy and solidarity.
- Each member of society is an active participant in a local community and is in turn committed to a global harmony reflective of the diversity of the human population.
- Each member of the global society must act individually and communally toward guardianship of our world as a whole, guaranteeing the right to a sustainable future

The implementation of this conceptual framework recognizes the practice of peaceful relations at all levels: personal, familial, communal, inter-cultural and global. It entails a process of knowledge acquisition and skill-building which affects the behaviour of individuals and groups and provides a model for the formal and informal curriculum of the school. Education for Peace is a process and condition which permeates all aspects of school life, with implications for learners, teachers, and administrators and it extends beyond the school to society as a whole.

Education for peace seeks:

- To conduct community and social development projects in any part of the world with a focus on creating a more peaceful and violence-free world;
- To provide the structure for the development and implementation of the peace education projects around the world;
- To offer both community-specific in-class and international web-based Education for Peace programs for school communities and leaders in various countries of the world where the ravages of war, prejudice, terror and rapid social, economic, and cultural change

have created conditions of insecurity and conflict in families, schools, and communities alike;

- To establish a comprehensive on-line library on issues pertaining to Education for Peace and make it available to educators and policy makers everywhere;
- To conduct research on the principles of Education for Peace and make the findings available globally;
- To develop curricula of Education for Peace based on established universal scientific principles and the unique cultural and social circumstances of each participating group, making the curricula accessible to all through the Web, in as many languages as possible;
- To train educators and Education for Peace specialists who would, in turn, use their knowledge and expertise in pursuit of peace through peace education;
- To offer expert consulting services to governmental and non-governmental agencies regarding issues of conflict, violence, and peace.

29.2 AIMS OF EDUCATION FOR PEACE

The overall aim of Education for Peace is to help build a peaceful world. To do so we aim to:

1. Understand the nature and origins of violence and its effects on both victim and perpetrator.
2. Create frameworks for achieving peace and peaceful, creative societies.
3. Sharpen awareness about the existence of unpeaceful relationships between people and within and between nations.
4. Investigate the causes of conflicts and violence embedded within perceptions, values and attitudes of individuals as well as within social and political structures of society.
5. Encourage the search for alternatives and possible non-violent skills.
6. Equip children and adults with personal conflict resolution skills.
7. Show people that violence and war are learned and not an intrinsic part of human nature and that it is possible to resolve conflict peacefully.
8. Create a more peaceful world where all of us may become agents for change. Education for Peace gives us the skills that will assist in achieving peaceful societies.
9. Correct the limited understanding of peace held by many people that it is the absence, however contrived, of direct violence, of wounding and killing.
10. Create a better learning environment where conflict and relationships may be explored.

29.3 KEY PEDAGOGICAL PRINCIPLES OF PEACE EDUCATION

Virginia Cawagas (2007) has identified four key pedagogical principles in peace education:

1. ***Holism:*** Demonstrating that all issues are interrelated, multidimensional, and dynamic. Holism stands in sharp contrast to the fragmented way in which school subjects are often taught. A holistic vision allows us to see the complex relationships of different issues. A holistic vision involves looking at the temporal (past, present, future, and how they interrelate) and spatial dimensions (from micro to macro, and across sectors of society) of an issue.

2. ***Values Formation:*** Realizing that all knowledge is never free of values, educating for a culture of peace needs to be explicit about its preferred values such as compassion, justice, equity, gender-fairness, caring for life, sharing, reconciliation, integrity, hope and non-violence. Peace education involves teaching for these values in all educational interventions.

3. ***Dialogue:*** A dialogical approach cultivates a more horizontal teacher-learner relationship in which both dialogically educate and learn from each other. Dialogue is a key component of peace education pedagogy. In addition to class discussion, the following are the tools for dialogic pedagogy:

Guest Speakers: For example, invite street children to a class to talk about their lives.

Web Charting: Make a web chart using a theme (in a circle in the center), and sub-themes connected to the center, and draw connections.

Role Play: Have students act out a cross-cultural conflict.

Simulation: Simulate a small-arms convention for a lesson on disarmament; have students play different roles, such as that of an arms dealer, arms buyer, protester, etc.

4. ***Critical Empowerment:*** In critical empowerment, learners engage in a personal struggle to develop a critical consciousness that actively seeks to transform the realities of a culture of war and violence into a culture of peace and non-violence. Thus, through critical empowerment, learners develop a deeper understanding of problems, and are also empowered to take action to solve these problems. Critical empowerment also requires an understanding of power; in a system of inequitable power relations, empowerment involves reconstructing this system to one of more equitable, horizontal relations.

29.4 IMPORTANCE OF EDUCATION FOR PEACE

Most disputes between people are solved without violence, but not all. If, we are to move away from violence as a way of solving disputes at home and abroad we must work together to help young people learn how deal with conflict creatively and non-violently.

To prevent continued cycles of violence, education must promote peace, tolerance and understanding to help create a better society for all. Disputes and conflicts may be inevitable but violence is not. To prevent continued cycles of violence, education must seek to promote peace and tolerance, not fuel hatred and suspicion. The General Assembly of the United Nations proclaimed the years 2001-2010 the ***International Decade for a Culture of Peace and Non-violence for the Children of the World***'.

It defines a culture of peace as 'all the values, attitudes and forms of behaviour that reflect respect for life, for human dignity and for all human rights, the rejection of violence in all its forms and commitment to the principles of freedom, justice, solidarity, tolerance and understanding between people'.

Essential for building a culture of peace is education for peace. The United Nations has called on every country to 'ensure that children, from an early age, benefit from education to enable them to resolve any dispute peacefully and in a spirit of respect for human dignity and of tolerance'.

Most disputes between people are solved without violence – but not all. If we are to move away from violence as a means to solve disputes at home and abroad we must work together to help young people learn how deal with conflict creatively and non-violently.

29.5 VALUES AND ATTITUDES OF EDUCATION FOR PEACE

Awareness of values and attitudes underpin peace education and need to be addressed through the curriculum and the whole school. Education for Peace is founded on the following values and attitudes:

1. Respect for others regardless of race, gender, age, nationality, class, sexuality, appearance, political or religious belief, physical or mental ability.
2. Empathy – a willingness to understand the views of others from their standpoint.
3. A belief in positive change by individuals and groups of people.
4. Appreciation of and respect for diversity.
5. Self esteem – accepting the intrinsic value of oneself.
6. Commitment to non-violence, equity and social justice.
7. Concern for the environment and understanding of our place in the eco-system.
8. Commitment to equality.

29.6 EDUCATION FOR PEACE ACROSS THE CURRICULUM

Each subject could help educate for peace and foster a culture of non-violence

English: Pupils could script and perform a play, or write a short story, about the experiences of a young refugee. Texts, such as military recruitment literature or the front pages of national newspapers in times of war, could be analyzed for the use of language and what is said explicitly and implicitly. These activities would increase understanding and awareness of war and peace issues; develop skills of empathy; illustrate links between the personal, local and global spheres; and promote honest talk and sensitive listening.

Maths: How about calculating the amount spent on the military in one particular country, region, continent or conflict? By using meaningful data pupils value the learning experience more and take the learnt skills and knowledge beyond the classroom. Military spending figures could be compared to GDP, education or health spending, or how much it would have cost to resolve a conflict non-violently. Graphs, charts and so on could be produced to display some of the relationships.

Science: A study of the effects of war on the environment could take in all three natural sciences. Lessons could consider how the atmosphere and water resources are affected by war and how this in turn effects plants and animals. A discussion of nuclear technology would provide an opportunity to examine the ethics of scientific research and development and how scientific knowledge is used. Alternative forms of energy production – wind, solar etc. – also have implications for the social and political world and for the location and type of future conflicts.

Design and Technology: Design and technology lessons could focus on technology for a better world. The project can be design an environmentally friendly house or clothing with built-in safety features and communications technology.

Information and Communication Technology: ICT has greatly increased the potential for global co-operation but has also changed the way wars are fought. Pupils could use ICT to research and present their hopes for greater co-operation and understanding in the future by producing a website or multi-media presentation. Pupils could examine the morality of killing people from a keyboard thousands of miles away, or the notion of a 'just' war in which some are armed with hi-tech equipment and others use military technology centuries old.

History: War is studied in History lessons – in fact probably too much. However, the focus is usually on the events that took place – battles, sinking of ships, declarations of war and declarations of peace. Visits to war cemeteries, battlefields and war museums tend to focus on sorrow, heroism and sacrifice. The really challenging questions of why, who was responsible and how can we avoid the same terrible mistakes in the future do not surface in the study of war in history lessons.

Geography: Famine, food distribution, refugees, under-development, environmental pollution, natural resources (oil, diamonds, water etc.), trade flows and migration are all concerns of the geographer. They are also intimately tied up with violent conflict and war, yet war is hardly mentioned in the geography classroom. The negative effects of war on the human and physical geography of the world should form a major part of any geography course.

Modern Foreign Languages: Amnesty International has produced some excellent packs on teaching human rights through French, Spanish etc. Pupils need to practice the language they are learning so why not focus the practice exercises around issues of peace and war. Being able to communicate across political and cultural borders easily is a good way of ensuring relations between and within states does not deteriorate to violence. Learning to listen is another key skill required for a more peaceful world.

Art and Design: The art world is full of images of conflict, death and anger but also of peace, serenity and co-operation. By studying 'peaceful' images and 'violent' images pupils can learn how thoughts and emotions can be expressed through image and form. Signs and symbols have been used for centuries to promote war or peace. Pupils could design their own symbol or logo to promote a culture of peace.

Citizenship: Human rights and responsibilities; the world as a global community and the role of the UN; the work of local, national and international voluntary groups and the importance of resolving conflict fairly all form part of the Citizenship curriculum.

Suggested Practicum

1. In the light of different schools of thought, plan a 'dream school' incorporating the best from all the philosophies.
2. Trace the role of a teacher from the ancient times to the present time in value inculcation among students. Reflect critically and write a report.
3. Design five activities for integration of peace education in elementary school curriculum. State the criteria for the selection of the activities.
4. Study the impact of family, peers, neighbourhood and media on children by understanding their problems, challenges, concerns, fears, joys and dreams. Interview 5 children in a class and prepare a report.
5. Interview 5 parents of elementary students to know the child rearing practices they are using and prepare and present a report in the classroom.
6. Role play and dramatization of issues relating to inclusive education.
7. Surveys to study condition of different kinds of schools and teachers and other staff working in them.
8. Surveys to study the environment of inclusive schools. Find out the problems and challenges of students, teachers and other staff working in them.
9. Action research to understand the implementation of government schemes for education of the challenging students.
10. Action research to understand the problems faced by challenging children of in inclusive schools.
11. Surveys to understand field realities relating to policy issues under discussion.
12. Action research to understand the problems faced by children of marginalised communities in schools of different kinds.
13. Compare the role of teacher in the light if Idealism Naturalism, Pragmatism and Humanism.
14. Observe 3 elementary classrooms and identify the teachers' philosophy that he/she is using in the classroom.
15. Plan a project to find out the elements of socialization of elementary students.

References

Adams, D. (2009). World Peace through the Town Hall. Self-Published. http://www.cultureof--peace.info/books/worldpeace/introduction.html.

Aggrawal, J.C. (1996). *Theory and Principles of Education.* Vikas Publications, New Delhi.

Aggrawal, J.C. (2001). *Basic Ideas in Education.* Shipra Publications, Delhi.

Aggrawal, J.C. (2005). *Education for Values, Environment and Human Rights.* Shipra Publications, Delhi.

Anand, C.L. (1993). Teacher and Educations in the Emerging Indian Society. NCERT, New Delhi.

Badheka, Gijubhai (1999). *Montessori Paddhati.* Vaagdevi, Bikaner.

Badheka, Gijubhai (2001). *Baal Shikshan Aur Shikshak.* Vaagdevi Prakashan, Bikaner.

Bajpai, Amita (1991). Fifth Survey of Educational Research, 1988-92, M.B. Buch, Volume, 2, Pg. 1333, NCERT, Sri Aurobindo Marg, New Delhi.

Banks, James (2008). *An Introduction to Multicultural Education.* 4th edition, Pearson, Allyn/Bacon.

Bhatacharya and Sriniwas (1977). *Society and Education.* Academic Publishers, Calcutta.

Brubacher, John S. (1962). *Modern Philosophies of Education.* McGraw Hill Book Company Inc., New York.

Brubacher, John S. (1978). *Philosophy of Higher Education.* Jossey-Bass, San Francisco.

Brunacher, John S. (1962). *Eclectic Philosophy of Education.* Prentice Hall, Engellwood Cliffs, New Jersey.

Campbell, Duane (2010). *Choosing Democracy: A Practical Guide to Multicultural Education.* 4th. edition. Pearson, Allyn /Bacon.

Central Board of Secondary Education (1997 and 2003). Value Education: A Handbook for Teachers. CBSE, New Delhi.

Coombs, Philips H. (1985). *The World Crisis in Education.* Oxford University Press, New York.

Dash, B.N. (2004). *Theories of Education and Education in the Emerging Indian Society.* Dominant Publishers and Distributors, New Delhi.

Delors, Jacques (1996). Learning the Treasure Within. UNESCO, Report of the International Commission on Education for Twenty first Century.

Dewey, John (1952). *The School and the Child.* Macmillan Company, Delhi.

Dewey, John (1961). *Democracy and Education.* Macmillan Company, New York.

Dhavan, M.L. (2005). *Philosophy of Education.* Isha Books, Delhi.

Durkheim, Emile (1956). *Education and Sociology.* Free Press, New York.

Education and National Development: Report of the Education Commission. NCERT, 1964-66, New Delhi.

Fields, Jason. (2003). Children's Living Arrangements and Characteristics: March

2002. Current Population Reports. United States Department of Commerce Economics and Statistics Administration.

GOI (2001). National Human Development Report. Planning Commission, Government of India.

GOI, MHRD (1993). Learning without Burden, New Delhi.

Govt. of India (1993). Education for All: The Indian Scene: MHRD Widentry Horizons, New Delhi.

Hanley, M.S. (1999). The Scope of Multicultural Education. www.newhorizons.org.

Hufstader, C. (2007). Building a Culture of Peace in Senegal. http://www.oxfamamerica.org/articles/building-a-culture-of-peace-in-senegal

Jaffee, Sara R., *et al.* (2003). Life with (or without) Father: The Benefits of Living with Two Biological Parents Depend on the Father's Antisocial Behaviour. *Child Development,* 74: 109-27.

Kar, N.K. (1996). *Value Education: A Philosophical Study*. The Associated Publication, Ambala.

Karst, Patricia. (2000). The Single Mother's Survival Guide. Freedom, CA: Crossing Press, Periodicals.

Kashyap, Subhash (1993). *Perspectives on the Constitution*. Shipra Publications, Delhi.

Kilpatrick, W.H. (1934). *Source Book in the Philosophy of Education*. McMillan and Company, New York.

Kincheloe, Joe and Shirley Steinberg. (1997). *Changing Multiculturalism*. Open University Press, London.

Knight, G.R. (1998). *Issues and Alternatives in Educational Philosophy* (3rd ed.). Andrew University Press, Michigan.

Kumar, Krishna (1988). *What is Worth Teaching*. Orient Longman, New Delhi.

Mayer, F. (1963). *Foundations of Education*. Ohio, Charles E Merrile Books Inc.

MHRD (1986). National Education Policy, New Delhi.

Mohanti J. (1987). *Democracy and Education in India*. Deep and Deep Publishers, New Delhi.

Mohit Chakrabarti (1997). *Value Education: Changing Perspectives*. Kanishka Publishers, New Delhi.

National Council of Educational Research and Training (2003). Values Education in Indian Schools: Experiences and Strategies of Implementation. New Delhi.

National Council of Educational Research and Training (2011). Education for Values in Schools: A Framework, New Delhi.

Nayar, P.R., Dave, P.N., and Arora, K. (1982) Teacher and Education in Emerging Indian Society, New Delhi.

NCERT (1997). Code of Professional Ethics for Teachers, NCERT, New Delhi.

NCTE (1998). Gandhi on Education, New Delhi.

Palmer, Joy A. *et al.* (2001). *Fifty Major Thinkers on Education from Confucious to Dewey*. Routledge, New Delhi.

Panday, V.C. (2005). *Value Education and Education for Human Rights*. Isha Books, Delhi.

Pandey, K.P. (2010). *Perspectives in Social Foundations of Education.* Shipra Publications, Delhi.

Pandey, R.S. *An Introduction to Major Philosophers of Education*, Vinod Pusatak Mandir, Agra.

Parents without Partners. 1650 South Dixie Highway, Suite 510, Boca Raton, Florida 33431. http://www.parentswithoutpartners.org.

Passi, B.K. (2004). Value Education. National Psychological Corporation, Agra.

Prem Singh, G.J. (2004). Towards Value Based Education. *University News*. Vol. 42 (45): pp. 11-12.

Rajput J.C. (2006). *Human values and Education*. Pragun Publisher, New Delhi.

Ram Murti Acharya (1990). Towards an Enlightened and Humane Society: A Committee Report, MHRD, New Delhi.

Rathore, Bharti. (2006). Beyond the Text: Values in Language Classes. *Learning to Teach,* Charutar Vidyamandal.

RIMSE (1999). Value Education: An Outline. Mysore.

Ross, James (1962). *Groundwork of Educational Theory*. George Harre and Sons, London.

Rousseau, Jacques J. (1979). Emile on Education, Basic Books: New York.

Ruhela, S.P. (1969). *Social Determinants of Educability in India*. Jain Publishers, New Delhi.

Ruhela, S.P. and Vyas K.C. (1970). *Sociological Foundations of Education in Contemporary India*. Dhanpat Rai and Sons, Delhi.

Saiyidain, K.G. (1970). *Facts of Indian Education*. NCERT, New Delhi.

Singh, Y.K. (2007). *Philosophical Foundations of Education*. New Delhi: APH Publishing Corporation.

Single and Custodial Fathers Network Inc. Web site: http://scfn.org.

Single Parent Central. http://www.singleparentcentral.com.

Sleeter, C. and McLaren, P. (2000). Origins of Multiculturalism. www.rethinking schools.org.

Steinberg, Shirley. (2001). Multi/Intercultural Conversations. NY: Peter Lang.

Stephenson, J. *et al.* (1998). *Value Education*. London: Routledge

UNESCO. (2010). Culture of Peace: What is It? http://www3.unesco.org/iycp/uk/uksum cp.htm

United Nations Educational Scientific and Cultural Organization (2001). Learning the Way of Peace: A Teacher's Guide to Peace Education. UNESCO, New Delhi.

Willace, O.P. and William, A. (1977). *The Elements of Philosophy: Compendium for Philosophers and Theologians*. Alba House, New York.